Surviving the Workpla

RENEWALS 458-4574

DATE DUE

GAYLORD			PRINTED IN U.S.A.

Psychology at Work

Series editor: Clive Fletcher

This series interprets and examines people's work behaviour from the perspective of occupational psychology. Each title focuses on a central issue in management, emphasizing the role of the individual's workplace experience.

Books in the series include:

Creating the Healthy Organization
Well-being, Diversity and Ethics at Work
Sue Newell

Impression Management
Building and Enhancing Reputations at Work
*Paul Rosenfeld, Robert A. Giacalone
and Catherine A. Riordan*

Managing Employee Performance
Design and Implementation in Organizations
Richard S. Williams

Managing Innovation and Change
A Critical Guide for Organizations
Nigel King and Neil Anderson

Managing Teams
A Strategy for Success
Nicky Hayes

Psychological Types at Work
An MBTI® Perspective
Rowan Bayne

Recruitment and Selection
A Framework for Success
Dominic Cooper, Ivan T. Robertson and Gordon Tinline

Surviving the Workplace
A Guide to Emotional Well-being
Ashley Weinberg and Cary Cooper

Surviving the Workplace

A Guide to Emotional Well-being

Ashley Weinberg and Cary Cooper

WITHDRAWN
UTSA LIBRARIES

THOMSON

Australia • Canada • Mexico • Singapore • Spain • United Kingdom • United States

University of Texas
at San Antonio

THOMSON

Surviving the Workplace
Ashley Weinberg and Cary Cooper

Publishing Director
John Yates

Commissioning Editor
Geraldine Lyons

Editorial Assistant
James Clark

Production Editor
Alissa Chappell

Manufacturing Manager
Helen Mason

Marketing Manager
Leo Stanley

Typesetter
KnowledgeWorks Global Ltd

Production Controller
Maeve Healy

Printer
Zrinski; d.d., Croatia

Cover Design
Stefan Brazzo

Text Design
Malcolm Harvey Young

**Copyright © 2007
Thomson Learning**

The Thomson logo is a registered trademark used herein under licence.

For more information, contact Thomson Learning, High Holborn House; 50-51 Bedford Row, London WC1R 4LR or visit us on the World Wide Web at: http://www.thomsonlearning.co.uk

All rights reserved by Thomson Learning 2007. The text of this publication, or any part thereof, may not be reproduced or transmitted in any form or by any means, electronic or mechanical, including photocopying, recording, storage in an information retrieval system, or otherwise, without prior permission of the publisher.

While the publisher has taken all reasonable care in the preparation of this book the publisher makes no representation, express or implied, with regard to the accuracy of the information contained in this book and cannot accept any legal responsibility or liability for any errors or omissions from the book or the consequences thereof.

Products and services that are referred to in this book may be either trademarks and/or registered trademarks of their respective owners. The publisher and author/s make no claim to these trademarks.

ISBN: 978-1-86152-999-2

British Library Cataloguing-in-Publication Data
A catalogue record for this book is available from the British Library

Library
University of Texas
at San Antonio

Contents

Figures

Tables

Case studies and exercises

Case studies

Exercises

Series editor's preface

Understanding the psychology of individuals and teams is of prime importance in work settings as rapid and far-reaching changes continue to occur. Organizational structures are shifting radically to the point where individual managers and professionals have far greater autonomy, responsibility and accountability. Organizations are seeking to reduce central control and to 'empower' individual employees. These employees combine in teams that are frequently cross-functional and project based rather than hierarchical in their construction. The traditional notion of careers has changed; increasingly, an individual's career is less likely to be within a single organization, which has implications for how organizations command loyalty and commitment. The full impact of information technology has now been felt, with all the consequences this has for the nature of work and the reactions of those doing it.

The capacity of people to cope with the scale and speed of change has become a major issue and the literature on work stress only increases. The belief in the importance of individuals' cognitive abilities and personality make-up in determining what they achieve and how they contribute to teamwork has been demonstrated in the explosive growth in organizations' use of psychometric tests and related procedures. Perhaps more than ever before, analysing and understanding the experience of work from a psychological perspective is necessary to achieve the twin goals of effective performance and quality of life. Unfortunately, it is the latter of these that all too often seems to be overlooked in the concern to create competitive, performance-driven or customer-focused cultures within companies.

It is no coincidence that the rise in the study of business ethics and increasing concern over issues of fairness paralleled many of the organizational changes of the late twentieth century. Ultimately, an imbalance between the aims and needs of the employees and the aims and needs of the organization is self-defeating. One of the widely recognized needs for the twenty-first century is for a greater emphasis on innovation rather than on simply reacting to pressures. However, psychological research and theory indicate that innovation is much more likely to take place where individuals feel secure enough to take the risks involved, and where organizational reward systems encourage experimentation and exploration – which they have signally failed to do in the last century. Seeking to help organizations realize the potential of their workforce in a mutually enhancing way is the business challenge psychology has to meet.

The central theme of the *Psychology at Work* series is to interpret and explain people's work behaviour in the context of a continually evolving pattern of change, and to do so from the perspective of occupational and organizational psychology. Each of the books draws together academic research and practitioner experience, relying on empirical studies, practical examples and case studies to communicate their ideas. The reader, whether a student, manager or psychologist, will find that they provide a succinct summary of accumulated knowledge and a guide to how to apply it in business. The themes of some of the books cover traditional areas of occupational psychology, while others focus on topics that cut across such boundaries, tackling subjects that are of growing interest and prominence. They are directly relevant for practitioners, consultants and students of HR and occupational psychology but much of what they deal with is of great value to managers, and students of management, more generally. This broad appeal is demonstrated by the fact that an earlier version of the series, the *Essential Business Psychology* series, was highly commended by the Management Consultancies Association book award. The *Psychology at Work* series shares the aims, and some of the titles, as the original series but the individual books have been substantially updated and the range of titles is expanded. Although the books share a common aim and series heading, they have not been forced into a rigid stylistic format. In keeping with the times, the authors have had a good deal of autonomy in deciding how to organize and present their work. I think all of them have done an excellent job; I hope you will find that too.

Clive Fletcher

Acknowledgements

I would like to thank my wife Anne for constantly helping me to realize the relative importance of work in the big scale of things, my children James and Lottie for inspiring and helping me whilst writing this book, my parents Martin and Risha for their unconditional support and encouragement; I would also like to thank my co-author Cary for his guidance, the series editor Clive Fletcher and Rose James for their helpful comments and all those people who were kind enough to ask 'How's the book going?' I dedicate it to all would-be survivors.

Ashley Weinberg
August 2006

I would like to dedicate this book to my closest personal friend, Alan Djanogly, who has always been there for me whenever I have been troubled.

Cary Cooper
August 2006

An introduction to survival at work

It is a truth universally acknowledged that an employee in possession of a winning lottery ticket will want to leave their job. Exclusive research for this publication showed that hardly anybody I asked would stay in their current work should they be presented with such a tempting escape route, and furthermore it seemed nobody would blame someone who fled the workplace for this reason. Having spoken to many people about their varied jobs and ways of earning a living, it has become clear that it is not the doing of the work itself which people would rather swap, but the near-compulsion to behave in a particular style or achieve certain goals in a manner prescribed by customers, managers and the wider organization. In a capitalist society, it is hard to do without work as to do so would often create financial challenges. However, if workers were given the chance to carry out their chosen task without the pressure of deadlines and of curious definitions of quality, it is conceivable that certain types of work could be redefined as a pleasant way to pass the time. Ah yes, I hear you say, but he hasn't tried to do my job has he? Er no, but I did say certain types of job, and this might depend on the level of satisfaction which doing the job would bring. Well that wouldn't make my business any money and we'd be unemployed, wouldn't we?! OK, but let's not take it to extremes. After all, there is a break-even point and I don't mean financially: I mean in terms of your health.

Let me put it another way: would you swap your winning lottery ticket for an extra ten years of life in good health? No one can predict these things with certainty, but enough research has been conducted which shows there are aspects of work which can do us harm. If we do try to act upon these, who is to say with equal certainty that we won't live to see the benefits?

In the event that we will need to wait at least one week, and most likely a lot longer, in order to get that winning ticket, those of us who need to work for a living face the daily task of making the most of things. This can mean we pursue one or more from a range of strategies: we might try to find a job we actually like, change that job to something more bearable, or even change our own approach to work – a sort of healthy delusion – or decide that it is time to dig in and change the workplace for the better. In real terms, it could be that you are hanging on by a daily thread of sanity from a job which brings you little satisfaction, and that the ability to keep your head above water is reward enough. Alternatively you might be looking for a first or second contract whilst developing the type of skills which will one day land you the ideal job. Perhaps you have escaped from a monstrous organization to set up business on your own where you can be boss and nobody can tell you what to do any more. It might be that you are mid-career and have been able to keep in work earning enough to maintain a home and tolerable family life.

All of this may add up to some kind of survival of the world of work. If that is the case, then it could mean the only way to be sure of having survived is that you have reached retirement age safely and are able to draw on your pension. But then it would be too late to know if your working life – not to mention the rest of it – could have been better!

Whatever the situation in which you find yourself, the common factor is that work for most people is a necessary evil, which gains us entry to the capitalist game of supply and demand. Without work, it is hard to lead the life we might choose, or to provide for ourselves or our families. This may seem like a forced choice, but is that a good enough reason to give up some or most of our waking hours in the pursuit of one type of activity for which we care little or not at all? The economic system relies on the ability of most to sign up to it and the attempts to elude this are many and varied. However, there remains one inescapable fact: humans were never designed, nor have they yet evolved, into animals which are suited to many of the types of work environment in which they are obliged to spend so much of their waking time.

Things were different in the times of hunter-gatherer communities. Now, as then, we need to eat and to continue the species via families or communities, yet this was, and in many parts of the world still is, at the mercy of the natural environment, which can be far deadlier than the human-made workplace. However, as shelter and technology have improved, we have given ourselves more choice over our living environments and the types of natural pressures we need to endure. Taking a long view, the human species has made a number of choices, some for better and some for worse, as we have made the equations of achieving a healthy living more complex for ourselves. It takes thousands of years to achieve evolutionary change and yet technologically developed organizations expect our bodily systems to adapt to new performance limits within months. One only has to look at the natural environment to see that this does not happen without costs and it is the same for human beings in the workplace. The feats of human endurance achieved in the world of sport represent peaks of physical performance, and as such are occasional and fleeting. Yet in the world of work, where there are arguably far fewer prizes, there is an expectation we can maintain our achievements over many years.

Workplaces seem more and more to reflect how life must have seemed to Charles Darwin when he first explored the Galapagos Islands. Employees, like splendidly coloured birds or cleverly camouflaged reptiles, have evolved to exist in an often inhospitable climate of demands and responsibility. The ones who are missing are those who have not been able to stand the heat or have developed the power of flight. Adaptation is the key to survival, whether in work or in nature. Careers, businesses and governments depend on the success of being able to change and meet the demands of the economic and political environment. We are faced with certain inevitabilities including the tide of instant global communications, the expectations of employers, consumers and stakeholders, the desire of market and world leaders to leave their mark and all in the context of a growing population. At the very least, survival at work can be described as the ability of the individual or organization to adapt as far as possible to changing employment environments in such a way that the costs to our health, performance and life outside of work do not outweigh the benefits. One simple strategy was explained to me by a mobile phone retailer: 'I hate mobiles . . . so I just sell them!'

At its best survival might equate with individual and organizational success in introducing change which is of benefit to one and all, and surviving to tell the tale. Written over 2000 years ago, Homer's *Odyssey* compares our species to that of ants whose individual efforts are not likely to make a difference to the world around us, but which when added together can exert huge and positive change. Occasionally one person captures the spirit of such change and is seen as representative of it, such as Winston Churchill or Nelson Mandela, yet anyone who has been part of a struggle can rightly claim a share in the deeds. Within the worlds of work where most of us exist, great deeds often go unrecognized, yet it is possible to derive personal satisfaction from the difference which we know we have made and occasionally an appreciative soul will say 'thank you'. For many of us, these flashes of light encourage our survival in psychological terms and arm us for future challenges. Maybe one day we will look back at those moments with a smile and even a warm glow, before we go to cash in that winning lottery ticket.

The meaning of work

Work can be a positive or negative experience for the individual, or a set of tasks which fluctuate in the level of enjoyment or personal sacrifice involved. A whole range of factors may play their part in shaping judgements of whether a job is positive or not, and this book aims to highlight a representative variety.

The twentieth century produced a consensus among the great philosophers that existence alone is not sufficient to justify our sense of being. Jean-Paul Sartre broadly claimed that 'to do is to be', and in this way we can claim that work provides us with structure and meaning in our lives. However, we should be clear what work really means, as there is a general assumption that this only refers to paid work. Yet for people who drive, wash clothes, care for the young or sick family members, clean dishes and houses, we know that these tasks are all types of work for which it would be possible to earn money if they were carried out in an official organization. It has been estimated that in the UK alone the total cost of paying for these unofficial work tasks would be in excess of £739 billion! (*Guardian*, 1997.)

Societies have long recognized the value of work, however defined, and whether one subscribes to the existentialist views of Sartre, or the Protestant work ethic, or other philosophical or religious advocates of human activity, work tends to be linked to the progress of the species. However, work can also lead to sinister outcomes, for example when work for a particular goal amounts to a giant step back for humanity. Above the entrance to Auschwitz concentration camp are the words *Arbeit macht frei*, which may be translated as 'work sets us free'. Within this phrase lies a cruel irony which finds echoes in the days of slave trading and in the times of workhouses and the abuses of child workers. The concept that work can somehow cleanse and purify was seen by Karl Marx as a useful propaganda tool for those who owned the means of production before the days of worker cooperatives. The sickening side of the misuse of industrial ownership was remarked on by Prime Minister David Lloyd George after the slaughter of the First World War, when he looked across the floor of the House of Commons and mocked the owners of the munitions factories as 'the well-dressed men who did well out of the War'.

For the most part, survival and work in its various forms are seen as inextricably linked. For many individuals and many reasons, this combination is not always a possibility, or it is simply not accepted. However, for the majority in a capitalist society this is the deal at some stage in our lives. This is not merely the case in evolutionary terms but also with regard to our own sense of identity. Most often, when introducing ourselves to others, it is the main work role in our lives which we describe, again whether paid or unpaid.

So how do we recognize work? It can be defined as any form of human activity which is meaningful to the person enacting it or to others who witness it. Hopefully this covers activities as diverse as parenting, gardening, managing, helping, cleaning, travelling, teaching and observing. Work tends to be characterized by the need for a level of individual effort, a pace at which one applies this effort and a frequency at which this takes place, aimed at producing a useful outcome which might be accompanied by rewards for the worker. Such rewards may be extrinsic, such as money, or intrinsic, such as satisfaction. Time away from work has also been valued by society. We should not forget that some religious teachings provide for time off from all types of work, and it is only comparatively recently in the UK that the potential to carry out work at any time on any day has become widely accepted and exploited.

Shrouded in the cloak of human awareness which allows us to make judgements and shape our attitudes and beliefs, lie the emotions. These are the lifeblood of feelings and the basis of our most vivid memories and learning experiences about the world. Emotions represent our most instinctive or 'gut' reaction to events, or indeed are the starting points for many of our actions. Emotions are controllable to a degree, depending on our individual personality and physiology and our perceptions of the environment around us. There is little doubt that emotions are powerful motivators and communicators and as such share a strong dependency on and a doubtless reciprocal relationship with our psychological health. The first chapter explores this relationship and the ways in which this is manifested in the world of work. In the early 1970s, Studs Terkel claimed that 'work is about violence, to the spirit as well as to the body'. With this in mind, we should not forget that emotions impact in physical and psychological ways and on others as well as ourselves. We should remember that survival is also about violence, in subtle or more obvious ways. Survival of the fittest is the quiet mantra of the workplace as well as Darwin's beloved Galapagos Islands, yet is ugly by comparison.

Part
One

The meaning of psychological and emotional health

This section of the book sets the parameters for the concepts covered in this text and aims to familiarize the reader with the context of work-based emotions and psychological health issues. Relevant models are covered and their relationship to the emotional challenges faced by employees in the modern workplace is examined.

- Chapter 1 – Defining and recognizing emotional and psychological health
- Chapter 2 – Prevalence and significance of emotional and psychological health problems
- Chapter 3 – Models of emotional well-being at work

1 Defining and recognizing emotional and psychological health

The meaning of psychological and emotional health

Psychological health

Most readers are likely to be familiar with the term 'mental health', even if its definition does not readily spring to mind. The terminology for anything relating to our mental well-being has changed over the last century and particularly in the last 25 years. From the derogatory terms which have been previously used to describe those experiencing poor psychological health, debate has progressed and at times raged about defining mental health and mental ill health. Newspaper headlines when a well-known celebrity experiences such difficulties still serve to demonstrate how such terms are still widely misunderstood and stigmatized.

In fact mental health refers to both ends of the spectrum of well-being, from the positive to the negative, from being well to being unwell. Until comparatively recently there has been a tendency to emphasize the negative side of the spectrum, and it is more helpful to consider the whole range of well-being. This is not an easy task: 'Anyone who has reflected on the many definitions of health, and of mental health in particular, will, I think, conclude that there is no consensus' (Sir Aubrey Lewis, 1963, p. 1550). A slightly more positive, although limited approach to definition is 'Mental health consists of the ability to live … happily, productively, without being a nuisance' (cited in Wootton, 1959). Anthony Clare's influential *Psychiatry in Dissent* (1980) considered that 'mental health appears to include an internal confidence of feeling and knowing, an ability to make the fullest use of mental powers and abilities, and a capacity for enjoyment and self-content'

(Clare, 1980, p. 17). From a more structured standpoint, Warr (1987, 1999) presents a five-factor model of mental health which includes the following:

- positive self-regard – how we view ourselves
- autonomy – the level of control we experience
- aspiration – how keen we are to interact with our environment
- competence – how good we are at carrying out tasks
- integrated functioning – how effectively the above factors interlock.

Furthermore, Warr draws the distinction between two types of psychological health: job-specific and context-free well-being, so as to avoid the confusion between individuals' feelings about themselves at work and in life more generally. This is reflected in the many types of survey used to assess well-being; some measures require answers in relation to our attitudes and functioning at work, others consider our health more globally. How easy it is to extract the necessary information for such research is considered later in this book (see Chapter 9).

It is worth bearing in mind that such definitions are Western in their orientation. In Chinese philosophy, the above model of mental health would not be complete without the factor of predetermined luck, wherein a birth sign can even influence the longevity of those born under it. Within a Western framework, psychological health may cautiously be defined as the conscious state of well-being which draws upon our mood, self-esteem, skills and abilities, physical health and our interpretation of internal and external events and environments. If one wanted to take the great risk of an even simpler definition, positive psychological health means feeling good about ourselves and what we are doing! As stated earlier, our experiences of this multifaceted phenomenon can be anywhere between the extremes of most positive and most negative, added to which everyone responds differently within the broadly defined understood limits of human capabilities. As a highly adaptive species, we have developed many ways to describe these responses, including emotional states as well as psychological and physical symptoms.

To further simplify things, the experience of mental health can be viewed as a continuum, along which various states of well-being may be registered (see Figure 1.1), but it is important to note that one stop along the continuum does not necessarily lead to the next (Jones and Bright, 2001). Figure 1.1 features terms developed and widely used in the twentieth century which relate to individual well-being.

Figure 1.1	**A continuum of well-being**				
Positive					Negative
Psychological good health	Eustress	Stress	Distress		Poor psychological health

Eustress

At the positive end, we recognize a state of positive well-being where we perceive and experience life in uplifting terms. This is close to the eustress described by Hans Selye (1956), one of the first theorists into the impact of psychological pressure on human functioning. Eustress is the positive sense in which we might enjoy challenge or obtain a positive 'buzz' from meeting a challenge, such as working towards a deadline, or handling a conflict situation. In this state, it is often the process itself which produces the positive 'high', which may be lacking when the task is completed. Alex Ferguson, manager of the Manchester United football team which won eight premiership titles in eleven years, has described how he felt elated during the championship campaign and then a sense of anti-climax at its completion, whether his team were successful or not. There is little doubt that many people are suited to involvement in challenging situations and are attracted to jobs which feature these aspects. Sales, politics, stockbroking, advertising, entertainment and broadcasting all dictate that you are only as successful as your last deal or show. The element of risk seems to get the best out of some of us, most notably those who only start to perform at an optimum level when the pressure is on. Thinking back to how successful we were at meeting our last deadline with a quality result is sufficient to tell us if we are one of those people!

Stress

The term 'stress' was first introduced by Sir William Ostler (1910) in his observations of medical patients. Selye's (1956) book *The Stress of Life* emphasized the body's physiological response to the actual or perceived demands of the environment, which formed part of our adaptation to survive. Subsequent theoretical models of stress have focused on the mismatch between the individual and their environment (French *et al.*, 1982) and the cognitive appraisal of events occurring around us (see Lazarus and Folkman, 1984). Since the 1970s our understanding of poorer psychological health has tended to encompass the term 'stress' and after decades of research into this phenomenon, there is a feeling that it covers such a wide spectrum of meanings as to be meaningless (e.g. Jones and Bright, 2001). Anecdotally people refer to stress as a fairly frequent experience, whether at work or outside of work, which suggests a daily grind or a specific event leading to negative feelings about ourselves and what we are doing. For example, a mother of two school-aged children working 30 hours each week in a paid job might experience stress when one of these aspects of her life comes into conflict with the other. Similarly the demands of a job with unrealistic deadlines, or having to give a presentation in front of a large audience, or trying to get to work on time, may all invoke the cry, 'I am stressed'.

The term 'stress' has been used to refer to environmental conditions, subjective perceptions, individual reactions, or to a process which includes a combination of these (Kasl and Amick, 1995). This could mean that stress is a cause or a result of the demands facing the individual, or indeed both! In search of clarity, some authors (e.g. O'Driscoll and Cooper, 2002) prefer to talk about 'stressors' as the causes, and 'strain' as the outcomes, of what we generally know as stress.

Distress

Distress refers to a situation where the individual's resources to cope are disabled, for example in the face of a major trauma such as bereavement or forced job loss. Such an acute situation predates a longer period of adjustment which has the potential to be problematic. A range of factors including an individual's personality, their manner of interpreting events, coping strategies and access to sources of social support will shape the nature of the outcome.

Poor psychological health

In this situation, the individual is failing to regain the ability to cope with their life circumstances and will tend to exhibit symptoms of psychological strain, such as fatigue, anxiety, loss of confidence, etc. The situation on the negative side of the continuum in Figure 1.1 is characterized by long-standing or persisting difficulties. Within people-oriented occupations, the term 'burnout' has been coined to describe a range of responses which distil into feelings of a lack of personal accomplishment, emotional exhaustion and depersonalization (Maslach, 1982) (see the Case Study on p. 18). Whilst this is not a diagnostic term, it is most certainly relevant to the consideration of the impact of a job on both psychological and emotional health.

Poor psychological health may or may not come to the attention of a health practitioner, whether a counsellor, GP or occupational health worker. However, where a referral to a mental heath professional is made, the range of symptoms and the ability of the individual to function on a day-to-day basis are assessed. The focus of the assessment will include the form of the symptoms, their severity, duration and the level of impairment experienced in daily activities. Based upon these, decisions about possible treatments can be considered.

Emotional health

To distinguish between psychological and emotional health may seem arbitrary, because there is little doubt the two are interconnected and often overlap. Both psychological and emotional health can each be located between opposite poles which represent positive and negative, yet the relationship between these types of well-being is often reciprocal, and we may not be sure whether emotions or psychological health outcomes are the cause or the result of the other in a given situation. Warr (1987) relates psychological and emotional states within a three-dimensional framework of feelings ranging along axes from displeasure to pleasure, anxiety to comfort and from depression to enthusiasm. Such a view highlights the interrelationship between emotional and psychological health.

Emotions can result from our experience of an event or an interpretation of events in our immediate surroundings, which in turn leads to a short-lived response (Reeve, 2005). This is different from our mood, which will influence the focus of our thoughts (Davidson, 1994) and which may persist for a longer period of time. Having said this, there are certain facets of psychological and emotional functioning which are independent of one another. For example, an employee genuinely reporting anxiety or misery over a period of time is likely to be in poor psychological health. However, this would be in contrast to an individual who appears positive and in good spirits, yet acts as though they are out of touch with their emotions or unable to express much regard for others, whose emotional health may be deemed poor. In this way it is possible to illustrate a real-world difference between psychological and emotional well-being.

Emotions have been defined as brief experiences which represent an attempt by the brain to coordinate four factors into an organised response: a feeling as we experience it (e.g. fear), our physiological arousal (e.g. rush of adrenalin), our sense of purpose (e.g. self-protection) and our expression (e.g. tense body posture) (Reeve, 2005). The difference between psychological and emotional health may therefore be more readily understood as the difference between internal thoughts and beliefs and external functioning, as shown by the way we harness emotions within patterns of behaviour. In this way an individual might be experiencing negative thoughts about their own ability and feel miserable (symptoms of poor psychological health), but manage to be present for work and maintain good relationships with colleagues (i.e. function well in terms of their emotional health). Alternatively an individual may feel keen to engage with the surrounding social environment and feel confident about their ability (symptoms of good psychological health), but fail to appreciate the impact of their behaviour and actually upset customers (an example of poor emotional functioning). The latter is particularly crucial in a workplace setting which requires the investment of emotional labour by employees (see Chapter 4), where an important predictor of successful performance is self-control.

The ability to be in touch with our own and others' emotions is known as emotional intelligence, a concept which has gained popularity and academic acceptance in recent years (Goleman, 1998; Higgs and Dulewicz, 1999; Salovey *et al.*, 2000). Emotional intelligence is dealt with in more detail in Chapter 6. Its main components highlight the importance of a range of features (Goleman, 1998):

- Self-awareness – how in touch we are with our emotions
- Self-control – maintaining a hold on the expression of our emotions
- Motivation – how we channel our emotion
- Empathy – how we can feel and/or display appropriate emotion for others
- Social skills – the expression of emotions to achieve social goals.

From this it can be seen that emotional intelligence is akin to an internal management system which has some level of control over those brief experiences known as emotions. It is believed that those exhibiting higher levels of emotional intelligence (EI) are more successful in work and relationships (Goleman, 1998), so our notion of good emotional health should refer to the optimum level of emotional functioning for an individual.

In arriving at a definition of good emotional health, it is useful to recognize that emotions are focused on feelings and what accompanies and contributes to them, as well as our knowledge and use of them for internal and external social experiences and exchanges. In the light of this, it may be prudent to accept that good emotional health means effective functioning in a given social context which does not contribute to psychological ill-health.

As a society we have always been intrigued by what makes us happy and after a century of examining behaviour, particularly those aspects which are viewed as negative, psychologists are developing the field of Positive Psychology to consider this equally important positive side of the way we are. Given the large amount of time which people spend in the workplace, it makes sense to consider the potential work holds for us to be happy and to enjoy positive emotions.

Positive and negative experiences at work

The world of work is a source of the good, the bad and the indifferent in terms of our personal fulfilment. There are aspects which we like and look forward to, bits we do not and therefore dread, as well as things we had not anticipated we would have to do, but which seem to have taken up all of our time. How often has this happened with the result that you did not do the very thing you had planned for? Our experiences at work have been studied under many headings, including motivation, job satisfaction, accomplishment, stress, burnout, etc. The aim of this section is to examine the components of these observable factors which contribute to our feelings about the workplace. Of course, it would be naive to suggest that these factors exist independently of ourselves, and obviously our view of what is 'hot or not' is influenced by a range of personal variables which are not always consistent. Such personal factors, which include mood, positive or negative outlook on life and personality, are examined in Chapter 3.

In addition, there has been a tendency to overlook how satisfaction with our lives outside of work affects us while we are at work. The distinction between job-specific and context-free experiences of well-being (Warr, 1987, 1999) is useful to a degree, as it encourages a view of what is both inside and out of the workplace. Many occupational studies of the workplace have laboured under the misapprehension that the employee

15

between 9 and 5 is somehow different or separate from the same individual between 5 p.m. and 9 a.m. when the next working day begins. Despite often exhausting data collection, this can mean that a research study fails to highlight a factor which explains high levels of a variable such as psychological strain.

Job satisfaction

Job satisfaction has been defined as a 'pleasurable or positive emotional state resulting from the appraisal of one's job or job experiences' (Locke, 1976). However, there is evidence which suggests that those employees who are generally happier are better at their jobs (Wright and Staw, 1999). There are a number of interpretations of this finding (Judge *et al.*, 2001), which include the possibility of a reciprocal relationship between job satisfaction and performance, once again with perceptions of one influencing the other. This view has echoes within the practice of sports psychology, where the role of a positive mental attitude towards a challenge is seen as crucial in attaining set goals (Weinberg, 1995).

The relationship between job satisfaction and wider satisfaction with life is well-established in the research literature: Tait *et al.* (1989) cite an average correlation of 0.35. Not surprisingly this relationship depends on the degree to which work is seen by the individual as a core component of their life (Steiner and Truxillo, 1989). Tait *et al.*'s (1989) review of four decades'-worth of findings highlights the growing link between work and non-work satisfaction for women as they have increasingly occupied roles in the paid workplace. Of course the direction of the relationship between work and life outside of work is not one-way traffic, as many of us would no doubt testify, and longitudinal research has shown a mutual influence, with life outside of work tending to exert the greater impact on our feelings (Judge and Watanabe, 1993).

The term job satisfaction is an umbrella term for our feelings towards many factors at work. These are likely to include extrinsic features of the job such as pay, the management, work colleagues, job security and the physical surroundings, in addition to intrinsic aspects such as the amount of work, the tools or software, etc. As mentioned above, the impact of any or more of these on job satisfaction can be complex and may be mediated by other factors. Despite higher levels of psychological strain found in UK academic employees than in any other any occupational group, 58 per cent claimed they were at least 'moderately satisfied' with their jobs (Kinman and Jones, 2004). It is possible to attribute this unexpected finding to perceptions of feeling rewarded by intrinsic job factors, for example conducting research and supervision of students: this is consistent with previous findings (e.g. Iaffaldano and Muchinsky, 1985). Yet the dissatisfaction with the extrinsic features of stagnating pay and poor promotion prospects is taking its toll on individual workers: 'No one seems to enjoy their work any more. I used to love teaching – now it is just what I do' (Kinman and Jones, 2004, p. 25). This in turn could affect the performance of students, as research into schoolteachers has previously shown significant associations between teachers' job satisfaction and pupils' academic performance (Ostroff, 1992).

In the same way, the link between job satisfaction and resulting employee behaviour is not always straightforward. One might reasonably expect workers to remain in a job they like, and turnover is certainly lower in such circumstances (George and Jones, 1996), yet this is likely to be moderated by the availability of work in the locality or within the occupational group, and indeed by the competence of the employee (McKenna, 2000). Similarly it is logical to expect absenteeism to increase where job satisfaction is low, yet this inverse relationship is also subject to factors such as family circumstances and relationships inside and out of work (see Stansfeld et al., 1998). For example, the link between the number of episodes of absence from work and job satisfaction is stronger for women than men (Hackett, 1989), possibly indicating the influence of family responsibilities (Warr, 1999).

Employee performance, turnover and absenteeism are official aspects of organizational behaviour. However, there is a range of voluntary behaviours, referred to as 'discretionary', which might be expected of employees and are likely to be linked to levels of job satisfaction. Such activities include voluntary overtime and adaptive behaviours, including participation in training (Birdi et al., 1998). The category of prosocial activities covers those behaviours which relate to being friendly and helpful in the workplace and again is significantly related to overall job satisfaction (McNeely and Meglino, 1994).

Burnout

The other extreme of our experience of emotions can be witnessed in the organization which relies on the trade of feelings between employees and customers to such an extent that its workforce is left emotionally drained. This in turn leads to symptoms of burnout, characterized by emotional exhaustion, the tendency to depersonalize customers and a lack of personal accomplishment (Maslach and Jackson, 1986). The term 'burnout' is most often used in connection with the emotional drain on employees working in the public and human services, where dealing with people, their problems and frustrations is part of the daily routine. For the fresh-faced idealist this is a combination of challenges on which one can thrive: however, after thriving on this daily challenge over a period of time, it is possible to recognize the 'used up' feeling which many such employees experience, despite feeling very committed to the job they do. The social and healthcare professions are perhaps the most researched for this phenomenon of burnout. In these settings, emotional exhaustion can refer to the feeling of not being able to give any more of oneself or one's emotional effort to deal with another human's genuine problems. This is different from the 'I can't be a*sed' approach and should not be mistaken for something similar. To experience emotional exhaustion is to feel psychological and emotional strain through working with others, as though the action of caring for another's predicament is too much effort to invest – almost a feeling of your heart sinking when a new client walks through the door. For some employees this can develop into a hardened attitude towards others, so that feelings of empathy and caring cease to be part of their considerations. In this depersonalizing situation, people appear more like 'objects' (see the case study below). The third symptom of burnout is a feeling of a lack of personal accomplishment, in which the satisfaction with the difference made by one's work is not evident to the employee. In this way a doctor may no longer experience a positive buzz from helping a patient and the sense of enjoyment in doing the work evaporates.

Case Study 1.1	**Depersonalization on a hospital ward**

Maureen was given the title of 'hostess' on the ward where she worked, looking after very ill patients. She had worked there for many years and was very efficient in carrying out her daily tasks of preparing and serving meals and drinks to the patients, which she would embark upon when the numbers of meals were passed to her. In her work, Maureen would find that much of her time was spent listening to patients talking about their problems, ▶

especially those who were not blessed with regular visitors. The toll of working with people, many of whom were close to death, had started to become apparent. 'You cannot imagine', she told me, 'the feeling of relief I get when they tell me that there is one less meal to prepare for lunch. It is a blessing to know that you can save yourself the trouble of making that extra one, because someone has died.' Swallowing hard at this apparently callous disregard, I knew I would not forget my first encounter with depersonalization.

(Based on a real interview with a hospital employee)

Symptoms of strain in the employee

There is a strong tendency for most of us to be able to recognize the symptoms of strain, particularly in other people. This often means we are not adept at doing so when we are suffering these tell-tale signs ourselves! Whilst there is little doubt our experiences of symptoms of strain are individualized, it is a change in some or more of these for the worse which can indicate that our ability to cope is being exceeded by the demands placed upon us. It is possible to divide the symptoms of strain into four categories: cognitive, behavioural, physiological and emotional.

Cognitive symptoms of strain

Cognitive symptoms include those thoughts and ways of thinking which reflect negative beliefs about ourselves, other people or certain situations. Psychologists and counsellors often refer to the little voice in our heads which provides a commentary on what we do as 'self-talk'. For those who talk out loud to themselves, this self-talk can be heard as 'There's just no way I can do this', or more commonly in the example of sports competitors such as national tennis stars, 'Come on!!' Where the self-talk is positive, it means we are adopting a 'can-do' approach, but where this is not the case, the common example of a lack of self-confidence rears its head. Losing one's usual sense of self-belief is as common in the workplace as it is in a sporting context, so that returning to work after a period of absence is like returning to a game situation following a physical injury (except there is unlikely to be a practice session first!). Similarly, for those who are in work, having to face one's manager and colleagues the day after committing a serious error is in effect no different from the experience of a goalkeeper who dropped the ball into an empty net when the team went on to lose the match. Very often the way in which we deal with setbacks, as well as the responses of those around us, can determine our ability to bounce back. A negative change in our personal level of self-confidence is therefore a sign of psychological strain, which can also manifest itself as difficulty in making decisions or a general worry about future performance. A study of hospital doctors' confidence in performing clinical tasks has shown that the workers with significantly higher levels of distress also reported significantly lower levels of confidence in aspects of their work (Williams *et al.*, 1997).

It is not uncommon for an individual's usual level of worry to become focused on certain ideas or events and this may or may not be helped by efforts to reassure them. It is also possible that the individual's focus on things which may not appear important to a colleague can betray anxieties about a much larger problem over which the individual has relatively little control and possibly little insight. The employee who constantly copies emails to all their colleagues about the state of the mirror in the cloakroom may not simply be interested in the company's well-groomed image, but might be indirectly expressing anxiety over the impending move of offices which has not yet been finalized.

Common cognitive signs of strain are a difficulty in concentrating and a tendency to forget. This can be an indicator of overload, where there is already too much information to be processed appropriately by a busy brain, or where the individual has depleted resources with which to deal with the usual incoming signals from the environment. The employee on the floor of the stock exchange is often viewed in awe by outsiders for their ability to hold many pieces of information in their short-term memory and to clinch financial deals as a consequence. In the same way the actions of a parent who is feeding a baby, whilst ensuring that their two-year-old toddler is safely and gainfully occupied, and considering the next action in relation to the state of the laundry basket, is also a feat of juggling tasks. It is likely that in each of these examples, some of the tasks will be prioritized and others will come at the bottom of the list and occasionally be forgotten. However, where the individual starts to mislay, misremember or forget important information, such as the price of a well-known trading commodity, or the need to feed a baby, then this indicates more than a problem with concentration and other cognitive performance. Such errors might be understandable in the context of a severe illness in the family, ongoing relationship problems, threat of redundancy, etc., but nonetheless constitute signs of strain.

Physiological symptoms of strain

What has been termed the 'stress response' is an adaptive reaction to the need for 'fight or flight', which makes sense when viewed as an evolutionary tool to help humans survive. This has served the species well, but our bodies have not adapted to respond in any other way. Therefore on perceiving a threat to ourselves, chemical and physiological activation occurs within the body which is designed to prepare us to undertake a physical response: the adrenalin rush is a necessity when trying to outrun a lion, but will not help us deal any more effectively with disagreement with a colleague or most other types of work difficulty. The repeated activation of this set of bodily adaptations in a way which does not match the real-life danger actually facing the average employee can pose a threat to well-being (Clow, 2001), so it is not surprising that there is a range of physical symptoms of strain which are evident when we are under pressure.

These types of symptoms may be experienced in the short or longer term. Problems with sleeping and related tiredness or even exhaustion are common signs of strain. Many of us will recognize the situation of having thoughts about work or some other problem running through our mind, so that it delays our getting to sleep or means that if we are disturbed at night we find it hard not to start thinking about such issues, and spend the early hours lying there hoping to get to sleep! Psychosomatic symptoms – physical signs of psychological issues – are also common and can include headaches, twinges, muscle trembling (such as a twitching eye), a tendency to sweat, lack of appetite, indigestion, sickness, shortness of breath and even a decrease in sexual interest (Cooper *et al.*, 1988). All of these are consistent with over-activation of the body's 'stress response'. Usually these are short-lived and may only be present over a few days or weeks: it is the chronic presence (over time) of physical symptoms which can lead to health difficulties.

Perhaps the most sinister of the physical impacts of strain in the workplace comes from research into the impact on the unborn children of pregnant working mothers. A Europe-wide study of over 10,000 employed women found that among those working in jobs with a high mental workload, such as busy administrative and clerical jobs, for forty hours each week, 40 per cent gave birth prematurely (Di Renzo, 1998).

The most serious health outcome as a symptom of strain is death. Clearly, to have a word which means 'death from overwork' is evidence of a serious problem in society, yet this is the case in Japan, where *karoshi* means just that. Given the cultural emphasis on the significance of work organizations in the lives of employees, there is considerable pressure on workers to adhere to expectations which in turn can result in serious health consequences. The death of a junior doctor in the UK after working over 120 hours without sleep demonstrates that overwork is a potential danger wherever it occurs. Netterstrom and Juel (1988) studied 2465 Danish bus drivers over a seven-year period and found that workload – as assessed by measuring the intensity of traffic on certain routes – was the factor most strongly associated with heart disease.

Behavioural symptoms of strain

The identification of Type A behaviour (Friedman and Rosenman, 1959) led to the acceptance that a particular style of interacting with others is a precursor of coronary heart disease. Individuals exhibiting Type A behaviour tend to be highly ambitious, impatient, intolerant of others' mistakes, aggressive when faced with frustration and generally lacking in insight into the impact of their behaviour on others (Cooper and Bramwell, 1992). This manner of behaviour has been implicated as a risk factor in coronary heart disease (Rosenman *et al.*, 1964) and ironically it is the same set of behaviours which is frequently reinforced by the working environments inhabited by business executives. As a theory this has some face validity, however, more recent large-scale research has confirmed the role of alcohol intake and smoking in predicting heart disease and found little role for such a set of behaviours (Sanderman, 1998). It may be premature to view Type A behaviour as a myth, but it is possible that this type of interpersonal style is symptomatic of an individual who is striving to gain control over a situation in which they have relatively little power, which in itself is a known predictor of poor health.

Changes in individual behaviour for better or worse can indicate that the employee is experiencing strain in some way. A phenomenon recognized since the decline in job security in many sectors is that of 'presenteeism'. This is where the employee feels that their future will be brighter if they play the macho game of arriving early and staying late at work, so that they can be seen as the person who works hardest: a strategy which is subject to the fallacy that presence at work is a guarantee of higher productivity. In one extreme case a publishing designer whose colleagues were used to seeing him at his desk for long periods without moving, died some days before anybody realized what had happened! Notwithstanding this unfortunate example, there is evidence from national productivity figures which show that employees in the United Kingdom work a longer week on average than counterparts in France and Germany, but this is not necessarily a guarantee of higher productivity. The issue of decreased work performance has been scrutinized in a major US study of 4115 employed people, which projected that on over 130 million working days per year employees' performance was impaired by psychological and emotional strain (Kessler and Frank, 1997).

Absenteeism has been considered a major symptom of employee strain, with stress-related problems ranked second only to musculoskeletal difficulties in the league of causes of absence from work. In the early 1990s, the UK Department of Social Security (1993) reported that 80 million working days were lost each year due to illness related to psychological and emotional strain: now overall sickness absence accounts for 66 million working days at a cost of £3.4 billion in the public sector alone! (CBI, AXA, 2006.) Absenteeism rates have been found to vary between industries, with the average figures in the public services (8.5 days per year) higher than that for the private sector (6 days per year) (CBI/AXA, 2006). The toll of mental health and stress-related problems has also been long recognized in the USA with up to 54 per cent of its absenteeism due to such causes (Elkin and Rosch, 1990).

Another common symptom of behavioural strain is an increased rate of errors in an employee's work, which is also consistent with poorer levels of concentration. Symptoms of tiredness and cognitive overload have been blamed for fatal mistakes on the railways. Of course it is not necessary to be feeling a strong emotion in order to commit an error, but feeling the pressure of a set of demands has been linked to mistakes whilst carrying out everyday tasks (Reason, 1988).

Emotional symptoms of strain

Within our affective well-being lie the emotional symptoms of strain. Affect refers to the presentation of our emotions and as has been described, this can range from the very positive to very negative. Strain obviously invokes the negative and here it is not uncommon for individuals to experience a depressed mood which can be linked to a loss of interest or even feelings of guilt. The exact reasons for an individual experiencing such symptoms are not always clear, and the relationship between causes and consequences can be complex, but the change in an employee's affect (outward emotional appearance) is usually apparent to others. A usually energetic or cheerful individual may be transformed into a person who conveys a gloomy, dejected or tense outlook. Not surprisingly their tolerance of challenging situations may be reduced along with levels of motivation. Difficulty in managing human interactions may be impaired and the individual may withdraw from such situations or display irritation or temper when faced with them.

Whilst this section does not provide an exhaustive list of symptoms of strain, it is designed to outline the range and variety of experiences, both psychological and emotional, which can arise. It is also important to remember that these will vary between individuals and their circumstances.

Emotions and organizational well-being

Organizations are human creations and as such are subject to the experience of emotions. This is not immediately apparent from the plethora of automated answer systems employed by a growing number of customer service organizations, yet behind these systems lie human motivations for growing an organization in a particular way. This may even be guided by a management desire to avoid employee involvement with customers. Following an automated route by which one can enquire about a particular service can occupy many minutes before the increasingly frustrated customer gets to speak to a real human being. Whilst off-putting, this development is not accidental. Human communication costs organizations money and, as an integral part of this, so does human emotion. The cheaper option, as perceived by the chiefs of such organizations, is to provide a series of recorded, emotionless options which answer an enquiry or eventually relay it to a real operator. It is hard to estimate how many potential customers are actually dissuaded from doing business by this impersonal approach. Consequently it has become the major selling point of many small or high street traders that they can actually offer a personal or one-to-one service. The dilemma facing many large customer service organizations is whether to invest in delivering human contact and emotion via their representatives or to avoid this wherever possible. Each carries a cost to the organization and the result has been a compromise: the introduction of scripted interactions which human employees are required to adhere to in their contact with customers. This takes us into the realms of emotional labour, which is scrutinized more closely in Chapter 4.

As we discussed in Chapter 1, burnout and its symptoms are not evident only in the individual, they also register on barometers of organizational well-being. This is because the symptoms, if they are not addressed, can develop into a climate of suboptimal functioning, in which it is accepted by co-workers that 'this is how the job makes us feel'. Gradually it can become the norm for people to express negative emotions about their work and their customers and to perceive things in a negative way. Low morale is often evident in the lack of discretionary activities in which employees engage, i.e. those behaviours which are carried out by workers, but are not enforced by employers. These include voluntary overtime, attendance on training courses and prosocial activity, which can range from simply being friendly to colleagues to making suggestions as to how to improve the workplace (Warr, 1999). Customers and outsiders to organizations who are not as influenced by such negative norms are sensitive to this absence of extra effort among members of the organization. For the receivers of the product or service, low morale can manifest itself in poorer quality, miscommunication and ultimately customer dissatisfaction.

One sinister expression of emotion with which organizations seem unprepared to deal is that of bullying, which is discussed in more detail in Chapters 3 and 6. It is less likely that organizations do not wish to combat bullying; rather they have not developed the strategies for identifying or indeed the tools for dealing with it. The reasons for bullying taking place are manifold and its prevalence is widespread. It constitutes a set of behaviours which are committed in many guises in many workplaces, with as many as 10.5 per cent of employees currently on the receiving end (Hoel, Faragher and Cooper, 2004). It is unclear whether bullying is related to organizational well-being, but there is evidence to suggest that the incidence of unacceptable behaviours is higher in sectors under pressure, such as higher education (Kinman and Jones, 2004).

Staff absenteeism and turnover, whilst dependent on a range of factors respectively including 'sickness culture' (Martocchio, 1994) and the availability of alternative employment, are high profile indicators of poor organizational health. An average correlation of 0.37 between emotional exhaustion and intention to leave one's job indicates the strength of the relationship between emotions and costs to workplace organizations (Lee and Ashforth, 1996). Lower productivity is another financial outcome, but this can be eclipsed for sheer drama by the impact of planned and intentional acts of negative behaviour. Industrial action is a clear way of registering discontent with a workplace situation, but sabotage is a clear example of a display of emotion on the part of the employees. The tale of the wordsmith whose job was to insert the greetings on sweet sticks of seaside rock lives long in the memory not only for its demonstration of innovation, but also for the clarity of the message from the employee about their feelings for the organization. At least this is the supposition, as it would be hard to imagine that the insertion of 'f*** off' was really a genuine invitation to the would-be purchaser of the rock! Either way, this is surely more imaginative than what seems to have become the ritual abuse of photocopiers around the time of the holiday season!

This emphasis on the negative should not detract from the widespread feelings of positive work attitudes abroad in many organizations. For example a whistle-stop tour of well-established UK establishments reveals a pattern likely to be repeated elsewhere in the world. For example, the *Sunday Times* newspaper's annual review of the top 100 UK companies to work for is compiled using workers' ratings of their employers' organizations. Not surprisingly many of these have featured high levels of satisfaction with supportive management initiatives which demonstrate a level of caring not always associated with the workplace. The Manchester-based and family-owned Timpsons has previously featured in the top 20. Despite there being over 300 outlets across the UK, staff reported that their views counted and that they felt valued – it is not surprising that autonomy is a major feature of the business, which places pricing initiatives and above all trust in local managers (*Sunday Times*, 2001). One cannot expect a successful organization to be shining in all its aspects, but when you are impressed as a first-time customer by the friendliness, humour and capability of the staff, this is as handy a guide to the emotional pulse of an organization as the negativity witnessed elsewhere in the world of organizations. How much an organization allows its real life to be visible to the outside world influences outsiders' judgements about emotional health. The House of Commons in the UK Parliament has long had a 'strangers' gallery' from which members of the public can exercise a democratic right to observe the workings of parliament and this has been supplemented by television coverage in recent years. However, it is a brave organization – or one bound by the law – which is keen to show its inner workings. In this way the smaller high street shops have an opportunity to impress customers, whereas the larger organizations run the risk of presenting a faceless side to the world by relying too heavily on recorded messages to capture customers. One could say that emotions can be used as the currency which helps to promote business, yet the gradual erosion in the UK of community-based post offices, banks and other shops deprives the ordinary customer of the opportunity to take emotional soundings from their chosen supplier. For the public-serving organization, as we have seen, this can come as a mixed blessing.

Summary of the chapter

This chapter has aimed to outline the meanings of psychological and emotional well-being and has hopefully provided you with a range of terms and examples which are helpful in discussing these concepts further. Some or many of the key words may be familiar to you and to help you understand them further relevant models of psychological health by Warr and Selye, and of emotional well-being by Reeve and Goleman, have been described. The contrasting experiences of job satisfaction and burnout have been explored and a whole range of cognitive, physiological, behavioural and emotional symptoms of strain have been outlined. Issues which may be used to assess the health of the organization, as well as the individual, have also been covered.

Key terms	
psychological health	burnout
emotional health	cognitive
eustress	physiological and behavioural
stress	symptoms of strain
job satisfaction	discretionary behaviours

Questions and answers

1 *What does surviving the workplace mean to you?* If you are not sure of an answer to this, we hope this book will prompt you to ask this

question in many different ways and in the process identify your priorities in your dealings with the workplace.

2 *What are the key components of mental health?* Based on Warr's model of mental health, these might include: affective well-being (in terms of positive emotions), autonomy (control), aspiration (to get involved with one's environment), competence (being able to do one's best and accomplish things) and integrated functioning (putting it all together).

3 *What do we mean by the terms used to describe the experiences of psychological health: eustress, stress and distress?* Eustress – the positive buzz obtained from meeting deadlines or fulfilling expectations under pressure, e.g. on the trading floor of the stock exchange.

Stress – the everyday hassle which is more helpfully referred to as stressors (sources of pressure) and strain (outcomes of pressure), where our capacity to cope with the demands made upon us outweighs the ability to deal effectively with these demands, e.g. getting to a meeting by 9 a.m., after dropping the children at school and preparing a presentation for the meeting, the success of which depends on the technology working OK and the traffic being kind to us!

Distress – the presence of a high level of symptoms of poor psychological health, possibly in response to an acute trauma or longer-standing set of stressors, e.g. an individual suffers depressive ideas and symptoms of anxiety after being told unexpectedly that they are to be made redundant. Alternatively, an employee is the victim of bullying in the workplace and feels so panicky when they encounter the aggressor that they have to take time off.

4 *What kind of symptoms might we associate with the experience of these types of strain: cognitive, physiological and behavioural?* Cognitive symptoms of strain include: difficulty making decisions, lacking confidence in one's suggestions, focusing on objectively unimportant details, poor concentration, forgetting important facts.

Physiological symptoms of strain include: problems in sleeping, persistent tiredness, lack of appetite, feeling sick, involuntary muscle twitching, headaches, raised blood pressure.

Behavioural symptoms of strain include: impatience, uncharacteristic irritability with colleagues, customers or family, presenteeism, increased intake of alcohol and/or nicotine, withdrawal from social contact, absence from work.

5 *How might we describe the three components of Maslach's syndrome of burnout?*

    a. Emotional exhaustion – a sense of being overwhelmed and feeling that you have no more energy to devote to dealing with others and their problems

    b. Depersonalization – loss of feelings for those with whom one is working, so that they are no longer perceived as individuals or even as fellow humans

    c. Lack of personal accomplishment – feeling that the job is no longer rewarding or fulfilling, which may lead to questioning whether it is even worth doing.

Suggested further reading

For a gentle introduction to the kind of events at work which might cause some of the symptoms highlighted in this chapter, *Who Moved my Cheese* by Spencer Johnson has gained both popularity and detractors: however, it is the kind of brief book which can get you thinking about what is worth fighting for in the workplace. For those who are ready to confront the ups and downs of what psychological and emotional well-being can mean, then Christina Maslach's books, *Burnout: The Cost of Caring* and Maslach and Leiter's *The Truth About Burnout* as well as Peter Warr's *Work, Happiness and Unhappiness* (2007), produce some interesting contrasts. Details of these publications are contained in the reading list for this chapter which appears at the end of this book.

2 Prevalence and significance of emotional and psychological health problems

Psychological health in the general and working populations

At some point in our lives, one in three of us will experience some form of mental health problem (Royal College of Psychiatrists, 1995). Psychological health problems comprise the largest group of health difficulties in the UK, which means that 'in any one week, 18% of women and 11% of men have significant psychiatric symptoms' (Royal College of Psychiatrists, 1995). Indeed these figures have changed little in recent years, although notably the proportion receiving treatment has actually doubled (Office of Population Census and Surveys [OPCS], 2002). The British Household Panel Survey, which routinely collects data on psychological health from a cohort of over 5000 adults resident in the UK, has found that the proportions experiencing poorer health are higher for parents than those without children and higher still for lone parents (OPCS, 1995). The prevalence of such difficulties is highest among the unemployed (23 per cent), compared to 10 per cent among those working full-time and 14 per cent of those working part-time (OPCS, 1995). Within each of these groups, the proportion of women is double that for men. Data collection based on socio-economic status show that workers in unskilled manual jobs are at much higher risk from poor psychological health than employees in other occupational categories, with the lowest risk in professional and employers and managerial groups (OPCS, 1995).

Case Study 2.1	**Where do the figures come from?**

It is important to consider how such figures are derived. The measures which are used are examined in more detail in Chapter 9, but for the findings presented in this section, it is useful to know that the British Household Panel Survey uses the Clinical Interview Schedule (CIS-Revised) (Lewis *et al.*, 1992). The responses to the CIS-R are rated on subscales which are totalled and a score above a certain threshold is recognized as demonstrating the presence of a psychological disorder. Using other questions from the interview it is possible to apply diagnostic criteria to the symptoms described. Due to the cost-intensive nature of gathering interview data, questionnaire measures are also widely utilized. The General Health Questionnaire is one of the most widely used and therefore this permits some comparability between studies. Once again a cut-off score is identified, above which a score is taken as indicative of high levels of psychological strain. For the GHQ 12 item version a cut-off of 3/4 is commonly taken to mean that a score of 4 or more indicates poor psychological health. Methodological issues related to this approach are covered in Chapter 9.

Using the approaches and measures highlighted in the case study, work carried out in specified occupational or organizational groups reveals a troubled picture for public sector workers, particularly in professional roles (see Table 2.1). Whilst 20.5 per cent of the general population report high levels of symptoms of strain, the figures are comparably higher among employees in teaching, health and social work.

The percentage of academic and academic-related staff in UK higher education institutions reporting poor psychological health is the highest (50 per cent) and is only 3 per cent less than the figure produced by an initial nationwide survey in 1998 (Kinman and Jones, 2004). However, the raised levels of strain which occur in comparable occupational groups, such as 43 per cent of one university's employees in Australia (Winefield *et al.*, 2003) and 57.2 per cent civil servants in local government in Japan (Nadaoka *et al.*, 1997) show that this is a global rather than national pattern. These raised levels of strain may well relate to changing expectations and increasing demands on employees in the public sector and a similar pattern was observed among healthcare staff following reforms to the UK

Table 2.1 **Prevalence of high levels of psychological strain among occupational samples in the UK, as measured using the General Health Questionnaire (GHQ)**

Authors	Occupational group	Sample size	GHQ version and cut-off score	Percentage of GHQ high scorers
British Household Panel Survey (2004)	General population	5000	GHQ-12 3/4	20.5
Wall et al. (1997)	Healthcare workers	11637	GHQ-12 3/4	26.8
Jones and Kinman (2004)	University lecturers	1108	GHQ-12 2/3	50
Weinberg and Cooper (2003)	Members of Parliament (post election)	66	GHQ-12 3/4	24.1–29.9
Huxley et al. (2005)	Social workers (in mental health)	237	GHQ-12 3/4	47
Butterworth et al. (1998)	Nurses	586	GHQ-28 4/5	28–41
Stansfeld et al. (1995)	Civil servants	10314	GHQ-30 4/5	21.6–24.8

National Health Service in the early 1990s. Cooper and Sutherland (1992) found raised symptom levels among general practitioners following the introduction of the fund-holding budgets. Weinberg and Cooper (2003) found that political party candidates showed raised levels of strain several months after their successful election as MPs, suggesting the job had a long-term impact on individual well-being.

It is possible to divide the abstract map of employee well-being in a number of ways, so that within the occupational groups studied to date, it is possible to highlight further trends which suggest the vulnerability of certain sections of the workforce, although this is not to say there are others which do not deserve scrutiny! Wall et al.'s (1997) survey of over 11,000 NHS staff suggested gender differences in its findings with women managers (41 per cent) and women doctors (36 per cent) registering the highest proportions of individuals in poor psychological health, although figures within nursing were comparable for men and women (30 per cent and 29 per cent respectively). Within the medical occupational group, 48 per cent of general practitioners (Caplan, 1994)

and 46 per cent of child psychiatrists (Littlewood *et al.*, 2003) constituted the highest proportions experiencing high levels of strain. Studies
of other subgroups of the medical profession have consistently found
levels in excess of the rest of the general population. Comparing occupational group samples between urban-based and more suburban hospitals
has also produced different rates among healthcare workers, e.g. 40 per
cent (Weinberg and Creed, 2000) vs 26.8 per cent (Wall *et al.*, 1997)
and outside of medicine the levels of strain between teams of social
workers exposed to different organizational cultures also differ.

Suicide is likely to be related to depression and therefore a comparison of the rates between occupational groups is sometimes considered
as an indicator of pressure. This should not be regarded as a straightforward comparison given the complexity of contributory factors. Among
occupational groups, suicide rates are higher among doctors than
among the general population (Lindeman *et al.*, 1996) and access to the
means of committing suicide has been found to contribute to the raised
number of incidences among farmers (Howton *et al.*, 1998).

Emotional challenges for occupational groups

This section highlights some of the major challenges facing various
groupings within the workforce. These challenges are not exclusive to
the groups identified, but are likely to be those linked to issues of strain.

Starting the day

> Begin each day by telling yourself: Today I shall be meeting with interfer-
> ence, ingratitude, insolence, disloyalty, ill-will and selfishness – all of them
> due to the offenders' ignorance of what is good or evil.
> *Emperor Marcus Aurelius* – Meditation (*Staniforth, 1964*)

When was the last time you woke up on a working day and leapt from
bed in anticipation of a fruitful and rewarding experience at your job
(whether paid or unpaid)? Hopefully it wasn't long ago, but if it is hard
to remember then this is likely to be an emotional challenge which is
shared with many other workers. In a job which is busy and carries
responsibility (and most seem to), it is not hard to feel that living has
been replaced by working, or thinking about working. In fact some

measures of psychological strain include the item 'Do you feel as though you do not want to get up in the morning?' The temptation to change to a job which can be put to the back of your mind until the next day is often tempered by the difficulty in actually changing to that job, or by other factors such as the rate of pay, career prospects or the travel involved. Either way the prospect of a busy day ahead has been shown to register not only at an emotional level, but also biologically. Around the time of waking, cortisol levels within the body naturally increase. This increase is greater for employees with high workloads after waking on work days compared to non-work days, which may reflect the body gearing itself up to face the challenges of an overloaded day (Schlotz *et al.*, 2002). For many the situation is not always helped by the journey to work, which has many pitfalls of its own whether related to trains, traffic jams, parking or a lack of consideration to cyclists or pedestrians.

Whatever one's feelings about work before getting there, most of the emotional challenges lie in wait. The timing of these may differ depending on the use of home-working, or communication by mobile phones and portable computers, but whenever the working day starts there is an expectation that the employee is at the call of the employer. A certain level of prescription of what the job will entail is important for the sake of clarity and for appropriate outcomes, but the process by which these are communicated is a focus for emotional effort on the parts of both employer and employee. The level of management support and the way in which this is delivered are key issues in the workplace. Because each employee can only have a certain level of control over their working environment, they turn to their supervisor or line manager to take overall responsibility. This may not always be a fair expectation by the employee, but, remembering that control is important for individual well-being, it means that the stakes on the actions of the line manager are often high. In fact the availability of support from a line manager has been shown to be a major predictor of psychological health (e.g. Weinberg and Creed, 2000).

Case Study 2.2	**Would you prefer to manage or be managed?**
	Interpersonal styles will inevitably differ between everyone, but in daily communications a manager needs to convey trust and a caring attitude, that they value the contribution of the worker, are willing to listen to ideas and concerns and can demonstrate a capacity ▶

to act to improve situations, collaborating where appropriate and ultimately ensuring that the group is able to achieve its goals as part of the wider organization. All of this must be done whilst avoiding language which may be perceived as inflammatory or acts which may be taken as aggressive, offensive or ineffectual and in working environments which are constantly changing and subject to external economic and political considerations.

From the viewpoint of the cynical employee being managed, it is plain that the only reason a manager wishes to gain favour with you is in order to get you to take on extra work when you already have enough to do. After all, the manager is usually paid more and they are not likely to offer more pay for the extra you are being asked to do. Despite their attempts to talk to you rather than at you for a change, this is not sufficient to get you to agree. On the other hand you do need to finish early one night this week and you are hoping to be sent on the training course which will help with your own promotion. So, 'Yes, I'll do this extra work if you want me to'!

The result of this interaction is a sort of emotional trading, in which the manager invests emotional effort into the interaction and the employee, whilst not convinced about the manager's genuineness, but feels that the deal is fair given their own agenda.

Organizational culture shifts

Whilst the manager represents the human face of the organization's goals, bartering and trading emotional justice with the employee, the employee in turn is expected to perform in a similar way with the customer. Nowhere is this more evident than in those organizations whose *raison d'être* is dealing with the public. Within the UK public sector, a huge shift in the ethos of all the relevant health, social, educational, tax, civil and police services took place following the NHS and Community Care Acts of 1990. The philosophy of a caring public-orientation was reprioritized in line with prevalent commercial approaches of the time, such that added value and financial accountability were hailed as paramount. For employees who had served and those who had been trained to serve the public in their chosen professions or occupations, the new culture did not fit easily with their knowledge of what served the public best. Time spent with the patient, client or pupil was forcefully eroded in favour of administrative targets which served political agendas rather than those immediately relevant to the individual customers. Relatively few studies have scrutinized the shift in the use of public sector employees' time since the community care reforms became law in the UK in 1993: however, one study of social workers has shown that the replacement of traditional social work with more administratively focused care management has resulted in less than one quarter of workers' time being spent with the users of the service (Weinberg *et al.*, 2003). This is echoed in the mixed feelings of carers towards the statutory health and social services, whose needs have been under-prioritized until relatively recently (Weinberg and Huxley, 2000). Not surprisingly the new emphasis on administration has provoked an emotional reaction in a range of public sector organizations which in the UK have shortages of those wishing to enter them as well as large numbers planning to leave their posts. These are in the order of 25 per cent in both nursing (Scott, 2002) and social work (Huxley *et al.*, 2005).

It is perhaps not surprising that research into public sector organizations has shown much higher rates of psychological and emotional strain and distress than in other sections of the working population. The impact of negative change can be to undermine employees' expectations of what their work involves, as well as their feelings of job security. During the last decade the higher education sector has consistently registered some of the highest and fastest rising levels of strain among its academic staff in a number of countries, including the UK (Kinman and Jones, 2004) and Australia (Gillespie *et al.*, 2001). Kinman and Jones (2004) found that almost half of their sample of 1100 university staff had seriously considered leaving and 69 per cent found their job 'stressful'. Among the major changes in higher education has been the renewed emphasis on carrying out both teaching and research roles which has resulted in increased workloads and pressures at the interface between home and work. Over one-third of UK academic staff report working in excess of the 48-hour weekly limit set by the European Union's Working Time Directive (Kinman and Jones, 2004).

The home–work interface

The home–work interface, where the boundaries between work and home meet, has received considerable attention in recent years and the impact that each of these domains has on the employee has led to work–life balance initiatives as well as further research (see Chapter 8). This is not unreasonable when one considers that most employees do not undergo a dramatic transformation on leaving work, or immediately prior to arriving, and therefore are likely to carry with them any unresolved issues from life outside of work. However, the direction of the impact can be two-way, i.e. from work-to-family or family-to-work, and it is worth considering each in turn. Either way there is considerable evidence to show that difficulties in either the domain of work or family life can spill over and cause strain in the other area (Piotrkowski, 1978). One disadvantage with the research so far has been its tendency to focus on 'nuclear' families (Barling and Sorenson, 1997), thus failing to represent the variety of family structures in society.

There will be occasions when the emotional effort to manage one's feelings about events in one's home life is considerable and this is likely to be challenging to the individual in a workplace where there is limited access to social support. On the other hand, a beneficial impact of being at work and having a different focus for one's emotions is also possible and can even serve a therapeutic function. At one time there was an inclination for people with mild depression to be automatically given leave from work, but counter-arguments have been presented given the potential of work to provide structure and meaning, as well as to ensure a positive outcome in the longer term (Royal College of Psychiatrists, 1995).

Life outside of work contains many aspects including health, relationships with partner and/or children, finances, housing and education, which naturally means that events or difficulties in these areas will carry emotional consequences for the individual. Brown and Harris's (1978) seminal work on factors likely to contribute to poor psychological health found that individuals experiencing a severe event or difficulty such as a marital break-up, financial hardship, dangerous housing or life-threatening illness in the family were much more likely to go on to experience an episode of depression. Not surprisingly studies of working samples have found significantly more stressors for an individual both inside and out of the workplace in the year prior to recognition of an anxiety and/or depressive disorder (Weinberg and Creed, 2000; Phelan *et al.*, 1991). Of the participants in a work-based counselling programme in the UK post office, 25 per cent reported that the source of their emotional strain was actually due to factors outside of work, yet a workplace employee assistance programme subsequently helped to improve their well-being and absenteeism from work decreased (Cooper and Sadri, 1991).

The spillover of workplace demands into home life are also commonplace. These draw upon the amount of time workers are available to their families, physically as well as emotionally. The events of a working day or shift can continue to play on our minds after we have left the workplace and may well mean that we are emotionally drained or distracted and not able to pay attention to the demands of family or friends. The increase in working from home, perhaps on the computer as a teleworker, is seen by many as a way in which both aspects of life can be harmoniously combined: the reality is one which offers some flexibility, but also demands self-discipline and the ability to shut off from family life at given points in the day. This is in addition to the capacity to deal with the frustration of technical computer problems and a feeling of distance from events in the main workplace. For the majority who still travel to work, there is the possibility of behaviours which are expected at work, but are not appropriate in non-work settings, becoming habitual and difficult to shake off. In this way the manager who has felt obliged to develop a forceful interpersonal style in dealing with colleagues, may well find that their partner and/or children do not respond kindly to be treated in a similar way!

Conflict between work and family roles can therefore mean conflict in terms of time, e.g. whether one is able to spend time cooking with the family, helping with homework, doing housework, fulfilling social engagements etc., and also in terms of the personal emotional resources and social support from others needed to deal with the demands from work and non-work sources. The success with which one can manage these demands depends also on our ability to assess role overload, where we are able to realize that we are taking on too much. However, realizing this and having the choice and control to be able to address it is often another matter, which again draws on our emotional energy levels, helping us to make sense of it all or fail to cope adequately.

Bullying at work

The act of bullying has been variously labelled and defined and is something that many people come across at some point in their lives (see Chapter 6). Hoel, Faragher and Cooper (2004) define bullying as where

> one or several individuals persistently over a period of time perceive them-
> selves to be on the receiving end of negative actions from one or several
> persons, in a situation where the target of bullying has difficulty in defend-
> ing him or herself against these actions.

Whilst it is referred to as bullying in the UK and Ireland, it is referred to as 'mobbing' in Germany and Scandinavia and 'workplace harassment' in the US and Canada.

A phenomenon widely recognized among children in the school playground, this is something which has only comparatively recently been highlighted in the workplace. Yet the potential for bullying activities exists in most social situations. A national UK survey of over 5288 people across many industries found that 10.5 per cent were currently bullied, and that overall one-quarter had been bullied in the previous five years (Hoel *et al.*, 2001). Together with the proportion of employees who had witnessed acts of bullying, almost half of the sample had been affected by this type of behaviour, which was reported as most prevalent in the prison, postal and teaching occupations, yet has been found across most jobs. Some studies report that bullying affects men and women employees equally, although women perpetrators tend to be co-workers and the males are likely to be either co-workers or supervisors (Vartia and Hyyti, 2002).

At an emotional level the potential damage to individuals is huge, often resulting in a range of responses not all of which make sense to the victim: hurt, confrontation, apathy in bystanders and, at worst, suicide. Yet the acceptable limits of behaviour in the workplace are now more clearly defined by the law than previously. Despite this, it is hard to legislate against the emotional abuse which goes on out of the sight of others. Employees on the receiving end may find it hard to report because of what they perceive to be management collusion or apathy, or a threat to their own career progression. In response to this and the Disability Discrimination Act, more than one attempt has been made to introduce the Dignity at Work Bill into Parliament, its aim being to protect employees from harassment and bullying. It is now widespread practice for organizations to at least have a policy which means there is a system which the employee and the organization can use to eradicate unacceptable behaviour from the workplace.

Expressing the strong emotion which employees naturally feel is often an important part of being able to deal with the emotional challenge of bullying. Sources of social support are obviously vital to the employee in this situation, but what is most needed is a direct solution by the organization. This may be done by confronting it at the organization level and/or via a union, or even through the act of 'whistle-blowing'. This is where a concerned employee will report an issue to the world outside of the organization, such as the local media, or an MP, or to external regulatory bodies. Partially in response to this a charity, Public Concern at Work, was established in the early 1990s and has recorded a doubling in the cases reported to it between 1998 and 2002 from 230 to 561. In the early days of whistle-blowing, an employee would often find themselves ostracized and bullied, but this has begun to change as massive financial scandals in the US, involving corporate giants Enron and WorldCom, have elevated the status of those who tried to do the right thing. *Time* magazine even dubbed 2003 'the Year of the Whistle-blower'. Protection for those standing up to be counted is enshrined in the Public Interest Disclosure Act and from 2003 new rules in the UK require all listed companies to introduce effective whistle-blowing schemes which are monitored by a financial regulatory organization.

Discrimination

Acts of discrimination are also evident in the workplace and can take on as wide a range as there are expressions of human behaviour. The motivation for discrimination is hypothesized in many texts on prejudice, but its targets can be drawn from anywhere in the workplace. What one hears justified in the name of a 'personality clash' may represent discrimination against an individual, whilst the phrase 'the glass ceiling' describes a systematic approach to denying members of whole demographic groups the opportunities to work or to progress in the world of work. In asking undergraduate students what a prospective job interviewee will do on entering an interview room, it is instructive to learn that most automatically expect the candidate to 'walk in', discounting wheelchair users. Whilst the equality of expectations in the workplace is enshrined in the law, it is often sadly lacking in the reality of organizational cultures. In addition there are varying degrees of subtlety with which discrimination is expressed (see the case study on p. 42).

Those on the receiving end of discrimination may find that it is due to prejudice towards their gender, ethnicity, religion, sexuality, age-group or disability. The term 'glass ceiling' (Davidson and Cooper, 1992) describes the invisible layer within an organization which prevents people from a particular group gaining access or promotion to the higher echelons of management. This can also extend to the creation of other outgroups within the workforce which also have little bearing on the job itself, such as those related to parental status, occupational background, level of qualification or even affiliation to a football team! It was an accepted maxim in one large manufacturing company that entrance to the management board would only be possible if the candidate was known to support a certain football club. Where this type of behaviour appears to be accepted by the organization – because it remains unchallenged or apparently unstoppable – it is deemed to be institutionalized discrimination.

For the individual employee this raises a raft of emotional challenges. 'How can you go into work, knowing that you are being treated in this way?' one colleague asks another who is experiencing discrimination. The key is to know whether one is going to challenge the situation, or to find ways around it, or to move on to more accepting surroundings. When Britain's first black police chief constable, Mike Fuller, was appointed in 2004, he was keen to stress that he had overcome any difficulties which may have been related to racism and that his promotion should be a signal to people from all ethnic groups. Within higher education, where one might expect equality of opportunity, reports have continued to show that women employees earn on average 80 per cent of the earnings of male colleagues performing the same job roles, and that members of minority ethnic groups are under-represented and underpaid in senior roles compared to the white majority (*Guardian*, 2004).

The pay differential which sees members of demographic groups paid systematically less than their counterparts is particularly pronounced between genders, where for example in the UK male pay averages around 19 per cent higher than for women (Arulampalam *et al.*, 2005–6). This gap is greater in the private sector where woman are paid on average 45 per cent less than their male colleagues (*Guardian*, 2005) and this discrepancy is further accentuated at the higher end of the pay scales. This contrasts with an average gender pay differential of 12 per cent in Denmark and 23 per cent in Finland, whereas in Austria the gap is widest at the lowest end of the wages spectrum – an example of the 'sticky floor' phenomenon, in which employees find it hard to move away from the bottom of the pay scale (Arulampalam *et al.*, 2005–6). The role of a financial management consultant played by Whoopi Goldberg in the film *The Associate* illustrates the desperate lengths taken to overcome such discrimination. Only by inventing a white male partner for the firm she has founded and which has produced ingeniously successful ideas does she find that doors open and clients arrive where previously there were none. When clients insist on meeting the male partner she has to invent and wear a disguise to play the role of the white, middle-aged businessman. Only when her new persona is accepted into an all-male businessmen's club does she reveal to the discriminators the reality and foolishness of their 'exclusive' approach to commerce. George Eliot was one of many real-life fiction writers who adopted this tactic and is evidence that emotional survival strategies can range from altering one's name to 'fit in', to trying hard to be twice as good as those in the favoured ingroup.

Case Study 2.3	**What can a manager advise in dealing with the cutting edge of prejudice?**

'I hate your country', she said, glaring intently. 'I have been here five years and I have realized that it is still stuck in Victorian times. I speak perfect English and yet I am treated as an outsider, because of my foreign accent. I keep applying for jobs, but they don't even invite me for interview, despite my years of experience.' As this was the first time they had met, the manager wondered if the right thing to do was apologize for 'his' country, or the behaviour of 'his' people. It was obvious that apologizing would be inadequate and yet he did feel responsible in some way. People do exhibit prejudice, whether deliberately or not, and rightly the behaviour leads to justified cries for help and of anguish. A colleague had told the manager of the high-ranking position he had held in his own country, yet he could not seem to achieve anything like that level of responsibility here in Britain in the same type of work, despite his skills and clear ability. The temptation was for his colleague to try and blend in as best as possible by behaving in the way the majority do, laughing in all the right places and by listening intently. But ▶

it is hard to carry on with this sort of behavioural spin, when you know that this is a pretence in the face of real discrimination. The manager concluded that the least he could do for the individual was to offer some advice and emotional sanctuary, someone who they could talk to in an emotionally safe environment. Outside of that he vowed wherever possible try to influence management to act in a way which tackles the root cause of discrimination. The key to this was to use the desired legal-sounding buzz-words in management meetings, like 'equality and diversity', or 'pay differential' and to refer to the latest guidance from the Health and Safety Executive or the Department of Trade and Industry. In this way he realized that if he could not get people to think fairly, it might be possible to get them to behave fairly.

Working conditions

It would seem that ever since the proposal of a ten-hour working day at the Manchester Quarter Sessions in 1784 (Federation of European Employers, 2005a), the United Kingdom has built a reputation for working the longest average working week in Europe. However, the adoption of a more Americanized approach to working times by some of its European partners, including newer European Union members, means that the average UK working week of 44.8 hours is now only 1.1 hours higher than the EU average (Federation of European Employers, 2005b). Given that this seems not to guarantee any higher productivity for the population – as suggested by the phenomenon of presenteeism (see Chapter 1) – the British Prime Minister has called for the country to work 'smarter' rather than harder. The longer than average working week may be due to the higher percentage of UK employees who work more than 48 hours per week. The introduction of the European Working Time Directive gave employees the right to refuse to work more than this, which may have played a part in a gradual decrease in the UK's average working week. However, 22 per cent of UK employees are working more than 45 hours per week, which is high by EU standards, although lower than the USA and Japan (Chartered Institute of Personnel and Development, 2006). An opt-out clause in the Working Time Directive meant that the UK could permit individuals to agree with their employer to work more than this legal limit: in 2003/4 the Department of Trade and Industry took action to decrease the number of exempted occupations by extending the Directive to more groups within transport and offshore industries, as well as to junior doctors. However, this allows for the averaging of working hours over a period of time, which means that employees can find themselves working more than 48 hours in a specified number of weeks. It is envisaged that the guidance will come fully into force in 2009.

The nature of work and its practice has changed dramatically with the spread of the information superhighway and the boom in call centres. Call centres have attracted considerable negative press for representing the new Taylorism. When Freddie Winslow Taylor carried out time and motion studies in Henry Ford's car assembly plants one hundred years ago, it heralded the introduction of job specialization designed to improve productivity and output for the organization: however, this also meant a lack of control as well as deskilling for the individual worker. This has found new relevance in the type of work carried out in modern-day call centres where – just as on the production line – the work is divided into component parts and operatives are required to follow conversation scripts, with little variety or control over their work tasks (Zapf et al., 2003). The challenges of call centres are covered in more detail in Chapter 5.

As work and family life change in their shape and expectations, the great emotional challenges are likely to be faced by part-time workers, those on low pay and those enduring obstacles or abuse in getting into or staying in the world of work. Within the human services, which include much of the public sector, the introduction of performance-related pay is likely to reinforce the uncertainty which is characteristic of the massive and apparently continuous changes. Given the pressure on organizations, the strategies we develop to help us survive the unrelenting environment of work are coming to be seen as those which are likelier to guarantee our long-term well-being. However, the next section serves as a reminder that where organizations fail, the law can act as a safeguard.

The legal and moral implications

It is essential that we ask the question 'Why is it important to study psychological and emotional well-being at work?' The answer has four aspects to it: employee health, organizational financial success, legal rulings and a moral imperative.

It is the last of these that gets the least coverage as the ethics of work are often overtaken by events: however, the advent of Fair Trade organizations and political acts which have written off the debts of economically developing nations suggest that where there is a will, real ethical change can be effected. The UK Labour Government elected in 1997 committed itself to ensuring that everyone who was eligible to work could take up this opportunity in some way. By signing up to the European Working Time Directive, introducing the minimum wage and increasing parental rights in relation to the workplace, among other legislation, the government has attempted to increase the rights of the individual worker. Bodies such as the Confederation of British Industry which represent UK business interests tend to oppose this level of intervention by government, but this also begs the question: whose responsibility is it to ensure the emotional and psychological welfare of employees? The answer to this is not so clear-cut. One could reasonably expect the employer to follow the law to ensure that they fulfil their 'duty of care' to maintain a safe system of work, whilst employees tend to be aware they need to exercise their rights in the best interests of their health. This is easier said than done when an individual worker is facing a workload which they consider unreasonable, but their employer does not.

Compensation for employees experiencing psychological ill-health due to work is not a recent phenomenon. At the start of the twentieth century, a coal miner (Eaves *v* Blaenclydach Colliery Company Ltd, 1909) who had suffered physical injury to his foot also successfully claimed compensation for the period in which he did not believe himself able to work, despite his injury having healed. However, the last fifteen years have seen rising numbers of legal claims brought by employees for stress-related illness caused by work. The Management of Health and Safety at Work Regulations (1992) require that all employers carry out assessments of their workplace to ensure that risks to mental and physical health are minimized. Not surprisingly this has produced a range of legal outcomes, the first of which was the landmark ruling in Walker *v* Northumberland County Council (1995), brought by a social worker who was responsible for dealing with a high number of child abuse cases. Following his second nervous breakdown, when Northumberland CC would already have been aware of John Walker's previous history of mental health problems, it was demonstrated that this should have been foreseen and his breakdown was likely to have been related to his high caseload and the emotional demands it placed upon him. The result, after an appeal by Northumberland CC, was that John Walker received £175,000 in compensation. This case highlighted the need for the employer to recognize the actual condition of their employee and therefore to exercise an increased duty of care where stress at work might adversely affect the individual.

The key factor in bringing a successful legal action in the UK has been the ability to show that the employer has neglected their duty of care. A number of large pay-outs have followed, but many other cases have failed to demonstrate the employers' neglect. Since the millennium, a teacher has been awarded £254,362 after two nervous breakdowns caused by her employer's failure to address causes of psychological strain, including a high proportion of pupils with special needs in her class. A travellers' site manager received £203,432 following a lack of practical and emotional support from his employers in dealing with serious and personally threatening difficulties in carrying out his job. Other large settlements have been awarded to victims of bullying in jobs ranging from housing benefit offices to the ambulance service, as well as to employees, for example in the police force, who were not provided with support by their organization following emotionally challenging events or cases.

The courts became increasingly wary of ruling in favour of employees, where it appeared that they might be awarding compensation to individuals who were suffering from doing the job because of the nature of the work involved. Previously awards had been made to a junior doctor (Johnstone *v* Bloomsbury Health Authority, 1991) who became depressed as a result of the long hours demanded by his contract. Similar cases led to the issuing of guidance by the Court of Appeal in 2002 (*Daily Telegraph*, 2002) which tightened the rules on compensation:

- That an employer will not be in breach of the duty of care where they permit an employee to continue in a stressful job, if the alternative is to demote or dismiss that employee
- That the duty of the employer to take action can be triggered where it is readily apparent that action needs to be taken
- That the employer is in breach of the duty of care only if he/she fails to take reasonable steps to prevent harm, taking into account the nature of the risks being faced by employees

- That a breach in the duty of care, not simply occupational stress, needs to be demonstrated for an employer to be liable
- That no occupations should be regarded as intrinsically dangerous to mental health
- That an employer offering a confidential counselling advice service with access to treatment is unlikely to be found in breach of the duty of care.

This guidance has shifted the responsibility for employees' psychological health firmly towards the individual, who could be expected by employers and the law to withstand the pressures of the job unless they had made it known they had a particular problem. Consequently the courts rejected on appeal a claim for compensation from one teacher who left her job with depression, because her workload was deemed to be no greater than others doing a similar job. Another case brought by a teacher was also lost at appeal, because the individual had not informed the school about his psychological symptoms until he became severely ill. Whilst on the one hand the law has taken steps to reduce compensation awards, the Disability Discrimination Act (1995) was introduced to prevent discrimination against anyone with a 'physical or mental impairment' which is likely to affect their long-term ability to perform their duties. Therefore the Act makes provision for the employer to reallocate duties and alter working hours to ensure that where the employee may be experiencing poor psychological health, they may also be protected by the law.

At the beginning of this subsection, four reasons for considering the psychological and emotional well-being of employees were highlighted. If the ethical arguments are not always clear and organizational success is seen as one-sided in favour of the employer, then legal reasons usually focus the minds of employers and employees alike. After all, compensation claims affect individual circumstances as well as corporate reputations, but the issue of prevention is the current focus for protecting employee health and has led to the issuing of standards by the Health and Safety Executive. Much of this is based on the large Whitehall II study involving 10,308 civil servants which was established to study the reasons for social inequalities in health and has produced many publications since its inception in 1967, e.g. Cabinet Office (2004).

Health and Safety Executive Management Standards for Tackling Work-related Stress

The HSE standards encourage employers to ensure that employees are working appropriately in six core areas:

- Demands – that workload and work patterns are adequate and achievable, employees' skills are matched to the job and that any concerns about the work environment are addressed.
- Control – the opportunity for employees to have a say over how they work, including the pace of work and the use and development of new skills.
- Support – that systems exist to ensure that relevant and appropriate information and support is available from colleagues and supervisors, with the provision of regular and constructive feedback for employees.
- Relationships – that systems exist to promote fair working practices and to deal with potential conflict and unacceptable behaviours, such as bullying.
- Role – to ensure that individuals clearly understand their role and their responsibilities and are not subject to conflict between roles. That systems exist which permit the employee to raise concerns over the clarity of their role.
- Change – that information about change is made available and decisions about change include consultation; that timescales and likely impacts are to be made known to employees.

Timeline of work-based legislation which impacts on workers' rights

1970 Equal Pay Act – equal pay and contracts for men and women carrying out like or equivalent work.

1974 Health and Safety at Work Act – safe system of work and to ensure as far as is reasonably practicable the health, safety and welfare at work of employees.

1975 Sex Discrimination Act – 'It is unlawful to treat anyone, on the grounds of sex, less favourably than a person of the opposite sex is or would be treated in the same circumstances'.

1976 Race Relations Act – equal treatment by employers of applicants from different racial backgrounds.

1983 Equal Pay (Amendment) Regulations (in effect from January, 1994) – for equal pay for work of equal value in terms of skill, effort and decision-making, without the need for similarity of the work.

1995 Disability Discrimination Act – to prevent discrimination against anyone with 'physical or mental impairment which has a substantial and long-term adverse effect on (the person's) ability to carry out normal day-to-day activities'.

1999 National Minimum Wage came into force and has been reviewed regularly.

2000 Human Rights Act introduced in the UK – everyone has the right to equality and redress may be sought in the UK rather than European courts.

2000 Race Relations (Amendment) Act – to protect against racial discrimination by public authorities and to reduce racial discrimination.

2003 Employment Act came into force providing parents and part-time employees with increased rights at work.

2004 Working Time Directive extended to include junior doctors.

Summary of the chapter

This chapter highlights the prevalence of psychological poor health in the working population and identifies the key emotional challenges facing employees. Some of these issues are not new, but their recognition and the legal steps to tackle them are indeed recent. The knock-on effects on individual employees of shifts in organization culture, particularly in the public sector, and of European work legislation are charted and the government guidelines on what the employee can reasonably expect are outlined.

Key terms	
prevalence	glass ceiling
emotional trading	Working Time Directive
home–work interface	DDA (Disability Discrimination
spillover	Act)
bullying	duty of care
whistle-blowing	management standards
discrimination	on stress

Questions and answers

1 *What does a prevalence rate for poor psychological health actually mean?* The prevalence rate refers to the proportion of a sample or population who are experiencing a particular health problem, in this case poor psychological health. This can be expressed as a percentage of the respondents to a questionnaire or participants in an interview who score above a given threshold, thus indicating the presence of a form of disorder or distress.

2 *How have reforms in the UK public sector affected the way people feel about working in health and social care organizations?* Since the reforms to the health and social care services in the 1990s, most aspects of the public sector have been subject to reforms which prioritize accountability and added value. The introduction of an 'internal market' in the UK National Health Service meant that organizations became providers and purchasers of patient care. This ethos, borrowed from the private sector, has spread across the UK public sector. Given that most people enter helping professions with a high personal value attached to caring for others, the stark reality of meeting paper and financial targets is inconsistent with their personal and professional priorities. The resulting role ambiguity and role conflict is a cause of much disillusion in a range of public sector occupations.

3 *How might the individual tackle bullying within an organization?* There are a range of personal, organizational and legal strategies for addressing these threatening and recurring issues. It should be remembered that bullying can appear in many forms, of which physical violence is less common. Tackling bullying is covered in more detail later in this book, but individuals develop a range of coping mechanisms. These may be characterized by personal determination, drawing on the support of others, developing strategies for deflecting the aggression expressed at them, or learning to spot the factors which lead to bullying incidents and thereby avoiding the behaviour. It is vital that the recipient of bullying behaviour records what has been said and done, so that this can be used against the perpetrators in due course. Many organizations have a policy on bullying which should be used and the personnel department and/or union office are usually able to offer advice and support. Where organizations fail to address the issue adequately, it is possible to go outside the

organization and raise concerns with agencies who would support those willing to 'blow the whistle'.

4 *What factors would you take into account in advising someone on the likelihood of success in suing their employer for work-related psychological and emotional strain?* The key to these issues is being able to demonstrate, to the satisfaction of the law, that the employer neglected their duty of care to provide a safe system of work. The law will take into account what the employer could reasonably have been expected to know about the employee and their mental health, as well as any existing support services offered to employees in need of support for this type of difficulty.

5 *As an employer, would you see any disadvantages in complying with the HSE guidelines on tackling stress?* Practical issues such as the time it would take to assess every type of job in an organization would be daunting for employers and if identified how easy would it be for less desirable working practices to be changed? Standardizing behaviour across the organization presents a challenge and may require training for staff with the emphasis on the need to comply with HSE standards, as is done with other workplace hazards. However, the risk of being highlighted as an organization which does not conform to the standards – with its economic ramifications – is likely to persuade those who are having difficulty in improving their workplaces to change.

Suggested further reading

Chapters entitled 'Workplace bullying' (by Helge Hoel, Charlotte Rayner and Cary Cooper) and 'Working time, health and performance' (by Anne Spurgeon and Cary Cooper) are to be found in *Well-being in Organizations* (2001) edited by Cary Cooper and Ivan Robertson. Marilyn Davidson and Cary Cooper's (1992) book *Shattering the Glass Ceiling – The Woman Manager*, analyses the difficulties of discrimination facing one demographic group and the organizational expressions in which these are made real. More on the Health and Safety Executive guidelines on assessing and tackling stress in the workplace can be found at their website: www.hse.gov.uk/stress.

3 Models of emotional well-being at work

Job characteristics and the Vitamin Model

Psychologists studying the world of work have made a number of attempts to identify the salient aspects of the workplace which relate to the well-being of the worker. These have resulted in models of job design which emphasize either objective or subjective factors, or a combination of both, in addition to factors which relate to the job itself (intrinsic) or to working conditions (extrinsic). Arguably objective characteristics are more easily measured as they reflect issues which are quantifiable, such as working hours, levels of responsibility, rewards and work practices. However, the subjective view of the workplace acknowledges the important role of employee perceptions as well as their individual differences, such as personality and coping strategies. It is probably fair to assume that nobody better understands a job and how it affects them than the person who is actually doing it. Indeed research which has gathered employees' ratings of job characteristics as well as independent assessments, has shown that both produce similar results (Warr, 1999).

Intrinsic factors include how the worker and the job interact, such as the pace of work and the amount of control over the job task, while extrinsic factors refer to those things which accompany a job, such as pay and relationships with colleagues. In an early model of the workplace, Herzberg and colleagues (Herzberg *et al.*, 1959) labelled these intrinsic and extrinsic aspects as 'motivators' and 'hygiene' factors. As we shall see, the approach taken by work psychologists has developed from this early distinction and research has tended to focus on the impact of motivators on employee functioning and well-being, particularly in relation to job enrichment (Parker *et al.*, 2001).

The job characteristics model

Adopting an objective view of work, Hackman and Oldham's (1976) job characteristics model (JCM) highlighted five job characteristics which were felt to lie at the heart of any job.

1 *Skill variety* refers to the range of abilities required to perform a job, which might be more evident, for example, in the work of a salesperson than in some types of factory work.
2 *Task identity* describes the requirement to finish a whole section of work which can result in the completion of a product, such as a plug, or the processing of examination marks for a group of pupils.
3 *Task significance* is the importance of a particular job.
4 *Autonomy* is the level of control which the job allows and can relate to the freedom of the individual to take decisions about how and where the work is carried out. Not surprisingly this can give rise to petty jealousies between occupational groups, such as the computer programmer whose job was tied to a workstation and could not resist shouting at a community outreach worker in the same department – 'you never do any work: you're never here!'
5 *Feedback* from others in the workplace and from the success or otherwise of the work carried out.

These factors were theorized to predict employees' experience of meaningfulness, responsibility and 'knowledge of results'. In turn, Hackman and Oldham suggested that depending on the worker's personal drive to develop ('growth-need strength'), these factors would affect the worker's motivation, job satisfaction, productivity and likelihood of remaining in the workplace. Considerable research into this model has shown that the relationships between these job characteristics and experienced emotions such as job satisfaction and motivation are largely justified. Criticisms of the model focus on the completeness of the list of characteristics, whether or not they might be reliably individually assessed and the mixed research evidence on their role in workplace behaviours such as performance and turnover (Parker and Wall, 1998).

Don't forget workers are humans too!

A defence systems senior manager who was attending a course on business psychology pointed out to a consultant that the most up-to-date models produced by occupational psychologists were indeed interesting. However, in carrying out the task of managing workers and listening to their concerns, the manager had noticed that people were far more concerned about their rate of pay, and the comfort of the workplace. 'Is there somewhere for me to park my car, what time is the canteen open and how far away are the nearest toilets?' Not surprisingly, in comparison to these burning issues, the significance of variety and task feedback seemed to pale away. It is hard to ignore Maslow's hierarchy of needs, where the basic assumptions of food, shelter and safety need to be addressed prior to the finer considerations of intrinsic job characteristics. How many team meetings with a success story at the top of the agenda have been hijacked by the announcement that there is a fault in the building, such as the heating isn't due to be put on until October or more bizarrely that asbestos has been discovered in the roofspace!

The job demands–job control model

This model (Karasek, 1979) is attractive to many for its simplicity and its potential to be assessed using objective measurement tools. First developed to include the factors of psychological workload and work control (labelled as job decision latitude by Karasek), the model was expanded to incorporate social support (Karasek and Theorell, 1990) and predicts that 'high-strain' work will feature high levels of psychological demands as well as low levels of job control and social support. Furthermore the increased challenge provided by the work environment can create more possibilities for learning and self-development (Kompier, 1996). On the other hand 'low-strain' work comprises low demands with high levels of control. Karasek (1979) presented evidence to support the job demands–job control theory, i.e. the interaction of these two variables, among large samples of American and Swedish workers, and showed an increased rate of depression for employees in the high-strain work situation (51 per cent of employees) compared to the low-strain environment (11 per cent of employees). Many subsequent studies have been unable to replicate these findings, with the exception of those which demonstrate increased rate of heart-related problems in the high-strain jobs (for a full review see Terry and Jimmieson, 2001). The difficulties in finding support for the findings have been attributed to a range of methodological issues, although the individual factors of workload, control and social support are still considered important in predicting employee well-being.

The Vitamin Model

Building upon the job characteristics model, Warr (1987b, 1999, 2007) has developed a twelve-feature model which encourages us to view these aspects of the workplace in the same way that we might view a source of nutrition. Too little of a particular vitamin, such as A, is bad for us, whilst too much produces toxic effects, whereas vitamin C – at least at the time of the proposal of this model – was seen as fine however much one ingested. Such a metaphor is readily understandable and has gathered pace in the amount of research being carried out to evaluate it. The model encompasses twelve job characteristics common to work environments which are significantly related to employee well-being (Warr, 2007). Warr considers well-being on three continua: displeasure–pleasure; anxiety–comfort and depression–enthusiasm. Warr divides the job characteristics into those which are unhealthy if we have too little or indeed too much (known as additional decrement – AD) and those which we tend to view as having a positive effect, however much we have of them (constant effect – CE). In this way the model suggests that there is an optimum level of certain aspects of the workplace to which we should be exposed. This promotes a curvilinear relationship between well-being and a chosen job characteristic (see Figure 3.1). For example having little opportunity for control can mean we feel helpless in the context of a job. Supposing we are then given more power over the work and how it is to be carried out, this view may change up to a point where we feel contented with our level of control in the job. However, being given more control beyond this may lead us to feel weighted down with the level of responsibility and not having the time to fulfil the role successfully. Tsar Nicholas II took personal control over most of the Russian Empire, only to find that this was impractical and contributed to the Russian revolution. Hopefully this is not a

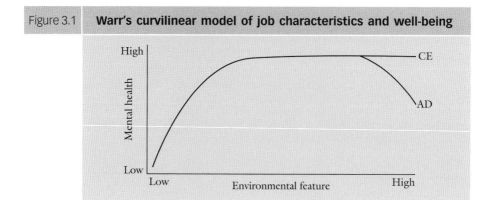

| Figure 3.1 | **Warr's curvilinear model of job characteristics and well-being** |

Source: Warr (1987a) Work, Unemployment and Mental Health.

daily occurrence, but there is no doubt that our experience of a job is likely to be influenced by our perception of the workplace (see p. 69).

Having said that, Warr's approach makes it conceivable that we can measure or assess job characteristics and therefore try to understand the likely demands on most employees. He states that the focus of the vitamin model is 'situation-centred' rather than 'person-centred', although he does acknowledge the influence of the interaction between characteristics of the individual employee and the work environment. In Warr's original presentation of the model these factors were described as baseline mental health, demographic features, values and abilities: more recently the focus has been on the role of positive and negative affect (Jeurissen and Nyklicek, 2001), which can be described as an individual's emotional style and how one feels about oneself (see p. 73).

Warr draws a distinction between intrinsic factors in the workplace – which describe the actual way in which we work – and extrinsic factors which accompany the role performed by the worker. The list of extrinsic factors has been increased to include supportive supervision (1999), career outlook and equity (both in 2007).

Intrinsic

1 Opportunity for control
2 Opportunity for skill use
3 Externally generated goals and workload
4 Variety
5 Environment clarity.

Extrinsic

     6 Opportunity for interpersonal contact
     7 Physical security*
     8 Pay/rewards*
     9 Valued social position*
   10 Supportive supervision*
   11 Career outlook*
   12 Equity*.

It is helpful to examine each in turn, drawing on relevant research, before considering the usefulness of Warr's vitamin model.

1 Opportunity for control

This is equivalent to autonomy as highlighted by Hackman and Oldham's model, and incorporates employee discretion as well as the absence of close supervision. Control tends to assume a different meaning when related to different parts of an organization's structure. When front-line employees are given more control over their work, it is often referred to as 'empowerment', when it is at the level of the workgroup it becomes 'autonomy': at the top executive tier it is known as straightforward 'power'. Not surprisingly, the subject of control in the workplace has been the focus of much research and organizational debate, the majority of which seems to show that empowering the workforce is good for mental health (Sparks *et al.*, 2001) and performance (Leach *et al.*, 2003).

A series of studies of machine operators in a computer-controlled working environment has neatly demonstrated this positive impact. Jackson and Wall (1991) investigated the frequency and amount of 'downtime' (when the machines had broken down) in a UK company and assessed training interventions designed to increase the control individual operators were able to exercise over their machines. From an initial level of 150 minutes lost each during each 8-hour shift when the machines were not functioning, the time lost dropped to 110 minutes after training had been introduced. Furthermore the decrease continued so that three months after training only 26 minutes were lost on each shift. Jackson and Wall emphasized the role of the employees in

---

*Indicates constant effect vitamins; the rest are additional decrement.

preventing faults via the tacit skills which they may have developed, enabling them to head off potential faults before they developed (as can happen when spending a lot of time with a particular machine, such as an old second-hand car!). The impact on production for the firm in Jackson and Wall's research is obvious and clearly demonstrates the benefits of empowering employees in an environment where previously specialist knowledge was protected.

Moving to the wider job context, it is important to consider control at the small group level. The idea of empowering individual staff to carry out their job can be seen as a gamble for some managers, for whom the thought of granting semi- or complete autonomy to a group of workers would be more likely to induce sheer panic. It depends on whether or not managers trust their workforce and this is boldly described by McGregor's (1960) X and Y Theory. Theory X states that we should not really trust the employee because they really only want to get away with doing the bare minimum – therefore they should be monitored as closely as possible and at best manipulated in order to ensure they do any work. Theory Y takes a much more positive view of the employee as inherently able to take on control for their work and suggests that given the appropriate forms of motivation by the organization, excellent results are likely to be achieved.

Whether or not you nodded knowingly at either of McGregor's philosophies, there is considerable evidence to support the efficacy of semi- and autonomous work groups in the workplace. Having received a cold reception for his ideas in the USA, Dr W. Edwards Deming (1982) took his theory of 'continuous improvement' to organizations in Japan following the Second World War. The resulting economic success of Japan in the decades which ensued was due in part to the adoption of the philosophy of empowering groups of workers to make decisions about improving the workplace. The concept of Quality Circles took off, and this was the name given to voluntary meetings between employees to discuss how the job or the product might be improved. Such an initiative is akin to the empowerment of individuals over their machines. Once the individual or the small group is given the opportunity to control aspects of the work environment, and is rewarded for an improvement in outcomes by increased rewards, then it is likely that the workers and the organization will benefit. The concept of autonomous work groups (AWGs) has gained in popularity and been used in diverse workplaces from car production plants for cars and aircraft to supermarket checkouts. The use of AWGs on the production floor of BAE Systems – which made the wings for the A380, the first 'larger than jumbo-sized' passenger plane – is evidence of the success of coordinated small teams deciding how to best to meet organizational targets. Similarly the introduction of project teams by selected Marks and Spencers' stores met the dual objectives of increasing job satisfaction and meeting organizational targets, as well as raising the confidence of supervisors to manage 'remotely' (Miller, 1994).

2 Opportunity for skill use

Again this is equivalent to the definition in Hackman and Oldham's model and refers to the range of skills and valued abilities which employees are called upon to utilize. The underlying assumption is that improved well-being will accompany greater opportunity for skill use and the research seems to bear this out. Kornhauser's (1965) oft-cited study of American car workers found particularly strong relationships between this vitamin and a range of emotional and psychological outcomes including freedom from anxiety and hostility, self-esteem, life satisfaction and sociability. Of the 40–49-year-old semi-skilled employees who had no opportunities for skill use, 53 per cent reported poor mental health at interview compared to 18 per cent of their colleagues who did have such chances (Kornhauser, 1965). Similarly research into 10,314 civil servants as part of the Whitehall studies found significantly lower well-being for employees in 'low-skill' jobs compared to colleagues in 'high-skill' roles (Stansfeld *et al.*, 1995). These and other studies demonstrate that even when one takes into account the influence of a person's occupation and accompanying status in society, opportunity for skill use remains a predictor of outcomes such as job satisfaction (Warr, 1987). Given the changing nature of the workplace, a portfolio of skills is likely to increase in demand in line with the fluidity of work organizations (Lawler and Finegold, 2000).

3 Externally generated goals

This refers to workload, either in terms of its quantity or its quality (the nature of the demands), and takes into account the resources at the employee's disposal. The goals may be work-related, but can also cover those at the interface between family and work, such as the workload of non-job roles. Either way, the impact of an excess of this vitamin on physical health is well documented. This is relevant to emotional well-being, because 'stressors are generally thought to influence the pathogenesis of physical disease by causing negative affective states, such as anxiety and depression, which in turn exert direct effects on biological processes or behaviour patterns that increase disease risk' (Cohen and Williamson, 1991, p. 7). Russek and Zohman (1958) reported that 91 per cent of sufferers of coronary heart disease reported strain due to work responsibilities, compared to only 20 per cent of those in the control group. They found that 71 per cent of the coronary patients in their study had previously worked more than 60 hours each week over a long period of time. In an attempt to measure the impact of job demands objectively, a seven-year study of 2465 Danish bus drivers found that the higher intensity of traffic on some drivers' routes doubled the risk of a heart attack (Netterstrom and Juel, 1988). Focusing on a different type of workload, premature births to 40 per cent of women working more than 40 hours each week in mentally demanding jobs again serves as a warning of the impact of overwork on health. In the wake of the death of a junior doctor in Britain after working over 130 hours without sleep, an editorial in the *British Medical Journal* concluded that 'Overwork can kill' (Michie and Cockcroft, 1996). In Japan the incidence of sudden deaths among younger adults is so high that there is a word in the language for 'death from overwork': *karoshi*. The relationship between longer working hours and increased psychological distress has been registered in many studies, e.g. among UK accountants (Daniels and Guppy, 1995), railway workers in Italy (Menotti and Seccareccia, 1985) factory workers in Japan (Ezoe and Morimoto, 1994) and national politicians (Weinberg and Cooper, 2003).

Although the link between factors such as workload and well-being is well recognized, the relationship between them is not always straightforward. For example it should be remembered that where external demands are high, it is likely that pressures other than workload will be found, e.g. spillover and conflict of work demands in the home environment and that overwork may reduce the employee's ability to cope with other sources of strain (Spurgeon and Cooper, 2000).

4 Variety

This refers to the variation in the nature and location of work, and in the tasks and skills performed, which may or may not be repetitive. As early as 1928, a study of assembly workers in a packing factory showed that an increase in variety led to increased output, but further variety beyond this disrupted the rhythm of employees in carrying out the task (Wyatt *et al.*, 1928). The significance of variety relates not only to jobs focused on the repeated performance of a given task, such as assembly work, but also to the repetition of more complex exercises, such as human interaction. The specialization of work tasks which characterized the Taylorist approach in Ford's motor car plants one hundred years ago seems to be making a comeback in the modern 'dark satanic mills' known as call centres (Wylie, 1997). Call centre workers are often provided with a script to which they are required to adhere in dealing with customers and targets for the length and number of interactions with customers are set. This can produce working environments where monotony as well as a lack of control are common difficulties facing employees.

5 Environmental clarity

Information related to clarity of expectations in the workplace, such as feedback on job-related performance and behaviour, as well as about future job demands and security, are covered under this vitamin heading. In general this relates to the level of assuredness experienced by an employee in a given work context. In a changing world of work, this is less likely to be guaranteed as organizational targets shift to meet new demands and as employees move jobs more frequently and encounter managers with different styles of supervision. The advent of electronic performance monitoring means that there is growing potential for timely feedback on performance (Stanton, 2000), but also the threat of less privacy and a link with increased strain (Aiello and Kolb, 1995). The monitoring of emails sent by employees has even led to employees being fired from their jobs. Despite this most people welcome feedback on their job performance where it is fairly and constructively presented and therefore this vitamin is particularly subject to the employee's perceptions. This not only relates to management style, but also job security.

The conflict of roles within the workplace is evident in new technology industries where workers are expected to fulfil selling, informative and intelligence-gathering functions (Frenkel *et al.*, 1999). Role conflict has been defined as 'the simultaneous occurrence of two (or more) sets of pressures such that compliance with one would make more difficult compliance with the other' (Kahn *et al.*, 1964, p. 19). Clear examples of role conflict are found in the UK NHS, where the introduction of an internal market meant that clinicians became responsible for financial budgets. This created a situation in which a senior doctor could be faced with making a choice between their professional code of conduct (the Hippocratic Oath) to do their utmost in terms of patient care, whilst being required by the organization to 'balance the books'. It is not unknown for doctors in this situation to experience role conflict on a grand scale when considering a choice of the best action for patient care. Unsurprisingly, a meta-analysis of sources of workplace strain has identified role ambiguity as a leading contender (Jackson and Schuler, 1985).

6 Opportunity for interpersonal contact

This vitamin incorporates the amount and nature of interpersonal interaction, which can include relationships with others, social space, social support and effective communication systems. It can be argued that the range of social aspects of the workplace are the most likely to give rise to emotions among employees. The potential for positive and negative aspects are ever-present. For example the open office which exposes the employee to colleagues they do and don't like, as well as opportunities to share problems and be constantly interrupted. Similarly the phone and email messages can bring positive rewards as well as increased work demands and complaints.

Within the occupational psychology literature, debate has proliferated over the role of social support as a possible buffer against the negative aspects of work, and although favourable conclusive findings have proved elusive (e.g. Stansfeld *et al.*, 1998). This is perhaps not surprising as it is hard to gauge the extent to which relationships inside and/or outside of work impact on well-being. The picture is also complicated by the apparently differing role of social support for men and women. Outside of the workplace, low levels of emotional support predicted poor mental health in men, but not women, whereas negative aspects of close relationships did result in poorer psychological well-being for women, but not men (Stansfeld *et al.*, 1998). Where the social support system is found to be weak, higher levels of burnout are evident among employees and consistent with this is the reduced incidence of depression where the individual experiences stronger social support (Nadaoka *et al.*, 1997). The importance of supportive relationships within the workplace is emphasized by findings which show that absence of emotional back-up from colleagues can mean increased likelihood of emotional exhaustion, psychological distress, dissatisfaction with the job and increased absenteeism (Littlewood *et al.*, 2003). Where organizations have taken action to promote beneficial social support structures, the introduction of teamworking in a community NHS setting has led to improved mental health and job satisfaction among the employees involved (Borrill *et al.*, 1998).

7 Physical security

Physical security for employees at work refers to safe and comfortable surroundings incorporating a well-designed physical environment as well as appropriate equipment. As we saw in the previous chapter, a safe system of work is enshrined in the health and safety at work legislation. However, there is also a need to consider behaviours, such as bullying, which threaten the well-being of individuals and undermine the wider working group (see Chapter 2).

Perceptions of who is responsible for appropriate physical security are related to ownership of safety issues. Where semi-autonomous working groups are introduced, and safe working – along with other aspects of the workplace – discussed in team meetings, the rate of accidents is likely to be lower than in work groups which are part of more hierarchical structures and therefore more dependent on external advice over safety issues (Pearson, 1992). However, the threat of job security, which is never far from the modern workplace, can also have a negative impact on safety attitudes and behaviours at work (Probst and Brubaker, 2001). This is effect can be moderated – and healthy working maintained – by the presence of a strong safety climate in an organization (Probst, 2004). A safety climate has been defined as 'a unified set of cognitions (held by workers) regarding the safety aspects of their organizations' (Zohar, 1980, p. 101). A review of safety issues on UK railways, which have been a focus for organizational uncertainty, shows that the target of zero workforce fatalities for 2002–3 was not reached and that 'the level of safety performance in this particular aspect showed no improvement over the previous year' (Cox *et al.*, 2003, p. 105).

Less than optimal physical conditions tend to expose workers to other deficiencies in the workplace environment. A rare longitudinal study into the impact of physical, chemical and ergonomic hazards found variations in employee well-being both inside and outside of the workplace, linked to increased exposure to negative factors (Kirjonen and Hanninen, 1986). This was despite controlling for the impact of other job characteristics.

The impact of the material environment on well-being can take its toll through a decline in employees' physical health, which in turn decreases workers' perceptions of well-being. The increase in recent years of work involving human–computer interaction, commonly in the form of desktop machines, has also given rise to new guidelines for their optimal use. Ergonomically designed chairs, footrests, computer screens, raised keyboards, paper holders, etc. are required to be everywhere in the modern office. However, it is unlikely that employees take the regular breaks from the screen which health and safety guidance recommends, and there is of course little legislation to protect the employee from the frustrations of hardware failure. The term 'technostress' (Arnetz, 1996) was coined to encompass the potential problems which a computer operator could experience and research has attempted to shed light on the relationship between physical and psychosocial factors, in physical injury cases, such as repetitive strain injury – a common problem among long-term intensive computer users. Similarly some consider 'Sick Building Syndrome' may be more completely explained in terms of psychosocial work factors, such as high workload and low levels of support, as well as control over the physical environment, rather than by physical phenomena such as humidity and bacteria (Marmot *et al.*, 2006).

8 Pay/rewards

Pay and level of renumeration are naturally often high in an employee's list of workplace priorities, but little work-based research has attempted to assess the impact of pay on psychological factors. One can envisage that the fairness of reward and the likelihood of its continuation are bound to involve emotional responses. The fervour with which industrial action has been pursued brings this into sharp focus, but action on this scale is not commonplace. The more frequent situation features the individual, or small group of workers, feeling and perhaps expressing discontent to or about the employer. The consequences for job satisfaction are likely to be negative (Agho *et al.*, 1993). It may be that underpinning the more overt display of emotion lies the impact of low or unfair pay on the employee's self-esteem. The level of pay conveys to workers how much they are valued by the organization, which can be taken to reflect on 'personal adequacies and worthiness as an organizational member which, in turn, influences employee performance' (Gardner *et al.*, 2004, p. 316).

9 Valued social position

This vitamin encompasses how the job is viewed within the organization as well as by society. This incorporates Hackman and Oldham's task significance as well as the meaningfulness of the job to the job-holder. Students of psychology are well-used to the stereotypical question 'So are you going to analyse me?' and this conveys a particular myth which has grown up around what all psychologists do and are capable of. The national census categorizes occupational groups depending on socio-economic, educational and vocational factors and this in turn relates to an indication of the esteem in which certain types of job are held. Anyone who has tried to get a passport photograph signed quickly realizes that the guidelines encourage ratification from certain occupational groups, which unfortunately reinforces rather simplistic views about the categories of work. In studying the impact of valued social position on well-being, it is likely that this is linked to other factors in the vitamin model, such as pay and opportunity for control, as these may improve alongside status. However, the application of Warr's model in a sheltered workshop for individuals with mental health problems showed that valued social position was the only vitamin to be significantly related to self-esteem (Dick and Shepherd, 1994).

10 Supportive supervision

Warr added supportive supervision to the vitamin model in 1999. Support and consideration from those with management responsibility, including the presence of effective leadership, are covered by this vitamin. At its fundamental level, supportive supervision relates to the availability and accessibility of the manager. In a cramped hospital kitchen where accidents, including burns and scalds, are commonplace, it might be expected that any type of manager would visit, take some action and monitor the situation. Similarly a professor's failure to acknowledge rapidly increasing staff turnover in a research team can represent a defensive reaction of denial so the manager is no longer accessible – in a psychological sense – to warnings of a deteriorating work environment. Both of these are examples of a lack of supervisor support and unfortunately most employees do not need to think too hard to remember their own bad experiences at the hands of a manager. Consistent with this is evidence from both sides of the Atlantic linking supervisor behaviour with poor psychological health among employees (Weinberg and Creed, 2000; Gilbreath and Benson, 2004). In both studies, absence of supportive management independently predicted psychiatric disorder.

At best, supervisors can act as role models to those for whom they are managerially responsible. They possess knowledge which is relevant to the job, have good listening skill, demonstrate commitment to their staff and are able to sustain supportive relationships (Sloan, 1999). Charismatic leadership is seen as providing employees with a vision (Conger and Kanungo, 1988) as well as the inspiration (Bass, 1985) with which to work towards it. This is somewhat different from the managerial scenario in the case study on p. 67.

11 Career outlook

The addition of this and the twelfth vitamin in 2007 recognizes the impact of changing economic and political environments on employees. As industries have blossomed and also fallen, the concept of job security has been a major preoccupation for many. Similarly the ways in which modern organizations are configured and increasingly deal with employees on a short-term or outsourced basis has meant that flexibility is a byword for individual survival at work, wherein the individual has to remain aware of the options before them and how best to ensure continued employment and/or promotion. This vitamin is particularly relevant to the theme of surviving the workplace.

Wherever there is change there is uncertainty, and ambiguity over the future of a job role is clearly linked to job-related dissatisfaction, anxiety and depression (Caplan *et al.*, 1975). The widespread practice of down-sizing, whereby organizations seek to flatten their structures and lay off staff, or even groups of staff, in order to save money or 'rationalize their operation', has proved a common cause for employee concerns over their job futures. The likely impact on emotional well-being is obvious, but can also be measured in terms of unexpected costs to the organization. An increase in the rate of long-term sick leave among those staff who 'survive' has been linked to downsizing (Vahtera *et al.*, 1997).

12 Equity

This concept, added in 2007, covers both the changing psychological contract at work which is shared by employers and employees (see Chapter 4), as well as the moral and procedural justice of the workplace, such as presence of fairness and absence of discrimination (see Chapters 2 and 6). The links between these concepts and emotional well-being are explored in more detail as indicated and fortunately are more widely recognized than was once the case. By acknowledging that every workplace has moral as well as statutory obligations, progress on such issues can be made.

Case Study 3.2	**Are power and supportive supervision mutually exclusive? (a true story of fear and loathing in a small sales company)**

Steve was new to the telesales office, but his boss promoted him within weeks, claiming that he would be a steady hand in a challenging work environment. Excited by this quick promotion, Steve was keen to prove his worth and felt it was now necessary to keep a close eye on the staff and ensure they behaved in a way likely to keep sales high. He banned talking between colleagues in the office while the phones were in use. Steve was not what could be described as a great physical presence, in fact he was rather self-conscious about his height. Fortunately he hit upon a solution which meant adjusting the height of his swivel chair so that when everyone in the office was seated, Steve appeared to be at the same level, if not higher. His colleagues had also noticed an unfortunate habit which Steve seemed to indulge in each time he went into the secretaries' office to give them work to do. This involved tucking in ▶

his trousers and readjusting himself in a rather disconcerting manner. One morning Terry, who was the most successful of the sales team, was late. He explained to Steve that his wife was in the early stages of pregnancy and was suffering with very bad morning sickness and Terry had stayed on at home to help her. A conversation ensued in which Steve revealed that his wife was also pregnant, but had not had any discomfort. Terry felt a little reassured that his manager would understand his situation, but as his wife continued to be unwell, this meant he was a few minutes late each day. At the end of that week, Steve gave Terry a formal warning letter telling him that if he was late again, he would be fired. Steve made no other mention of the letter or its contents to Terry. Despite making the effort to work extra hard and stay late, breaking sales records for that month, Terry was invited by Steve to meet him at a local hotel one morning before work. Steve told Terry he was fired and left him in tears before going into work and taking over the sales leads Terry had been developing, which meant Steve would get the commission.

Would you help Steve to become a more supportive manager or would you demote him as quickly as he was promoted?

Evaluating Warr's Vitamin Model

Peter Warr would probably be the first to acknowledge that drawing up a definitive list of 'vitamins' is bound to lead to omissions, and he has revised the model on two occasions to fill in some of the more obvious gaps by adding three variables: the role of management, long-term job prospects and the concept of justice at work. The idea of an optimum level of a job characteristic within the workplace is likely to be in tune with most people's thinking about how we feel about our jobs. After all, as humans we are complex beings and life is therefore rarely about straightforward cause and effect between one thing and another. For example, one would not be quick to say that so-and-so who does a repetitive job in the office is dissatisfied with work because of a lack of variety, if one also knows that so-and-so has been obliged to work late recently and is struggling to juggle the job with family commitments. Most scenarios are likely to have more than one facet to them and the vitamin model provides a framework within which it is possible to take these into account. This does not mean that the list of job characteristics is complete. Working with new technology may deserve its own vitamin, as indeed may the home–work interface. Despite the acknowledgement of personal characteristics, one criticism is that sufficient account may not provided for the subjective factors specific to the employee, such as job satisfaction. Warr does, however, emphasize the potential role for negative affect, and this is discussed in the next section.

Support for the vitamin metaphor as a curvilinear model has been mixed. De Jonge and Schaufeli (1998) investigated three components of Warr's model – goals, control and interpersonal contact – in a nursing setting, using 1437 healthcare employees in Holland. The results found curvilinear (inverted U) relationships between these job characteristics and both job satisfaction and job-related anxiety. A similar relationship was demonstrated between emotional exhaustion and both goals and interpersonal contact, leading the authors to conclude that 'the fit of the non-linear model is superior to that of the linear model' (de Jonge and Schaufeli, 1998, p. 387). Such findings have not proved consistent (de Jonge et al., 2000) and have even been contradicted (Jeurissen and Nyklicek, 2001): however, the negative impact of job demands has been demonstrated, even when controlling for negative and positive affect. Warr (1999) also claims that intrinsic factors are more closely tied than extrinsic factors to overall job satisfaction, but a major study which focuses on all of the vitamins and person characteristics and covering a range of occupational settings is awaited. Given the large potential for application of Warr's vitamin model and its recognition of the complexity of job situations, such research is certainly warranted.

Perceptions, personality and emotional health

Moderators and mediators

One of the more comforting moments in our efforts to understand how the world works is the realization that one event directly causes another: for example when clouds gather, it rains. Of course on reflection we might also realize that the world is not really that simple. For example the temperature, season, presence of hills and air pressure all play a part, but they do not always appear the most obviously relevant factors to the casual observer. In the same way there are likely to be background

Figure 3.2 **Michigan Organizational Stress Model**

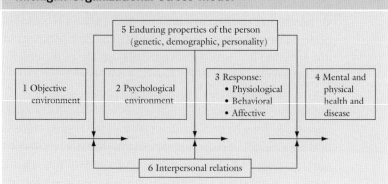

Source: J.R.P. French, Jr and R.L. Kahn (1962) A programmable approach to studying the industrial environment and mental health. *Journal of Social Issues*, 18(3) 2, Blackwell Publishing.

variables which will influence well-being in the workplace. The one which we might take for granted is that everyone is different: but this does not prevent incorrect expectations being raised.

Mediators are those factors which act as a filter, through which an aspect of a job can pass in order to influence the well-being of the employee. For example an individual who is generally of a positive disposition will usually deal well with a source of pressure, and this approach to life means that there is little negative impact on the person's psychological health. In this case the personality acts as the mediator between the stressor and strain.

Moderators are factors which can alter the relationship between a stressor and strain, perhaps acting as a positive or negative influence. An example is social support, which can act as a buffer enabling an employee to deal more effectively with sudden extra demands, perhaps because they have the opportunity to discuss this with colleagues and therefore feel in a better frame of mind than if they had to face the situation in isolation.

Having looked at models of the workplace which focus on the environment and examine relationships between job characteristics and the individual, the remainder of this chapter will scrutinize the role of psychological mediators and moderators which are likely to differ between each of us.

The Michigan Organizational Stress Model

An influential model which emphasizes the subjective view of the employee is the Michigan Organizational Stress (MOS) Model (French and Kahn, 1962; Caplan *et al.*, 1975). This has also inspired considerable research, and focuses on the employees' perceptions of the work environment. The way in which the worker interprets the workplace can mean that they view certain aspects as sources of pressure, which in turn can lead to stress-related outcomes. Caplan *et al.* (1975) emphasize roles at work and the difficulties which can arise when the job role is not clear (role ambiguity), does not match the expectations of the employee in that role, or requires two different sets of expectations to be matched (role conflict). The constantly changing nature of the workplace means that many of us can identify with these concerns. Universities provide a good example of role ambiguity, where lecturers are told they are required both to teach and to carry out research, yet the importance of either receives different weighting depending on the type of institution. Role conflict has the potential to cause even greater concern. The introduction of a marketplace into the National Health Service of the United Kingdom in the early 1990s meant that clinicians could manage their own budgets. In one sense this might seem sensible, until doctors realized that they could be faced with the choice of whether or not to treat a patient, depending on the financial situation of their service: in other words challenging their ethos and training. This could result in a case such as that of a psychiatrist faced with a suicidal patient, with no alternative but send him away due to a lack of money to run the ward. This is a clear example of a role conflict likely to put strain on the committed health professional and one which the UK has come to recognize in many areas of its National Health Service.

In addition to the problems created by roles, the MOS recognizes the impact on the employee of perceptions of lack of involvement in decision-making, having responsibility for groups of workers, unmanageable workload, threats to job security and experiencing challenging work relationships. For example, it does not take long for rumours of redundancy to gather pace and credibility among a group of employees or in the wider organization, and even where these are unfounded they still play a role in individuals' perceptions of the workplace.

The subjective nature of the workplace experience is logically extended by the MOS to include factors which are related to the individual employee. Therefore the demographic background and personality of the worker are acknowledged, alongside their physiological, behavioural or emotional response to the perceived aspect of the work environment. This increases the appeal of this model to many, as there can be little doubt that a worker's outlook on life and their repertoire of coping strategies will affect their chance of dealing effectively with a situation.

Lazarus and Folkman (1982) have played a major part in highlighting the role of perceptions in our daily lives and exploring the relationship with emotions and coping (see also Chapter 10). In describing the 'shifting pattern of cognitive appraisal and reappraisal' (p. 143), they explain the way we interpret the world in a two-stage process: through primary appraisal, the individual assesses the potential threat posed by a potential source of pressure. This is followed by secondary appraisal whereby the individual weighs up the advantages and disadvantages of a shortlist of coping strategies. This can be likened to a cognitive version of the physiological response to stress described by Selye (1956). The obvious link between our thoughts about a situation and our emotions has surprisingly received little serious attention from researchers and theorists until recent times. Daniels *et al.* (2004) have proposed an extension of the approaches of Lazarus and others to suggest how cognitive categorization of events might influence employees' appraisal of the workplace in both an unconscious and conscious manner. This is explored further in the next section of this chapter.

Personality

The field of research into personality has focused in recent years on the five factor model which features five main traits that are considered to be enduring aspects of personality, reflect the disposition of the individual and remain relatively unchanged over time. The 'Big Five' traits are well-established in personality research and are considered to be extraversion, neuroticism, openness to experience, agreeableness and conscientiousness (McCrae and Costa, 1990). In relation to emotional well-being, neuroticism naturally seems to attract the most attention, as it reflects a more anxiety-prone and worrying approach to life in general. However, in understanding the underlying mechanisms by which we experience and deal with our working lives, much attention has also focused on concepts such as negative affect, locus of control, hardiness and Type A behaviour. These are defined and considered in more detail below, but rather than being separate personality constructs, it is possible that these may actually reflect aspects of neuroticism, which has also been referred to as 'emotional stability' (Payne, 1988). Finally in this section, research which has looked beyond neuroticism or related traits is revisited under the umbrella of the five factor model.

Negative and positive affect

This particular trait describes a disposition in which the individual with high levels of negative affectivity will be more likely than others to experience increased distress and lack of satisfaction in a given situation (Watson and Clark, 1984). This is reflected in the tendency of the individual with high negative affectivity (NA) to focus on the disadvantages and pitfalls of their work, life, relationships, etc., such that they experience greater worry and appear over-sensitive, negative in mood, lower in self-esteem and over-emphasize the significance of routine bodily sensations (Watson and Pennebaker, 1989). In comparison, an individual who is low in NA will tend to feel greater satisfaction and more secure in a given set of circumstances. NA is similar to neuroticism, is consistent with the five factor model of personality mentioned above (Costa and McCrae, 1992) and can be viewed as a stable trait. Positive affect is not the opposite of negative affect, but it does reflect an enthusiastic and energized approach to life in general (Watson *et al.*, 1988). Therefore individuals whose overall approach is highly positive will tend to report their situation more favourably than a slightly positive colleague. A significant relationship between positive affect and higher levels of extraversion has been noted (Costa and McCrae, 1980).

Due to the reliance on cross-sectional designs and self-report measures in occupational psychology research, concerns have been expressed by many researchers that employees' responses to stressors at work may be influenced by other factors, such as personality traits (e.g. Spector *et al.*, 2000). Negative affect has been proposed as a likely candidate and this suggestion appears valid when one considers that high negative affectivity will mean an individual tends to highlight and prioritize the disadvantages of events inside and outside of work. How this happens is not as straightforward as it first seems. Negative affect can have an effect on the individual employee in a number of ways. First it can mean that the perception of strain by the individual who is high in NA is inflated and therefore results in 'over-reporting' of symptoms of strain (known as 'the confound model') and/or second it can mean the individual with high NA is simply more likely to succumb to strain when a source of pressure appears (known as 'the vulnerability model'). Consequently research into how

NA biases our perception of stressors and influences how we feel afterwards has been limited by the methodology used and has produced inconsistent findings. Certainly NA has shown significant statistical correlations with a variety of stressors and strains, both inside and out of the workplace (Jones and Bright, 2001). However, through the use of more sensitive research designs, such as the longitudinal study carried out by Spector et al. (2000), it has been shown that negative affectivity can influence employees' responses to measures of job stressors, e.g. on questionnaires, whilst having very little effect on the impact of those stressors on subsequent psychological strain (see also Barsky et al., 2004). In addition, some features in the work environment, such as job demands, have been shown to be more strongly linked to well-being than either negative or positive negativity (Jeurissen and Nyklicek, 2001). These findings would seem to indicate that despite a predisposition to view one's surroundings negatively, there is an effect which is independent of NA on the emotional well-being of the individual. In summary, the lack of research designs using a variety of approaches to assess the role of negative affectivity means it is hard to draw hard and fast conclusions. We might draw comfort from the confirmation that people are indeed more complex than can be encapsulated within some traditional research designs. In a real world context it is to be hoped that an acknowledgement of such complexity can only help to shift attitudes away from the simplistic view taken by sceptical managers that 'stress is for whingers'.

Type A behaviour

This pattern of behaviour was mentioned in Chapter 1 and represents an approach which is impatient, aggressive, ambitious and controlling (Cooper and Bramwell, 1992). 'Ironically these stress prone behaviours are the very behaviours that are rewarded in our western industrial society: particularly in males, they portray the stereotype of the dynamic executive' (Cooper et al., 1988, p. 13). Research into Type A behaviour has suggested that it is more of a risk factor for negative physical rather than emotional health outcomes (Ganster and Schaubroeck, 1991), although this has also been called into question (Jones and Bright, 2001). It is suggested instead that the presence of negative emotions may hold the key to Type A behaviour and therefore may predict it. Consequently hostility has been highlighted as a predictor of heart disease (Miller et al., 1996), as have other negative emotional states such as depression (Steptoe, 2006; Nemeroff *et al.*, 1998). It is likely that an employee experiencing negative emotions will contribute to stressors in their working environment or equally that they will respond more extremely when faced with sources of pressure. This spiral of emotion can be broken through interventions aimed at reducing the incidence of certain behaviours and such interventions have been shown to produce health benefits for patients already diagnosed with coronary heart disease (Gidron *et al.*, 1999). However, it is not surprising that what has been referred to as Type A behaviour is strongly linked with negative affect (Payne, 1988).

Hardiness

If there is one trait which is linked to emotional survival, then it is hardiness (Kobasa, 1979). Hardiness has been described as a trait whereby an individual seems able to cope effectively with a range of stressors, which might cause others to succumb to poorer psychological health. Hardiness can therefore act as a buffer. It is a cognitive appraisal system which consists of three components: 'commitment' which is similar to Warr's concept of aspiration and reflects a feeling of worth for one's actions and involvement in life. The second component, 'control', refers to the perception of events as determined by the individual's efforts rather than by the environment and is similar to the concept of locus of control (Rotter, 1966). The third factor is 'challenge' which illustrates a positive view of change, potentially as a route to enhancing self-fulfilment. Where individuals possess higher levels of each of these three components, they are less likely to suffer burnout. A study of nurses in both intensive and non-intensive care settings found lower levels of burnout in nurses with higher levels of hardiness (Keane *et al.*, 1984). Once again it is possible to view the hardiness trait as a component of negative affectivity, whereby an individual with high levels of this positive attribute is likely to be one with low levels of NA (Funk and Houston, 1987).

Other personality factors

Studies which have assessed each of the Big Five personality traits – openness to experience, conscientiousness, extraversion, agreeableness and neuroticism – in relation to psychological strain in the workplace are relatively few in number. However, once again, neuroticism stands out as the major personality trait involved in psychological strain. A study of 333 doctors found statistically significant correlations between higher levels of neuroticism and of work strain (Deary *et al.*, 1996). Specifically this showed the strongest relationship between neuroticism and strain caused by 'assessing relationships with colleagues and feedback on one's own performance' (Deary *et al.*, 1996, p. 12). This link was supported by further statistically significant correlations between neuroticism and emotion-focused coping (coefficient = 0.71) and between neuroticism and aspects of burnout, i.e. emotional exhaustion and depersonalization. These results suggest that an individual who is predisposed to negativity is less likely to manage the impact on their social functioning of their feelings in the workplace successfully. (This is explored further in Chapter 10 on coping.) For anyone who has found themselves or colleagues caught up in a spiral of negativity, this may sound familiar, i.e. bad things happen which seem to cause other bad things to happen.

Bearing in mind patterns which seem to repeat themselves, longitudinal research into the predictors of well-being in doctors has highlighted the importance of experience in early family life (Firth-Cozens, 1992). Findings have shown that doctors' relationships with their parents and the role of self-critical behaviour impact on their psychological health in their adult working lives. There is also the possibility that certain occupations attract individuals with particular personal dispositions, which may in time leave them vulnerable to emotional strain. Pursuing the medical theme, a 25-year study of American physicians revealed significant correlations between burnout and low self-esteem and low self-confidence (McCranie and Brandsma, 1988). Deary *et al.*'s (1996) study of medical specialties reveals that the personality traits of consultant psychiatrists differ significantly from physicians and surgeons, with psychiatrists scoring higher than their colleagues on the traits of neuroticism, openness and agreeableness. Although work stress did not differ between the medical groups in that study, psychiatrists reported significantly higher levels of depression (Deary *et al.*, 1996). This would seem to indicate the influence of a predisposition. It has been reported that the health and social care professions consist of a high proportion of Jungian 'helping types', who exhibit higher emotional competencies, as well as a preference for harmony and belonging (Garden, 1989). It would not therefore be surprising in an organizational climate of change, characterized by shifting priorities in healthcare, that individuals who are more likely to experience negative emotions are also more likely to be personally sensitive to the negative impact of some of these changes (see also Chapter 2). Consistent with this, a longitudinal study of bank employees and teachers highlighted the additional impact of negative affect and emotional exhaustion (Houkes *et al.*, 2003).

Case Study 3.3	**Personality as primary colours among infant school teachers (based on real events)**

Jill and Sean had both worked as senior teachers in a local school for fifteen years. Over the time they have been there, each has had to take occasional breaks to be at home with their family, such as when Jill took maternity leave to have her youngest daughter or when Sean's wife was very ill. During these periods, they have assumed full responsibility for running the school and have done so in ways which reflect their personal approach to life. Sean is a very dynamic and enthusiastic person, whose attitude to work is 'we can do this' – an embodiment of positive affect and hardiness! He is well known as a good ambassador for the department and is adept at handling a whole range of problem situations without too much bother, although staff sometimes feel he is not in tune with their feelings. Jill is a rather careful individual who always takes time to meet with colleagues and work out the fine detail of any new project before getting things going. She also tends to worry a lot about how things will turn out and coming across as negative: this has led her and Sean into conflict when the schools' inspectors have announced an imminent visit.

This week has seen the latest government brainwave, which encourages experienced teaching staff to apply for bonuses based on performance. This is bound to cause ill-feeling among some of the staff who have struggled in recent months. To top things off, the new education boss for the region is sending a team at short notice to inspect the school's effectiveness. Although Jill and Sean have been working 70-hour weeks for some time, and know that the pupils' results have met expected targets in recent months, they are both preoccupied with the latest developments. Sean is chatting to some of the support staff about it, when Jill arrives in the ▶

office. She looks pale and tired: 'I don't know what we're going to do: everything's going wrong.' Sean sees she is upset and reminds her: 'It shouldn't be much of a problem, we've always managed to meet our targets before. We'll just have to work through it.' Jill flops into a chair and with tears in her eyes, begins to shout at Sean. She accuses him of being unrealistic about his expectations of his colleagues and announces that she feels she cannot carry on. Faced with the prospect of losing a key member of staff, Sean takes Jill into a side office and after a long chat, persuades her to take a few days off. She is concerned that this will leave the department short-staffed at a crucial time, but he reminds her that if things at work are making her this upset, she needs to step back from the situation, until she feels better able to cope.

Applying models to the modern workplace

Models of the workplace are always going to be based on theoretical approaches and prioritizing whatever the researcher(s) feel justified in prioritizing. This is unlikely to match perfectly with the practice experienced by employees and their managers in organizations. There will be factors which the researcher has omitted, under- or overestimated, and interactions between factors which are not readily apparent from scrutinizing published research and one's own experience, or indeed are specific to the organizational context. 'You should try doing my job, instead of watching me do it', most people will want to say to a university researcher, but are usually too polite to do so. This is not to say that researchers get things wrong a lot, but so many findings are published which are contradictory or leave the reader thinking, 'Did they really need to spend money looking into this – I could have told them that already!' This section attempts to bridge the gap between the real world and the so-called 'ivory tower', by highlighting applicable aspects of relevant models covered as well as looking at others which have recently been developed to address the role of our emotions in our daily experience of work.

Until comparatively recently, emotions have been relatively ignored by those who study the workplace (Fineman, 2000). The emphasis on scientific research is not always a useful ethos under the influence of which to scrutinize fluctuating and sometimes irrational aspects of human behaviour. However, it seems that academic work psychologists have chosen to acknowledge the fundamental importance of emotions at work (e.g. Ashkanasy *et al.*, 2002). This section will present two models which have been proposed to aid understanding of the role played by emotions in our daily work and then highlight how a model can be used to help us analyse and understand our own work environment.

Affective events theory

This approach emphasizes how our emotions act as filters through which work events impact on our attitudes and behaviour at work (Weiss and Cropanzano, 1996). This type of framework can be useful for understanding the influence of mood as well as of individual emotions, such as anger and delight, on our experience of work. Utilizing this approach it is possible to see why an employee who seemed content in their job two weeks ago is now miserable and demotivated. On the face of it, efforts to produce a work environment which is conducive to encouraging the individual and indicative of a caring management style should be motivation enough. For example making sure that the worker has a pleasant office or workspace, a good level of pay and a path towards promotion, may on the surface seem sufficient and likely to get most of us going. From the perspective of the individual trying to enter the world of work, this might even sound particularly brilliant. However, from talking to individuals already in the world of work these factors are important, but on a daily basis are not uppermost in their minds, unless there is an ongoing grievance in relation to such important issues. If you ask someone in the corridor, photocopy or staff room what is on their minds that working day, the response might be a pressing deadline, the behaviour of a particular manager, the lack of support from certain colleagues, or what's gone wrong despite that person's best efforts to prevent it happening! Accompanying these concerns will be a level of emotion which, depending on that individual's personality, coping style and preparedness to be honest, will indicate how much the work event or difficulty is affecting them.

During the writing of this section, one colleague has approached me to say through the deafening roar of drills and machinery that the office roof is once again leaking on to one of the computers, while another colleague has informed me that the guest speaker was shown to the wrong room and the presentation equipment was faulty, causing time to be lost and embarrassment to be incurred. I have to say that neither colleague expressed anger, although their frustration mixed with a grudging acceptance of the situation was evident. If they were presented with a questionnaire asking about their level of job satisfaction and organizational commitment later today, I suspect they would be tempted to reflect lower levels than might have been the case on another day. In other words, emotions are variable and can influence how we interpret and interact with the world around us. In this way the workplace is no different from other domains of our lives. Therefore the regular repetition of similar challenges to our functioning at work is likely to contribute to an accumulation of emotion and feeling in relation to our job. The frequency and build-up of negative events, which taken individually seem minor, can even outweigh the impact of isolated but more major events at work (Fisher, 2000).

Having emphasized the negative aspects of a working situation, it is also important to acknowledge the role of events which positively impact on our emotions. Despite an accumulation of regular mishaps, it would be most unfortunate if there were no items in the positive side of the emotional weighing scales. These might include a colleague paying a compliment, a task being successfully completed or an invitation to join a particular work group. Fortunately such happenings can help to redress the balance in emotional terms (Grzywacz and Marks, 2000).

In attempting to understand how emotions determine our attitudes and behaviour, we are aware that we are grappling with a dynamic set of factors. These incorporate both the positive and negative aspects of the work environment which are experienced at the level of the individual employee according to the relatively malleable nature of their emotions. There is never likely to be an end point in satisfying once and for all the criterion of job satisfaction or any other set of employee's cognitions about work. Very much like the successful functioning of organizations, the achievement of a positive emotional state among employees is like building a sandcastle near the shoreline. We would like to think that it will last forever, but know that unless the world stands still, it will be eroded. We must then wait for another day to begin our efforts once again. Perhaps the lesson is to expect each day to begin anew with the emotional slate wiped clean and thus avoid the complacency which comes with relying on yesterday's good work.

Programming the emotions

Affective events theory maintains that our emotions are experienced in response to events in the work environment: the mechanism by which these various emotions are aroused underpins the whole process of experiencing our environment. Cognitive appraisal acts as the filter through which we interpret the world around us. Through this process we perceive actions and behaviour and categorize them in accordance with our previous experience of similar events. Consistent with this approach, an employee who is asked to take on a project for which they work very hard and receive little acknowledgement is unlikely to take on another such opportunity given their treatment on the first occasion. This seems straightforward enough, but it does not really shed any light on how we deal with new situations on an emotional level.

Daniels *et al.* (2004) suggest that there are parallel ways in which we process information: controlled processing which is flexible and under our conscious control, and automatic processing which occurs without conscious awareness and is therefore faster and proceeds whilst other cognitive tasks are being carried out (Schneider and Schiffrin, 1977). The theory utilizes the concept of mental models which are simplified cognitive representations of an event and the accompanying behaviour. In other words, we gather information from past and present experience to produce guidelines for our thoughts and actions.

Controlled processing involves using information available to us from our surroundings, to make judgements about whether a work event is likely to help or hinder us in achieving our stated goals. If it is felt that an event will impede progress towards a goal, then negative emotions are likely to be experienced. Not surprisingly, the more important the goal, the more extreme the emotional response. In this way getting negative feedback from colleagues about a new product idea is likely to be frustrating for an employee, but is more likely to turn to anger if it is considered this product would have been helpful in getting the employee a promotion.

Automatic processing is more readily understandable by first considering the process of learning how to drive. Initially we need to focus on how we carry out this new set of driving skills, such as turning the wheel, changing gear, braking, etc. At this learning stage, driving and talking at the same time is not easy at all, but having learnt how to drive, the skills become almost second nature to us. By becoming automatic, conscious thinking about specific driving tasks is not necessary, allowing us to focus our conscious attention elsewhere, such as on a conversation with a passenger in the car. Daniels *et al.* propose that we process information about our work situations in a similar way.

Referring back to the concept of mental models which act as guidelines for our responses to situations based on our previous experience, these are stored in the long-term memory and have links with a range of emotions which we experienced when we faced those similar events. Daniels *et al.* cite the impact of a manager shouting at an employee, which unconsciously reminded the employee of how they felt when this happened on a previous occasion in a past job. This caused the employee to respond using the same mental model or guidelines as on the previous occasion. This is comparable to the process of classical conditioning, wherein a response is provided automatically, based on an association between two stimuli. Comparable with Pavlov's famous study of dogs salivating to the sound of a bell, the workplace provides numerous examples, ranging from our behavioural response to the ringing of a telephone to our emotional response to a challenging situation. The employee may not appreciate why they experience certain feelings in such situations, but Daniels *et al.*'s approach represents a rare attempt to explain the functioning of emotions in the workplace.

Assessing my own workplace

Many measures are marketed as useful in assessing the workplace, but most of these are available at considerable cost or require scoring and interpretation expertise. Without wishing to undermine these, this section adapts Warr's vitamin model for user-friendly application in your own work setting. Notwithstanding the limitations of the model, it does provide a framework for ready use in appraising the highs and lows of the workplace and for enabling us to take a step back and assessing objectively what it is we do and do not enjoy at work.

The following grid can be used for any job – paid or unpaid – and produces a score which should not be taken as an absolute, but rather as a balance of advantages and disadvantages at work. The higher the score the more positively we view the workplace. For those characteristics which Warr states should be at optimum levels for our mental health, lower scores are given where there are too little or too much of a job

Exercise 3.1	**A rough guide to assessing your workplace**											
Work characteristic	Too little					Just right						Too much
	0	2	4	6	8	10	8	6	4	2		0
Opportunity for control												
Opportunity for skill use												
Goals												
Variety												
Environmental clarity												
Supportive supervision												
Opportunity for interpersonal contact												
Pay												
Status												
Physical security												
Career outlook												
Equity												

feature in the work environment (additional decrement). Five aspects are regarded here as having a constant effect on our mental health and therefore the higher score is roughly proportional to its availability. Using the information on Warr's vitamins, take a few moments to assess your own workplace.

What's the total score for your job? . . .

You might like to see how this compares with the score obtained by your partner/colleague/friend in relation to their own job. See if you notice any specific differences on particular job characteristics.

So which is the best job in the world?

A good place to start when you are considering the best way to survive the world of work is your choice of career. It is therefore of little surprise that when people come across a work psychologist, a question they often ask is 'Which is the best job to work in?' As a work psychologist this is arguably the most crucial question of all, and there is a temptation to say 'a work psychologist', but that might not go down so well. The things you might consider are which jobs will provide clear expectations, peaceful relationships, fair rewards and above all job security. On the surface it might appear that only one job meets these criteria: the undertaker. The requirements of the job are clear, customers will tend to have little choice but to trust you and there is always likely to be a supply of work. Having said that there are aspects of most jobs which not everyone will find satisfying, and being an undertaker is probably no different. We all have different priorities and we will want to choose a job which permits a suitable level of control over our time and the rest of life outside work, as well as providing satisfaction and fulfilment within it. Having arrived at your own score in assessing your own workplace, you might feel that there are things which you value which are not featured in Warr's list of vitamins – in which case feel free to add your own. No model is perfect!

Summary of the chapter

This chapter has provided an overview of key models related to furthering our understanding the interrelationships between the work environment, the individual employee and their personality and emotional functioning. The complex nature of these important factors is examined and a framework for attempting to objectively assess the workplace is suggested as a tool for use. However, readers are encouraged not to overlook the significance of taking a more holistic view of the work environment.

Key terms	
affective events theory	mental models
hardiness	Michigan Organizational Stress
intrinsic and extrinsic work	Model
factors	moderators
job characteristics model	negative and positive affect
job demands–job control model	Type A behaviour
mediators	Vitamin Model

Questions and answers

1 *How complete is the list of environmental characteristics in Warr's vita-min model?* It is always interesting to see how different theorists pri-oritize different factors in the work environment. Warr's model does build on the previous work of Hackman and Oldham and shares some of its factors with Karasek's job strain approach, but no set of job characteristics is likely to be complete. Partly in recognition of this, Warr added supportive supervision to the list of vitamins, although it could be argued that new technology and the home–work interface deserved a higher priority within the further extended model, which now also features career prospects and justice in the workplace. In addition, whilst Warr acknowledges the role of individ-ual factors, such as negative affect, it is hard to ignore the role of other mediators and moderators in the equation which describes how our work environment affects our well-being.

2 *How significant is the research support for Warr's vitamin model?* Comparatively few studies have evaluated every aspect of the vitamin model, but there is a considerable weight of research which has looked at some aspects of the work environment on which Warr and supporters of the model have drawn. De Jonge and Schaufeli (1998) demonstrate the appropriateness of the curvilinear relationship between some job characteristics and well-being: Jeurissen and Nyklicek (2001) present contradictory evidence. Despite the incon-sistency of these findings, they do suggest that the approach adopted by Warr in recognising the complexity of the relationship between work and well-being is warranted. Perhaps what is missing is the role of individual differences and non-work factors in predicting health outcomes using such an objectively-based model.

3 *What might be the role of negative affect in determining our emotional well-being at work?* Negative affect is the tendency in an individual to experience negative mood, poorer self-esteem and higher levels of worry. Negative affect shares a close resemblance to neuroticism and can be viewed as an enduring trait, and therefore unlikely to alter. This could mean that changes in the workplace are likely to be per-ceived by the individual as more anxiety-provoking than for others who do not possess negative affect, or than is objectively the case. This response can give rise to further negative emotions, as the

individual is less likely to make prudent decisions over how best to cope with this apparently threatening situation. However, it does not follow that negative affect will explain all of the emotional strain experienced by the individual with this predisposition: rather it can be an independent predictor of well-being, as some studies have shown. This means that despite the consistently negative response of an employee to changes at work, managers should not fall into the trap of attributing this solely to that individual.

4   *How do events at work guide our thoughts and emotions about a job?* Affective events theory (Weiss and Cropanzano, 1996) suggests that our emotions act as mediators through which our thoughts about work can be determined. In this way work events can have both positive and negative effects, which may balance each other. This theory is seen as advancing how we understand job satisfaction, which does not seem to be predicted by conventional models of job characteristics. As emotions are not fixed, but constantly dynamic, it is reasonable to conclude that our attitudes towards a job, which in turn will influence our productivity and quality of output, are likely to change too. By monitoring the frequency, accumulation and intensity of events at work, we may be better able to understand the attitudes and behaviour of individual employees. Daniels *et al.* (2004) go further to suggest that past events at work contribute to patterns of behaviour which are unconsciously linked to emotions. This can mean we are not consciously aware of why certain events at work make us feel so happy or uptight.

5   *Who has the best job?* As you may have gathered by now, the answer to this will depend on the work environment, the personality of the employee and the emotional and physical resources available. With any luck the answer to this question will be you, but if it is not, is there anything in the workplace or in how you approach it which can be changed to help improve your experience of work?

Suggested further reading

Warr's original book featuring the vitamin model is less easy to get hold of these days, but the updated version of the model is contained as a chapter in the book *Well-being: the Foundations of Hedonic Psychology*, which is edited by Kahnman *et al.* (1999), and in *Work, Happiness and*

Unhappiness by Warr (2007). For a useful overview of workplace design models relevant to mental health, Kompier's chapter in the *Handbook of Work and Health Psychology* (edited by Schabracq *et al.*, 2002) is a handy companion. For an insight into the quality systems approach which inspired a number of post-war economies, you might like to view some of W. Edwards Deming's original work, such as *Quality, Productivity and Competitive Position* (1982).

Lucy Cooper and Jim Bright offer a detailed and thoughtful analysis of the role of negative affectivity in Chapter 6 of the book edited by Jones and Bright *Stress – Myth, Theory and Research* (2001). *Managing Emotions in the Workplace* by Ashkanasy *et al.* (2002) is a book featuring members of the Emonet group which began as an email discussion list for those interested in emotions in organizational life and contains a range of analyses of aspects of emotional functioning at work. Stephen Fineman has edited a second edition of *Emotion in Organizations* (2000) which focuses on the topic in a variety of occupational settings.

Part Two

Identifying sources of emotional challenge in the modern workplace

Factors salient to understanding emotional and psychological health are highlighted in this section. Particular focus is given to the changing nature and perceptions of work by individuals and organizations, inside and outside the boundaries of experiencing work. The ability to cope with the evolving demands of the workplace and the emotional challenges facing employees are scrutinized.

- Chapter 4 – The psychological contract
- Chapter 5 – New technology
- Chapter 6 – Relationships at work
- Chapter 7 – How we manage people
- Chapter 8 – The home–work interface
- Chapter 9 – Measuring and assessing emotions in the workplace

4   The psychological contract

The psychological contract represents the unwritten set of mutual expectations held by organizations and their employees which can play a major role in determining attitudes and behaviour in the workplace. This chapter defines what we mean by the psychological contract and charts the changes in expectations which affect the way we feel about work in today's context.

Debate is ongoing over how the psychological contract should be viewed, and theorists have taken different stances accordingly. Argyris (1960) first used the term to describe 'the perceptions of both parties to the employment relationship ... of the obligations implied in the relationship'. The omnipresence of the psychological contract in workplace life has also been emphasized as 'an unwritten set of expectations operating at all times between every member of an organization and the various managers and others in that organization' (Schein, 1980). Denise Rousseau (1995) is arguably one of the most influential writers about this topic and a fierce proponent of the concept; however, her initial views emphasized a written aspect to the psychological contract, suggesting that something which existed in the minds of the workplace parties could only dubiously be labelled a 'contract' and may not even be reciprocal. Guest *et al.* (1996) has countered this assertion, highlighting the defining role of the psychological contract in the day-to-day experience of the employment relationship, which is therefore less likely to be restated in writing and more likely to be subject to renegotiation: he considers the role of fairness and trust as central to the concept, as well as the reality of the deal between employees and their organizations. As part of the ongoing evolution of the perceived meaning of the psychological contract, Rousseau (2003) has acknowledged this need for focusing on 'the dynamics of mutuality' (p. 229), including a fuller range of the psychological factors involved in shaping individual expectations. Whatever the configuration of the concept, there is general agreement that the psychological contract shapes our understanding of careers and influences the investment of our emotions in our work.

Shaping the new deal at work

Leaders of the business world 'have set in motion a revolution in the nature of the employment relationship the like of which they have never imagined. For they have shattered the old psychological contract and failed to negotiate a new one' (Herriot and Pemberton, 1995, p. 58). This plaintive cry suggests that the rules of engagement at work have been turned on their head and the assumptions under which employees operate have been erased. Some might consider such a statement as extreme – after all the world is always changing – so perhaps the reason for the underlying emotion is related to the manner and pace at which change in the workplace has occurred. As outlined above, influential writers have viewed the concept of the psychological contract differently, as constituted by a written rather than verbal or unexpressed contract, and the area has attracted increased attention from researchers. This distinction is likely to matter little to the worker, whose feelings are shaped by expectations in either form. So a change in working practices or rate of pay, the introduction of new technology with which to carry out a work task or the removal of a social space for staff to eat, all represent shifts in the psychological contract at work. These may have far-reaching consequences for how we feel about our jobs in the long term as well as giving rise to emotions which are short- or long-lived. Either way, it is desirable that the organization initiates consultation in order to renegotiate the likely change in mutual expectations. As Guest (1996) points out, failure to do so can have repercussions for employees' commitment to their organization, their well-being, performance in job tasks and desire to engage in citizenship – in other words going that extra mile to ensure smooth running of things at work. Unfortunately the necessary consultation is not as common as it should be and employees are left to deal with their emotional dissatisfaction or the line manager is left to face the music on the organization's behalf. Not surprisingly interest is growing in the concept of violation of psychological contracts, as this type of scenario is shared by workforces in both public and private sectors. So just how has the psychological contract changed in recent times?

It is often thought that the 1970s in the UK were characterized by difficulties in industrial relations in which conflict between the government, employers and trades unions representing workers were commonplace. Despite this, the psychological contract for most was said to be one in which the workers expected a job for life, incorporating job security, promotional career and a caring employer: in return they were expected to remain loyal and conforming to the organization's goals. This relational exchange which assumed trust, mutual respect and a long-term investment by both parties in the employment relationship was rocked by the industrial tribulations of that decade. The reforms to the National Health Service introduced by the Conservative Government in the 1990s under the economic influence of business leaders signalled an end to this type of psychological contract in UK public services. Alongside this the development of new technology, which UK workers had been encourage to embrace, had changed working practices in some sectors beyond recognition, from the printing of newspapers to an assessment of need interview with a social worker.

By the turn of the millennium, the basis of the understanding between employee and organization seemed to have reverted to the transactional exchange which had been so familiar to the workers in the distant past. Whilst many recognized the need to consider budgets and financial constraints, there were complaints of too great a focus on short-term economic plans and with this the new psychological contract came to resemble something which felt imposed rather than agreed. In practice the individual was expected to work longer hours, to tolerate change, to be accountable at all times and to offer a portfolio of skills. In other words the employee was required to demonstrate the 'added value' they could bring to the organization. In return it became reasonable for the employee to expect higher pay, rewards for good performance and some form of employment contract (which may be time-limited), but the idea of a career or permanent line of work was unlikely to be something fixed in the minds of those embarking on their first or even second job. Flexibility had become the key to survival at work where psychological contracts can be altered at short notice to include 'any other duties considered appropriate by the line manager'! In the world of employment this did not need to be all bad news, and many have benefited from retraining or gaining new types of qualification and experience. Indeed some would argue that such change has been a feature of work over the last 100 years, but there can be little doubt that the impact of the new psychological contract has been unhelpful in particular types of job. This may not be due to change itself, but the way in which change is managed (Giga and Cooper, 2003).

The revolution which Herriot and Pemberton (1995) describe has been felt most acutely in the UK public sector, where an ethos of providing care as paramount has been replaced by one which dictates provision of care where it is primarily affordable and justifiable in economic terms. In other words the priorities of the commercial sector were imported into public services from the private sector. Whilst this has appealed to successive governments, it has resulted in the introduction of market forces into areas of our lives which do not easily lend themselves to being treated in this way. Therefore the decisions as to whether or not to fund new cancer treatments or the placement of an individual with multiple care and financial needs in a nursing home are influenced by the amount of money social and health services have been allocated to spend, based on previous forecasts. This shift in how key decisions are made about the daily lives of the sick and needy is anathema to many who are committed to helping others. However, it is not simply a question of economic accountability, as things do generally need to be paid for, but also to do with a way of approaching these difficult types of work and ensuring the best possible care for those in need. Similarly teaching, hospitals, policing and even Inland Revenue operations, which are all public services, have altered the way in which employees are required to think about their jobs and the types of work they are doing. This is not to say that the 'caring' aspect of the caring professions has disappeared, rather that the definition of how we care has been reshaped. For example, before the NHS Community Care reforms in the UK, social workers could realistically expect to spend time sitting with a new and often distressed client finding out about their life situation and providing one-to-one support. Now this encounter has been moulded to emphasize the completion of paperwork. Whilst this can be incorporated by skilful practitioners into presenting a caring face to the client (i.e. writing and appearing to listen at the same time), this does represent a shift in the job from providing care to arranging care. Meanwhile in the commercial sector, the need to make customers feel valued and cared for has made a comeback, and the building of relationships with clients is a focus for many of today's successful businesses. This

rather ironic swap of positions has not surprisingly brought large numbers of employees to conclusions about where they would rather invest
their working time!

This type of change to the psychological contract can be seen as a
major one, but of course this depends on whether the individual views it
as essential and integral to their relationship with their job. The study of
violations of the psychological contract has become a growing area for
research. From an objective standpoint, this focuses on how the mutual
expectations between employer and employee have become unmatched.
Sometimes this can happen as a result of 'interpretations of patterns of
past exchange ... as well as through various factors that each party may
take for granted' (Robinson and Rousseau, 1994, p. 246). Violations
often come about as the result of broken promises, which can carry with
them far more emotion than a simple mismatch in expectations. A diary
study of managers' daily experiences revealed that 69 per cent of the
sample of 45 reported violations during one 10-day period, with an average of one broken promise per week (Conway *et al.*, 1999). The negative impact on employees of breaches in the psychological contract has
also been documented, with both emotional exhaustion and job dissatisfaction recorded as a result of this in financial sector workers (Gakovic
and Tetrick, 2003). The effect of violations has also been found to live
up to theorized expectations (see Guest's suggestions earlier). In a sample of over 800 managers involved in organizational change scenarios,
links were found between psychological contract breaches and subsequent job performance (e.g. dodging duties, wasting time), but violations were more strongly related to employees looking for another job
and displaying less organizational citizenship (e.g. volunteering for extra
duties, defending the image of the organization) (Turnley and Feldman,
2000).

As an employee facing what are perceived as unacceptable violations
of the psychological contract shared with an organization, what is the
way forward? Herriot and Pemberton (1995) outline three possible
courses of action: 'Get safe, get out or get even!' Given that the psychological contract is seen as a key motivator where employees are confident
the employer will maintain their end of the deal, this survival mantra
shows how undermining the failure to uphold this contract can feel. So
how do such strategies work in practice? 'Getting safe' is likely to see the
employee trying to conform to what the organization seems to want
and avoiding challenging the current situation. Either by not 'rocking

the boat' or 'keeping one's head down', the individual tries to remain inconspicuous and thus is hopeful that they will not be singled out for organizational punishment. It is hard to imagine that this would not lead to simmering resentment on the part of the employee, yet that for many is the extent of the psychological contract: 'Well, it's a job!'

There is certainly an argument for 'putting up or shutting up' as the aggrieved former British Prime Minister John Major once said, and in a similar vein surely it is better to have a job rather than face the alternative of unemployment? This sense of perspective is not a bad thing. Indeed by looking through the relevant appointment advertisements workers can get the refreshing feeling that the world does not revolve around this particular job and that there may be other opportunities, or alternatively that the current job is not so bad after all! The implied threat of leaving is a tactic which some employees use when they know their skills are valuable to an organization, but they wish to show their displeasure – in this situation a casual glance through the jobs pages may become a much more public affair, and copies of job adverts are left in strategic places for key people to see!

'Getting out' is what many employees instinctively feel like doing when the organization breaks its promises (see Turnley and Feldman, 2000), but in reality it is not easy to move to another job with similar or better pay. However, in a world of work characterized by increasingly sophisticated expectations among employers and employees, should the only choice be between working under particular conditions or not working at all? Not everyone is fortunate to have such a choice, but the International Labour Organization, which among its many activities observes working trends such as health and safety, is alive to the need for appropriate quality as well as quantity in our working lives. For example, a quick glance at the UK's top-rated employers reveals high performance linked with employee satisfaction (*Sunday Times*, 2006). Obviously things do not always run so smoothly, as evidenced by the need for a directive from the European Parliament to get UK and European employers to provide advance notice of any major organizational change (Giga and Cooper, 2003).

'Getting even' is one strategy which is more likely to give the disgruntled employee a greater sense of retribution in redressing the perceived imbalance between them and the organization. This can amount to doing as little work as possible without the line manager finding out, or withdrawing from discretionary behaviours in the workplace. These are prosocial activities which may not be strictly required by the job, but assist in the smooth running of the organization, such as voluntary overtime, undertaking training, organizing social events for staff, etc. However, it would be easy to underestimate the emotion which some employees feel at experiencing violations to their psychological contract. One employee working at a firm which supplied sweet sticks of rock to a seaside resort became so resentful with their lot that they tampered with the lettering which is imprinted into the rock. But for the intervention of an eagle-eyed quality controller, a host of holiday-makers would have missed out on the usual welcoming greeting from their chosen destination and received instead the contrary message: 'F*** off'!

So how important is the psychological contract? As a source of both motivation and demotivation, fulfilment and resentment, trust and misunderstanding, there can be little doubt that it does shape positive as well as negative emotions in the workplace, which in turn will have an impact on employees' behaviour as well as their long-term commitment to the work they do.

Full-time and part-time careers

Over the last 100 years there have been great changes in the nature of the workforce, featuring the increased role of women in work since the Second World War and the ongoing increase in the proportion of part-time employees across the European Union to almost one in seven of the continent's population (Brewster *et al.*, 1997). 'Most part-time jobs are occupied by women, and many part-time workers have two or more part-time jobs' (Arnold *et al.*, 2005 p. 521) The gradual increase in the average age of the workforce (as birth rates slow) and the plans to change the statutory retirement age, along with the drive in some countries, including the United Kingdom, to provide a better qualified workforce, are further factors which are likely to change the expectations of current and future employees. The globalization of commercial and service activity, the need for organizations to remain flexible in the face of the resulting worldwide competition and the ever-changing nature of economic and political circumstances mean that organizations will continue to expect added value, 'something extra', from their employees.

Case Study 4.1	**We can find you anywhere...**

The global village made possible by the advances in mobile phone and Internet technology means that organizations are able not only to compete across the world, but also to promote their services on a more personal level than before. Marketing via phone can be seen as more effective than via the mailshot. Consumers' emotional responses to this total marketing approach are varied. While standing on the Skye road bridge at 4 a.m. one August morning waiting for an annular eclipse of the moon, the silence was broken by a mobile phone going off among the small huddle of tired yet expectant astronomers from around the world. 'Who was it?' one asked. 'It was a courtesy call from the company who fitted me a new tyre last month', he paused, 'in Singapore!' The development of sophisticated computer links has also meant the exploitation of cost-effective opportunities to use cheaper-paid employees in countries in the same time zone as the UK to undertake a range of manufacturing and other work. In this way security firms in the UK can employ workers in Nigeria, with whom they are in contact via computer, to monitor live surveillance equipment. The employment of labour in the much-criticized call centre environment can combine with up-to-date technology and computerized information to promote the intimidation of customers, who feel that there is no escape from unsolicited sales phone calls in their homes. The pressure on telesales workers to produce results can mean that in an effort to get that sale, they will ring up to twenty times to get hold of their target customer even when they have been threatened with police action, because 'we know where you live'!

Charles Handy's (1989) influential writings have informed thinking about the shape of modern organizations. His 'shamrock' model (see Figure 4.1) serves as a useful illustration of how the relationship between employees – both full and part-time – and employers has altered as a result of organizational strategies for survival. In fact the shamrock provides an allegory for how we are coming to view the notion of work.

The core component of the shamrock represents those aspects within the organization which are essential to its identity and functioning, for example the role of lecturers in universities or of dentists in dental care

Figure 4.1   **An illustration of Handy's 'shamrock' organization**

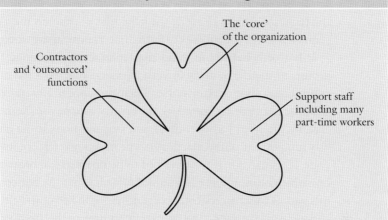

practices. The idea of sticking to the core business to enhance organizational success was a key motto for organizational gurus in the 1980s (e.g. Peters and Waterman, 1982) and with it came a need to view other non-core functions as additional and therefore subject to new ways of being engaged in the running of the organization. It was no longer seen as a necessity for a hospital to employ its own security or laundry staff, as these were not 'core' to the operation of the organization, although nonetheless important. The idea of contracting out ('outsourcing') such functions became commonplace. In other words, the hospital would retain its core employees, including doctors, ward staff and administrators, but would no longer channel resources into the employment of staff in non-core functions. This would seem to hold benefits in economic terms for the organization and in terms of freedom for the contractor, who could retain autonomy from the administrative structures of the hospital in this case. A potential disadvantage could, however, arise where the contractor's employees might not feel compelled to fit in with the core organization, either in terms of behaviour or expectations. To combat this potential mismatch, some building firms take pains to advertise their 'considerate' nature to reassure the core staff of organizations with whom they are fulfilling a contract. Sometimes the strongest bidders for such a contract are individuals who have previously performed the function which is to be outsourced, as they are already familiar with the cultural norms of that organization and can be seen as in tune with what is required. The example of school canteen staff who, with no previous experience of bidding for a contract, rebranded themselves as a new provider of school meals and were successful in winning the tender illustrates not only the harshness of this new reality, but also a survival strategy for employees facing uncertainty in the workplace.

It is worth bearing in mind that contractors can range from whole groups to specific individuals with relevant skills, as in the management consultant, office clerk or nurse. Their presence in the outer leaf of the shamrock is often facilitated by the agency, whose rise has been accelerated by the need for individuals and organizations to be matched in a way reminiscent of the matchmaker in traditional tales of love and marriage. The match may turn out not to be one made in heaven, or indeed one which blossoms into a beautiful romance, but the bottom line is that this part of the shamrock suits organizations in keeping their costs down and can suit the individual worker who prefers the freedom not to be confined to one leaf in a veritable garden of employment opportunities.

Another way in which employers and employees share a work relationship signifies the importance for many in balancing work and non-work roles. The increasing prevalence of part-time employment has been mentioned already and again can appeal both to employers, who require only a certain amount of input from certain staff, and to employees who wish to juggle the demands of family, finances, education and/or employment. The hourly paid lecturer who is called upon to deliver a specialist aspect of curriculum by a number of colleges, the office worker who wants to fit work around their children's school hours, the factory or retail employee who is also a student taking a qualification, are all examples of typical part-time work situations. Within these contexts there is an assumption that the individual has a choice and some level of control over their opportunities in the workplace; however, this is often not the case. A part-time job may represent a toehold for the individual in the workplace who aspires to a full-time job, or a stop gap because opportunities are limited, or a step out of the workplace as the pressures of full-time work have proved too onerous. In these scenarios, the relationship with the shamrock organization places the power firmly with the employer, who may be inclined to cut back on expenditure. It is only comparatively recently that part-time employees have been accorded the same employment rights as full-time workers in the European Union, including the United Kingdom. It can be hard for the part-timer to feel valued in the same way, simply by not being present for as many hours in the week. Yet the demands on part-time workers can exceed the number of hours for which they are employed and the psychological contract of pressure to perform whilst not perceiving fair treatment can give rise to resentment. The concept of boundaryless careers (Arthur and Rousseau, 1996), whereby the traditional barriers within organizations and between areas of our lives are seen to be more fluid, suggests that individuals with a marketable portfolio of skills will find more opportunity to express themselves in the world of work (Arnold *et al.*, 2005). The reality is that opportunities for individuals to 'call the shots' is likely to be tempered by the demands of the core of the organization in Handy's model.

It is worth bearing in mind that most UK employees are not part of large organizations – almost half of the UK workforce are self-employed or work in small organizations numbering fewer than twenty individuals (Arnold *et al.*, 2005). This represents an added consideration in the battle for control over one's working life.

So you thought you'd have a career?

Should a visiting management consultant (MC) with time-travelling capabilities descend from a far-flung galaxy to see how we plan our working lives, there are a number of things which would intrigue them. Knowing that time is relative and therefore permanence cannot be guaranteed, our MC would be impressed with how we seem to have surrounded ourselves with reminders of impending change. However, as mere earthling employees, we might simply have learned to ignore or habituate to such signs. For example there are the departmental nameplates which are attached with Velcro, or the blasé attitudes of staff when management announce a new suite of offices ('Because we'll all be moving offices again in twelve months' time'), or indeed the offering of a timepiece to a long-serving employee on their retirement. The table below is designed to get you thinking about how best to protect yourself in the career wars.

Challenges in the world of work	Weapons in your armoury
Global competition	Keeping skills up to date
Pressures on time, including workload	Learning to network effectively
Organizational changes and upheaval	Dealing with uncertainty
Constraints on pay and pensions	Managing personal finances well
Fewer promotional prospects	Developing entrepreneurship

The battle for control

Our understanding of the workplace and the deal we have with it as workers has received much attention from political theorists for over 150 years and it would be convenient for psychologists, researchers and students of work psychology to think that this is not an area of immediate concern to the discipline. However, as employees everyone has the right, although not always the opportunity, to influence the environment in which we spend so much of our adult lives and which can shape our emotional well-being well beyond those hours, weeks and years. The idea that work is a battle for control has been examined by Marx and Engels and cited as the inspiration for changing whole societies, yet the meaning of control automatically begs the question – who has it? Or for the more apathetic among us – who really wants it? Yet however we view control at work, we readily understand the emotion which accompanies the feeling of being forced, obliged or cajoled into doing what we do not want to do. It is no surprise that control is a key component of good psychological health both inside and outside the workplace (see Chapter 1).

The history of psychology – including occupational psychology – in the United Kingdom was traditionally linked with politics, particularly in the late nineteenth and early twentieth centuries. The link between politics and work is based on the exercise of power, or control as it is referred to more euphemistically inside the world of work. The moral stances of large-scale employers such as Cadbury and Rowntree were predated by the Victorian social philanthropists Robert Owen and William Morris, and astute business people such as Josiah Wedgwood, who realized that the human condition was not best served by treating people as machines and that their well-being actually influenced the quality and scale of their work. Wedgwood's decision to move his pottery production and his workforce from the polluted centre of Stoke to the nearby rural setting of Barlaston was a direct result of this type of thinking. One imagines that apparently benevolent employers such as he won the respect of their workforces more readily than those more obviously focused on profit, although his approach can also be viewed as an astute business move in the modern tradition of winning employees' 'hearts and minds'.

The advent of the production line at Henry Ford's car plants in the early twentieth century in the United States and the working conditions in munitions factories during the First World War prompted more structured investigations into how work was designed to achieve the best outcomes. In the United States, the Hawthorne Studies conducted by Elton Mayo at the Western Electric Company were prominent in the foundations of research into work psychology. Similar evidence could be seen in the UK with the founding of the Institute of Work Psychology in 1921 and the appointment of the first occupational psychologist (Morrees) at Cadbury's. These events did not occur in isolation from the political mood of the time and the notion of best outcomes rather depended on one's perspective.

In the UK the first Labour Government came to power in 1924 and there was real hope that the rights and well-being of working people would be placed at the top of the political agenda. The psychological impact of work was arguably the closest it has been to a general election issue. This was in part due to well-founded concern, but more significantly it reflected a battle for control of how the workplace was run, culminating in a General Strike in the UK in 1926. Over time this struggle became secondary to the issue of mass unemployment which dominated Western economies up to the Second World War. The subsequent human relations and organizational culture traditions reflected a more considered approach to the issue of how management control is exercised in the workplace, while unions came to the fore as representing employees' workplace concerns. The use of hard-line tactics in undermining union power by 1980s Conservative UK governments shifted the balance, and the negative impact of working hours became the bread and butter of academic researchers as stress took on the mantle of the employees' plague. Throughout this time the distance between politics and psychology has grown, yet the battle for control in the workplace is alive and being waged on a daily basis.

The psychological contract represents our understanding of this daily battle for control. Our aspirations may not be to take over the workplace, but rather to retain our sense of self-worth whilst earning a living. It is here that the skirmishes occur, as employers and managers try to exert influence over what we do and how it is done. It is a sort of micro-politics where the individual, either alone or in small groups, tries to fend off what are perceived as unreasonable challenges from the job, the tools required to do it or the organization. The weapons may be emails, phones, memos or verbal instructions and the tactics may range from ignoring the messages, for example by leaving the mobile phone switched off, to confronting the colleague one sees as responsible for the attack. Both are reminiscent of Herriot and Pemberton's (1995) concept of 'getting even'. A manager in a well-known manufacturing organization would relieve pressure situations in which he found himself by answering the phone when others present were convinced it had not rung! Of course there may be many occasions when the individual is happy to meet the challenge of carrying on with the job and feels that the enemies are those who represent obstacles to doing the job well. In fact the depiction of the workplace as a battlefield may seem curious, but by using a caricature of work-based behaviour it is possible to see the more salient aspects of what is important to the people involved. Two shiftworkers who were obliged to hotdesk – use the same desk, but only for the length of their own shift, therefore they never met each other – resented the lack of permanence which they were obliged to feel by the sharing arrangement. This led to their setting traps for one another, such as blocking access to the computer, removing one another's family pictures and soft toys and removing the key to the desk drawer!

A contrasting view to focusing on the negative is to consider the depth of trust and justice present in the work environment. Logically it follows that colleagues who one trusts and managers who behave fairly should not really pose a threat to emotional well-being. In this situation the psychological contract stands a lesser chance of being challenged, as our expectations of respect, feeling valued and good treatment are more likely to be met. A trawl of the 'Best Companies to Work For' (*Sunday Times*, 2006) confirms that these are recurrent themes which employees prize in organizations ranging from manufacturers to jewellers, law firms to hospices. The ways in which these are conveyed follow a familiar pattern.

- Communication which tries to involve all staff
- Flexibility to carry out the job in the best way (including working hours)
- Feeling cared for by the organization (conveyed via effective and hands-on managers)
- Bonuses which reward hard work
- Healthy work–life balance
- Opportunities to build healthy social ties with colleagues

- Believing that their organization makes a positive difference
- Energetic and inspirational leadership
- Ethos of the organization
- Opportunities for personal growth.

The reason for the success of organizations in such a survey is based on the sound principles of treating people well, sometimes in very challenging economic and work environments. It follows that employees who are happy with their psychological contract are more likely to invest themselves in their work. It is not surprising then that the *Sunday Times* survey of top organizations shows that the greater the proportion of employees who feel inspired by their boss, the higher the average number of hours worked. The next section examines how willing we might be to act in the way the organization would like us to – a phenomenon which is increasingly recognized as emotional labour.

Emotional labour

Emotional labour was first defined by Arlie Hochschild (1983, p. 7) as the 'management of feeling to create a publicly observable facial and bodily display' and consistent with this, has since been described as 'managing feelings to create an impression that is part of a job' (Smither, 1998, p. 43). Following on from Goffman's (1959) recognition of the 'invisible hand' of organizational expectations which influence employee behaviour, Hochschild's original work, *The Managed Heart*, detailed a study of how airline hospitality crews were trained, particularly in response to challenging behaviour. This involved teaching new recruits cognitive strategies for dealing with 'air rage' incidents which focused the employee's thoughts on the reasons for the passenger's anger rather than their own response to this challenging emotion. Similarly a smile can convey confidence to passengers that everything is running smoothly, even when weather conditions outside the window communicate a quite different picture. In this way the concept of emotional labour is about investing one's feelings in a work situation, in a parallel way to which we might devote bodily labour to the accomplishment of a physical task.

The concept of emotional labour has been further developed to emphasize the 'effort, planning and control needed to express organizationally desired emotion during interpersonal transactions' (Morris and Feldman, 1996, p. 987): in other words, how often, how much and for how long? Once again the answer to this depends on who has control in the workplace, but it is likely that the employee and organization will not always agree on this. Emotional dissonance is the probable outcome. This is where the employee is required to 'express organizationally desired emotions not genuinely felt' (Morris and Feldman, 1996, p. 986), such as when a doctor is obliged to turn off the life support system of a patient for whom they have cared.

This begs the question of how much of our emotion we should invest in a job. To a large extent it is assumed that the answer to this is within our conscious control and therefore depends on how we view the task in hand. No doubt there is a role for our satisfaction with the psychological contract in making this decision, but whatever the outcome, Hochschild and subsequent writers have viewed it as a form of acting. Furthermore this acting is differentiated into the ability to put on a front, i.e. surface acting, or 'exhorting feeling ... making indirect use of a trained imagination' (Hochschild, 1983, p. 38) to convince ourselves we actually believe the way we are feeling is genuine, i.e. deep acting. Given this view of emotional labour, it would be possible to see all of our interactions in this way, whether in the workplace or outside of it. There are likely to be times and situations when we are more motivated than others to invest in an appropriate emotional display, such as within personal relationships, or meetings which might impact on our financial or housing status, or indeed in key workplace situations (see the case study below). Most workers can recall hearing themselves or a colleague say at some point, 'I'm going to tell that manager where to get off', only to think better of it when confronted with the individual concerned. In this way we are denying the true expression of our emotions in order not to say anything controversial.

Case Study 4.2	**Emotional labour in action**
	In collecting data for an applied social psychology project, one undergraduate witnessed the regulation of emotional display whilst working in her part-time job on a hospital ward. When her ▶

fellow nurses believed that a visit from the ward manager was pending, she recorded how many times they toured the ward and found the total to be significantly higher than at other times when no visit was planned. Given that the nurses were checking that the patients were comfortable, emotions were being invested by the staff much more than usual. Another project in the class noted the difference in customer behaviour in a DIY store depending on whether or not the employee behind the complaints desk wore a jacket and tie. It was found that customers were much less likely to use abusive behaviours, leading the student to conclude that 'power-dressing' caused customers to invest greater emotional labour in a complaints scenario. Echoes of these findings are to be found in the experiences of emotional labour in a remarkable range of service professionals, including undertakers, referees, dentists and taxi drivers. Ashforth and Tomiuk (2000) found that in over two-thirds of the interviews analysed individuals felt they were required to act in the way Hochschild originally described. Around a quarter of these employees stated that their behaviour was so different from usual that 'a close friend would not recognize them in the role' (p. 189)! The main factors which affected the workers' investment of emotional labour were the behaviour of the customer, the need to uphold organizational credibility, how the employee is feeling at the time and how long they have known the customer (Ashforth and Tomiuk, 2000).

Studs Terkel's (1972) famous quote that 'work by its very nature is about violence to the body, as well as the spirit' indicates that emotional as well as physical labour is invested at a price to the individual. Indeed one of the reasons why emotional labour has become an area for research is its increasingly routine use and exploitation within the rapidly growing service sector workplace. Whilst it has always been evident, such as within the work-based examples included in this section, emotional labour is an obvious feature of life in the ubiquitous call-centre environment, where conversations are scripted for use by employees and deviation from these is likely to incur penalties as a result of any increased amount of time spent on each call. This represents one of the more obvious ways in which employees' emotions are shaped, risking the result of either suppressing what the employee would really like to say, or ignoring the wishes of the customer. This type of standardization of workers' social behaviour in the early twenty-first century is reminiscent of the specification of tasks on assembly lines over one hundred years before. It is perhaps not surprising that call centres have been dubbed the new satanic mills. Given the need for quality in the services provided by an organization, which rely heavily upon the behaviour of its employees, the concern for successful and productive interactions is warranted. However, reflecting the focus of the previous section in this chapter, the level of control which organizations should exert over employees' behaviour is open to question.

Morris and Feldman's (1996) hypotheses that the frequency, intensity and variety of emotional labour all lead to increased emotional exhaustion have met with mixed research findings (Brotheridge and Lee, 2003, Hartel et al., 2002). However, the tensions created by the dissonance between felt and expected emotions have been linked to poorer psychological health and reduced job satisfaction (Hartel et al., 2002). Significant relationships between surface acting – wherein the employee is portraying the image required by the organization – and the components of burnout (emotional exhaustion, depersonalization and lack of personal accomplishment) have all been found (Brotheridge and Lee, 2003). In this way studies have shown that emotional labour can impact on employees' psychological health and performance in a range of job settings, ranging from health (Wharton, 1993) to hospitality (Adelmann, 1995; Van Maanen and Kunda, 1989), buying (Rafaeli and Sutton, 1990) to barristers (Harris, 2002). The negative impact on barristers has been found to include mental and physical exhaustion from presenting a case in court, not feeling able to discuss their emotions with colleagues for fear of being perceived as unprofessional and even taking the surface acting role into their home lives (Harris, 2002). Nevertheless, the use of emotions is a key aspect of the barrister's job, as it is in many others, and the ability to simulate emotions can be viewed as a strategy for remaining detached and therefore able to present a 'professional demeanour' (Harris, 2002, p. 569). On balance some authors are keen to point out that emotional labour can have both positive and negative effects on employee well-being, ranging from healthy self-expression to emotional exhaustion (Strazdins, 2000).

One factor which has been largely underestimated in seeking to understand the impact of emotional labour is the context in which the organization operates. In this way the values which underpin an organization convey norms and expectations to the workforce as part of a wider psychological contract. It is possible to go further and state that cultures which require employees to invest emotional labour should routinely recognize this is the case and acknowledge and act upon employees' needs accordingly (Hartel *et al.*, 2002). Unfortunately this is an approach which has bypassed key aspects of the UK health and social care sector. The enduring changes to this sector, which began in the early 1990s, are a powerful example of how the psychological contract has been torn up and a new one has not been negotiated, resulting in implications for the use of emotional labour by employees. Many social workers who entered this arena expecting to spend time working directly with individuals who needed their help have found that their job has been transformed into that of a care manager, who instead is required to organize and administer packages of care (Weinberg *et al.*, 2003). Consequently 'the cost to the worker and potentially to the user of services ... relates to the worker relinquishing control over how the work is to be done' (Gorman, 2000, p. 154). In terms of emotional labour, here is a group of employees who are prepared to invest these personal resources, but instead are constrained from doing so by the need to adhere to administrative requirements. The resulting emotional dissonance and lack of control clearly have the potential for a negative impact on the well-being of this occupational group. Similarly the occupational domain which has found itself at the top of the list for the highest prevalence of psychological strain is the higher education sector, particularly academic staff (Kinman and Jones, 2004). Consistent with these findings is the expression of views by lecturers which allude to a sense of helplessness in meeting the needs of both the customers (i.e. the students) and of financial growth for the organization (increased admissions, etc.) (Constanti and Gibbs, 2004). Emotional labour is invested by those engaged in teaching, among others, who are required by their job tasks to 'either conceal or manage actual feelings for the benefit of a successful service delivery' (Constanti and Gibbs, 2004, p. 243). As with health and social care, the educational sector has undergone huge change and in higher education this has also been characterized by a shift towards a more managerial culture which conflicts with notions of academic freedom.

It is in such scenarios of dissatisfaction with the psychological contract that one finds ready examples of 'getting even'. It is almost as though the phrase 'Life will find a way' – used so poignantly in Steven Spielberg's *Jurassic Park* – can be applied to strongly felt emotions. Just like the dinosaurs in the film who were so keen to escape from captivity, our feelings tend to find ways to be released. So rather than shout at an angry customer and attract complaints, a call centre employee might channel their emotion along a more socially acceptable path by 'accidentally' disconnecting the caller or scrunching up paper into a ball with a clenched fist. For a number of good reasons, the need to avoid upsetting a waiter or waitress who is serving you a hot frothy drink is perhaps the most important consideration any customer with a short fuse should try to remember!

Measuring emotional labour

There has been a growth in the development of questionnaire scales which measure emotional labour (e.g. Brotheridge and Lee 2003; Glomb and Tews 2004), and given that this has the potential to become an area for increasing research and organizational focus the trend is likely to continue. The measures which have been developed usually employ Likert scales and contain items which emphasize the frequency with which employees engage in emotional labour, as well as the expression of emotions which are fake (equivalent to surface acting) or genuine. Based on this format, the following scale is not a validated instrument, but is designed to help you assess the role of emotional labour, particularly surface acting, in a role of your choosing: the higher the score (out of 50), the greater the investment of emotions you are making. It might be interesting to photocopy the scale and compare your answers with those of a colleague or friend. Use the numbers in brackets to help you calculate a score on the ELIAS (Emotional Labour in Activities Schedule).

Exercise 4.1	Emotional Labour In Activities Schedule (ELIAS) – assessing your ability to express or hide emotions which are not consistent with how you really feel

In my chosen role, I do the following:

		All of the time (5)	Frequently (4)	Sometimes (3)	Rarely (2)	Never (1)
1	Pretend to be happy					
2	Put on a brave face					
3	Make it look as though I care					
4	Stop myself saying what I feel					
5	Hide my dislike of someone					
6	Use a false smile					
7	Say things because it seems right					
8	Pretend to look interested when I am not					
9	Try not to show my real feelings					
10	Work hard to appear in control					

Summary of the chapter

This chapter has scrutinized the concept of the psychological contract – the set of expectations and assumptions – which exists between employees and the organizations for which they work. This unwritten deal between the workers and employers has changed both in its general shape and in its daily experience by the two parties. This is set against the backdrop of changes in the way we view work and the notion of careers. The modern organization – as exemplified by Handy's shamrock model – encourages a view from within of dividing human resources into core and non-core staff, whereas from the individual's perspective this represents a reshaping of our psychological contract with the workplace. In fact the psychological contract can be an allegory

111

for the battle for control over the workplace which is waged, whether unofficially or officially, and this is traced back over time to include progressive movements such as social philanthropism and occupational psychology. The success of employers who work hard to establish a satisfactory psychological contract is highlighted. The concept of emotional labour is examined and a measure suggested and the sources of strain for employees are identified against the shifting psychological contract of public sector life.

Key terms	
psychological contract	control
part-time work	emotional labour
shamrock organization	surface acting
outsourcing	emotional dissonance
boundaryless careers	call centres
occupational psychology	

Questions and answers

1   *What does the psychological contract mean to you in your workplace?*
Try to bear in mind the issues raised by the relevant writers, e.g. expectations, fairness, violations. Consider the ways in which the psychological contract may have changed in the type of work you do and in terms of your personal strategies, try to be honest with yourself about what is really going on – in the words of Herriot and Pemberton, are you getting safe, out or even?

2   *Try applying the shamrock model to your own workplace or place of study. Identify the component staff groups and consider the nature of their psychological contract with the organization.* Within a university, the core staff are often key lecturers, researchers and administrators, who are supported and supplemented by part-time and/or temporary staff in similar job roles, while tasks which are seen as less integral to the organization, but still vital, such as catering, car parking and security are often contracted out (outsourced) to specialist firms. Within a small building firm, the core staff would often include the owner, supervisor and a few long-term and experienced labourers,

while the supporting role of administrator and extra labour might be in the shape of temporary/part-time staff, offered work as required. Specialized roles such as electrician, plumber and accountant could be contracted out to those when the work was needed.

3 *Looking forward to the coming years, or looking back over the recent ones, how much control do you expect or recall having over the development of your career (including part-time and full-time roles)?* This is likely to depend on the type of job and the size of the organization you are with. For some these types of career question are predetermined and for many more they seem to just happen. This is not to say that we must have control, although the self-employed and those with considerable influence are likely to be in that position, but do consider how important autonomy is to you. If you have too little, can this be changed to your advantage, or if you have too much, should this be shared around?

4 *How satisfied are you with the level of influence your staff or student group has over the running of your place of work or study?* It would be surprising if there was not something you would like to see changed in your organization. If you are fortunate, there is a listening style of management which acts in the best interests of justice. If this is not the case, how could you get positive change to take place?

5 *How much do you feel you need to be a good actor to do your own job? If a friend were watching you at work, would they recognize you as the person you are outside of work?* Being at work can be like playing a role – in fact this is considered by some to be our life's work; playing a series of parts and showing to others what we would like them to see. How many of us can really say we are aware of being in these roles most of the time? Certainly we can look at others actions and think, 'How false!' while yet more may impress us with how genuine they actually seem. This is likely to be influenced by how much someone enjoys their work as well as by the kind of person they are, so can we really say we are consistent between these different aspects of our lives?

Suggested further reading

In 1995 a number of authors battled over the psychological contract, with books from Denise Rousseau, Herriot and Pemberton and Guest *et al.* Rousseau remains one of the most influential American writers on this topic. Arnold *et al.* (2005) present a fine summary of theoretical perspectives on careers, including part-time work, while Langan-Fox (2001) writes authoritatively on gender and work in *Well-Being in Organizations* (eds. Cooper and Robertson). Morris and Feldman's (1996) paper on emotional labour raises the key issues on this topic and it is a theme within the book *Managing Emotions in the Workplace* (2002; eds. Ashkanasy *et al.*). Fans of politics in the workplace might like to track back to Marx and Engels' *Das Kapital*, although for a more psychological insight into how psychology has served the workplace and its development Shimmin and Wallis (1994) provide an informative text.

5 New technology

The term 'new technology' deserves definition, as it is likely to mean different things to different generations and cultural contexts. In fact anything which can be seen as a machine-operated innovation has the right to be labelled new technology. Hence computer- or microchip-run machines, communications systems including mobile phones and video-conferencing facilities and transport systems from the wheel to time travel are all eligible for this ever-enlarging category. The adjective 'new' is continually revised of course, but this simply highlights the pace of change. Tape recorders were once relatively new technology, but within 20 years have been superseded by compact disc players. The advent of email and the Internet has made the world more accessible for those with access to computers, while the invention of the pocket-sized mobile phone means that we can contact others around the world at any time, regardless of where we are.

There is no doubt that new technology is heralded as time- and labour-saving. This chapter sets out to scrutinize the reality of this proposition and the psychological impact of new technology on the employees and organizations who are expected to work with it. The continuing theme of the battle for control of the workplace will be evident: however, within this context new technology, the changing nature of work and the implications for employees emotional well-being will be highlighted. After all, while the technology is being adapted to our needs, our own hard-wiring as humans remains relatively unchanged and therefore our capacity to deal safely with the new pace of work is likely to be limited.

New methods of working – the way we work

As the nature of work has changed, so have the ways in which we carry it out. Our lives both inside and outside of work are subject to technological developments as one can easily see from counting the number of people who pass by in the street using mobile phones, i-Pods, or motorized transport. Not only have communication and travel been revolutionized, but also food production, power supplies and indeed many procedures in today's workplaces. In supporting an increasingly consumer society, the thrust of new technology has been towards improving the speed and delivery of essential resources. Communication via computers means that email, the Internet, videoconferencing and virtual environments cut down on the time taken, while computer controlled manufacturing and voice-recognition systems reduce the need for people to be involved in every step of design or service delivery.

The shift from manufacturing to service work has been a dominant theme in the commercial world, and within each of these areas, as in life outside of work, new technology has assumed an increasingly greater role. All of this means that the importance and flow of information in our world has quickened, and with it the expectations we have of each other have similarly been raised. As information is provided in a speedier manner than before, it is expected that we will respond to it equally speedily. Within the workplace this means that new technology has not only changed the way we work, but also the expectations held by employers and organizations of their employees. One result is we can be told to respond quicker to the demands of the workplace and in theory we can be available to our employers at any time. Taken to its logical conclusion, this can lead to wider social changes where teams and offices can be virtual, linked across geographical space and time zones, and the working week becomes a 'waking week' instead (Parker *et al.*, 2001). Herein lie the potential dangers of new technology for the well-being of employees. On the one hand the mobile phone means ease of communication, while on the other it means no employee who has given their number to their workplace is ever away from it!

The main advantage of new technology for organizations is its promise of improving efficiency and productivity. Coupled with this shift in demands on workers, employers are increasingly tapping into the potential for new technology to save costs. Savings can be made in terms of the physical workplace by cutting financial overheads such as heating, lighting and rent for office space by encouraging staff to work from home. Alternatively organizations may increase their chances of hanging on to valued staff (and cutting recruitment costs) by offering them greater flexibility to work from home from their computer and thereby juggle their work and home lives. The flexibility afforded by this type of 'remote' teleworking is increasing dramatically, with surveys showing a 28 per cent rise in just one 12-month period (*Guardian*, 26 May, 2005). However the network can equally be used to disempower employees by encouraging them to work from home where they are physically isolated from their colleagues (Symon, 2000).

This change in the specifics of how we work has taken place over a relatively short time and in the context of the evolution of our species, new technology is a latecomer to human existence. In nearly 300 years since the Industrial Revolution, the history of the workplace has seen those in charge of work using technology to improve products and services, changes which have not always met with the approval of the workforce. This is reminiscent of the battle for control outlined in the previous chapter. It has often led to conflict between governments and trades unions or bands of workers. The Luddites were early examples of this struggle. They were anti-technology protestors in the 1800s who set out to destroy manufacturing machinery in the UK, burning factories and smashing their contents. The protests of the Luddites were both politically motivated as well as symptoms of anger against the rapid advance of new technology which changed the nature of work and signalled the erosion of the rural lifestyles of the majority of the population. Anyone who has sat helplessly in front of their computer as it failed to work properly might find themselves sharing some of this frustration!

When Labour Prime Minister Harold Wilson encouraged Britain in the 1970s to embrace the 'white heat of technology', he envisaged that new inventions would change the way we work for the better. However, the question of whether such change would actually improve our working lives has not been satisfactorily answered: instead new technology has been taken for granted as a sign of progress. Unlike the evolution of humankind, new generations of technology have continued to evolve and doubtless will continue to do so. This begs the question: at what point do we as humans reach our capacity to function in step with the new pace of work which is only likely to increase as the speed limit on the information superhighway increases? Governments tend to focus on the fairness of the economic exchange which takes place between employers and employees, but there is still no broad framework for assessing the impact of new technology on our employees and the wider public. To take Harold Wilson's reference to the white heat of technology, we all know that it is accompanied by the ability to burn and destroy, as well as to forge new and exciting materials. As scientists have often discovered to their regret, it is the use of technology by its human owners which poses the threat. Fears of global nuclear war haunted the public from the 1960s to the 1990s, however, the potential dangers of new technology are changing and will probably have a more personalized impact. Very much as is the case with the Daleks who haunt Dr Who across time, this is despite the impersonal nature of the machines involved and their apparent lack of emotion! (See the case study below.)

Many people do not want to be left behind in the adaptive drive to survive, and certainly examples of our willingness to use new technology are all around us. If this is true of individuals, it also applies at the organizational level. New technology appeals to business operations because it appears at first glance to lead to increased productivity, to improve longer-term flexibility and also to cut back on labour costs (Arnold *et al.*, 1998). In reality, it is thought that less than half of projects combine technology effectively with desired business outcomes (Clegg *et al.*, 1996). The main reason for this staggering figure is the lack of involvement at the design stage of those front-line employees who are expected to work with the new technology. In this common organizational scenario, the range of emotions experienced by individual employees is likely to include puzzlement, frustration, anger and resentment. Taken objectively, workers are obliged to respond to the change which new technology has produced often without their consultation. As if to worsen the situation, these so-called 'improvements' mainly serve to simplify jobs rather than to enrich them (Arnold *et al.*, 1998). The impact of new technology on the workplace is therefore deserving of further analysis.

Case Study 5.1	**The machine is never wrong . . . !**
	● 'I am sorry your postcode does not exist according to our computer.' ▶

- 'I am sorry, I pressed the wrong button and that's why your car failed the exhaust emission test on its MOT.'
- 'We cannot complete your purchase of your new home in time because we are waiting for a prompt from the computer screen.'
- 'The computer does not understand what you are saying – could you speak more clearly?'
- 'According to our computerized records, you only have one lung and so we didn't perform the operation as planned.'

The emotions likely to have been experienced by the human recipients of the above true examples can only be imagined (not to mention the consequences for the employee!). Whilst there is no doubt that the applications of computer-related software have abounded, it is also essential to bear in mind the impact on real people of relying too heavily on the false certainty which can accompany new technology. No mechanized system is likely to be better than the contributory designs and processes which went into planning it! Coupled with this are spiralling costs and the inevitable teething troubles which accompany the introduction of new computer systems to the workplace. Salient examples were those highlighted by the delays which followed the computerization of the UK passport service and the introduction of air traffic control software at the turn of the twenty-first century. It is no surprise that the prospect of an identification system in the UK which is designed to recognize such unique physical characteristics as fingerprints and iris colour in every citizen is a cause for nail-biting. Especially should it turn out that according to the computer system you don't actually exist!

Innovation, expectations and strain – the impact of how we work

An example of everyday use of new technology highlights how life has changed and with it the expectations of people, both inside and outside of work. The act of purchasing of a newspaper or magazine is as common today as it was 30 years ago, and the financial transaction with the shopkeeper continues to be a major feature. However, changes have occurred at a range of levels throughout all the processes involved.

Scrutiny of these will help to highlight both the advantages and disadvantages for employees and consumers.

Let us begin with the production of a newspaper, tracking the impact of new technology from the collection of news items to its purchase. While travelling to carry out an interview, a news reporter might receive a mobile phone call and a text message with vital information about a breaking story. Having arrived at the destination and gathered the rest of the relevant news, the article is written on a laptop computer before being emailed to the news office. The newspaper editor receives the article and amends it on the desktop computer and shapes the relevant page layout. Following this process for the rest of the paper, the editor emails the whole publication to the publisher who is relying on computer-aided design and advanced manufacturing technology to publish the finished product. Any difficulties are resolved via a videoconference link which saves time on travelling to meetings. The printed publication is mass produced overnight using laser printing technology and then transported to distribution outlets where the quantity of papers and magazines are logged on to the waiting shops' stocktaking software. In this way retailers can keep track of how many newspapers have been sold and how many are left in stock, as well as calculating revenue from newspaper sales.

The time taken for the above to happen should be a fraction of the time once taken to produce a newspaper, when communication relied on landlines rather than mobile phones, on postal services rather than email and networked computers, on manual typesetting rather than laser printing, and on stocktaking by hand rather than via the computerized till. For the employees engaged in the above production process, including journalists, printers and retailers, one would normally expect that their tasks are made easier. For the customer there are changes in how they purchase the newspaper which are also designed to aid convenience. They can decide to download the publication from the Internet or pay for it using a bank card which immediately transfers money from their bank account to that of the shop, thus saving them a trip to the bank. These innovations mean that the behaviour of the consumer, the shop worker and the banker is also affected by new technology. This smooth process is doubtless how the pioneers of new technology imagined modern life.

Where technology may give us the capability to achieve new heights, it can also work against us. What happens if the smooth process is derailed? Taking a slightly different view of the above example, this might begin with the journalist's mobile phone failing, running out of credit or simply being out of range. The reporter may not be able to call back the editor who is annoyed that his journalists always seem to cut him off when he rings them with an important lead. While compiling the news story on the laptop, there is a power failure or a computer virus causes the system to crash and two hours' work is lost. The videoconference with the newspaper publisher may convey ambiguous messages and result in misunderstandings and mistakes, or the unintentional downloading of a computer virus or the advent of an electrical fault might halt the production of the newspaper. This sort of bad technical luck may seem unlikely, but there are many other reasons why the new technology involved in the above process might not work – nearly all of these are likely to be human and a large proportion can be traced to the way in which we work, i.e. not like machines.

Taking each of the commonly used aspects of new technology in turn from the above example, it is possible to understand how people utilize and feel about them, including our emotions when things do not match our expectations.

Common gripes about working with new technology

1 The amount of work doesn't seem any less since we had the technology which was supposed to make things easier and save us time!

2 The number of emails waiting on the computer when you arrive back at work after a holiday always takes hours to sort out.

3 Anything which is that important will result in a phone call anyway, so why not wait for that instead!

4 Using capital letters in emails is taken to mean the same as shouting at someone.

5 Email means people in the same office don't feel the need to communicate by walking over and saying hello, but send a computer message instead!

6 Downloading porn from the Internet is such a problem that organizations are having to monitor their own staff.

7 Computer hackers can break into any system they like, including American military databases.

8 Self-service supermarket checkouts where you scan in the barcodes yourself don't seem to work and need a supervisor to be on duty to help as things are always going wrong!

Mobile phones

A fertile area for future research surrounds the use of mobile phones. In theory a mobile phone can make us available to the workplace at all times, it can act as a convenient way of getting things done and it means we can be reached by our loved ones and friends at any time. Each of these scenarios has the ability to blur the boundaries between our work and non-work lives. Anyone receiving a phone call or text message outside working hours or hundreds of miles from the office will testify to this. In this way, the use of the mobile phone increases the individual's perception that they are 'on call' and therefore subject to the control of their line manager, while on the positive side the receiver may perceive a phone call as a form of social support from either inside or out of the workplace.

Concerns about the psychosocial impact of the mobile phone in employment situations may be offset by positive characteristics associated with its use at work. These include the potential for greater flexibility for the employee and the opportunity to optimize their use of time, e.g. utilizing what would otherwise be 'waiting time'. This type of task-related control can act as a buffer against experiences of stress (Terry and Jimmieson, 2001). Due to our fairly ingrained and conditioned response to the phone, we are subject to feeling that we should deal with whoever is at the other end. This conditioned response is reinforced by subsequent interactions, but with mobile phones, there can be the added factor of 'self-importance' for the receiver of the call, which is imbued by taking that call while in a public place, such as a train. The attention which the receiver attracts by talking out loud in a social situation, when they are the subject of the conversation, may be a positive factor and provides one explanation why mobile phone use has been recognized as habit-forming, even to the point that it can become a positive addiction (Cassidy, 2002).

Alternatively considerable annoyance is caused when someone else is talking on a mobile phone in a public place and this intrudes upon your own space and thoughts. Indeed the sound of the ring tone – which itself ranges from the tacky to genuinely humorous – can be unwelcome in a number of work-based situations, either as a disturbance (e.g. during a presentation or exam hall) or as an interruption which breaks up a face-to-face interaction (e.g. in a meeting) or private time (e.g. whilst eating lunch). To be subject to the potentially controlling influence of the phone in this way can be a clear sign that the organization has the upper hand and the individual employee feels helpless to resist the conditioned response of answering, or that the worker is content to deal with incoming communications on a minute-to-minute basis. In either situation, the individual has a low level of control over their time which, as we have seen, has negative connotations for well-being (Sparks *et al.*, 2001). The need to switch from one situation requiring emotional input to another is an additional demand on the individual, which can result in having to deal with conflicting feelings. The use of vibrating rather than ringing phones introduces greater discretion as to when and how to answer a mobile phone, but there are a number of unanswered physical health issues about keeping them so close to the body (e.g. Wilen *et al.*, 2002).

Visual display terminals

Laptop and desktop computers have been a tremendous aid to the preparation of written material – at least where there have been no electrical or networking problems! – but there is a need for much more research in this area. This is emphasized by indications of a long-term negative impact on employees who are seated for prolonged periods at computer terminals. These range from musculo-skeletal difficulties (Aaras *et al.*, 2000) to psychological stress (Ekberg *et al.*, 1995). Where computers have been introduced to an office environment, clerical employees have reported raised workloads, with one-third experiencing increased symptoms of stress (Liff, 1990). The prospect of greater mental workloads without automatic outlet for frustrations again raises the spectre of reduced autonomy over one's job. The accompanying emotions are likely to take a toll either in how they are expressed or even controlled. Sending a 'flame mail' or switching onto the Internet for non-work related tasks may relieve immediate frustrations, but in the longer-term repercussions are probable. Keeping our emotions under control demands the need to find a suitable release in a socially acceptable manner, e.g. at the gym rather than at fellow drivers on the way home, or on one's family when one gets there. Similarly for the growing proportion of teleworkers or telecommuters (working from computers at home) the potential pitfalls include technological breakdowns, the anxiety caused by dealing with these, conflict at the home–work interface and social isolation from colleagues. It has been suggested as a positive factor that there will be a reduced need for face-to-face meetings. However, teleworking is likely to have an impact on the number of people involved in organizational decisions and thereby has an implication for the exercise of control in the workplace (Arnold *et al.*, 1998), e.g. 'We didn't want to trouble you at home, although someone was supposed to send you an email'!

There is no doubt that email has made the distribution of documents easy and the process of written communication much speedier than by post. This depends on when the receiver has time to switch on their machine and can distinguish the significance of certain messages from that of many others arriving at the same time. Furthermore the nature of their reply is subject to the time available to deal with the incoming workload, their ability to write in a socially acceptable manner, the effectiveness of their system to decode any attached documents and the visibility of their computer screen or its contents to co-workers and line management. All of these possibilities will depend on the emotional state of the receiver at the time of replying. The significance of this is twofold. First, employees are likely to develop a range of strategies for maintaining some level of control over their work which can mean simply ignoring much of the information (Finholt and Sproull, 1990), although this increases the likelihood of vital knowledge being missed (Symon, 2000). The second factor is highlighted by the advent of electronic performance monitoring (EPM), where managers can see what is on the employee's screen. In the UK employees have been fired from their job for sending emails the organization deemed inappropriate and public sector organizations have announced steps to stamp out illicit use of the Internet at work. EPM can however result in different outcomes, conversely providing feedback for employees on their performance (Stanton, 2000) or resulting in decreased privacy and increased workloads (Carayon, 1994).

However control is exercised and by whom, it is the case that social interaction via email is different than in person. A range of social signals, including non-verbal cues cannot be transmitted and this can lead to the removal of inhibitions (Arnold *et al.*, 1998) or simple misunderstandings

(Symon, 2000). The apparent absence of social barriers to sending certain types of communication can create in managers and employees alike a sense of false security, from which they feel comfortable about emailing what they would not normally say. If we can actually see the person down the line, via a videoconference for example, this can help build the communication on a more human level. While this is closer to a more usual interaction, it can be subject to time delays and a range of assumptions about the other person which are quite distinct from face-to-face encounters (Parkinson and Lea, 2005).

Advanced manufacturing technology

Advanced manufacturing technology (AMT) usually means computer-numerically controlled machinery, robots or software applications in design and manufacturing. These are involved in the mass production of many items, for example magazines or drinks. AMT is seen as producing speedier and more flexible working (Chmiel, 1998), with the added value for the organization of saving labour and guaranteeing standardized products and quality. However, this implies again that new technology, driven by management concerns, moulds the working lives of those responsible for the daily operation of the machinery and may be more trustworthy than human performance levels. The introduction of new technology often results in failure as the role of the employees has not been adequately consulted or considered. Not surprisingly a whole range of emotions are experienced by those involved, including frustrated employees, irritated managers and exasperated technical staff who are striving to make the system work. In dealing with these emotions, the following points are worthy of consideration:

- *The perception of new technology by the employees on the shopfloor or on the front line.* It may not be the actual change in working practice which creates hostility: it is more likely to be the workers' perception of the underlying motives of the management (Arnold *et al.*, 1998): is this another of management's bright ideas which have helped someone gain promotion, will my working life become easier or more importantly, is this the end of my job? Insult is occasionally added to perceived injury as those (often contract staff) who have been brought in to make new technology function are placed on better rates of pay than existing employees.

- *Lack of employees' involvement in the design or implementation of technology.* Training may well be provided, but the parameters of the technology have already been set by that stage and employees are obliged to work within its confines. UK universities have invested heavily in new and improved systems for administering students' marks and records, but still find that these expensive software solutions cannot deliver basic material such as average scores. In a manufacturing setting, Wall and Davids (1992) highlight the link between poorer psychological health and jobs entailing high cognitive demand for monitoring new technology, where the employee is in a more passive rather than interactive role, observing the technology in action.

- *Lack of autonomy for employees who use the technology.* This includes the ability to fix the technology or troubleshoot problems for themselves, which in turn leads to increased downtime and decreased satisfaction. Where increased control over the new technology is encouraged, these trends are reversed (Jackson and Wall, 1991). In fact where autonomous work groups take responsibility for new technology, increases in sales of almost one-fifth have been recorded (Batt, 1999).

Much of the research has tended to show that AMT has produced job simplification (Kelly, 1982) rather than enrichment (Arnold *et al.*, 1998), yet a number of studies clearly support the logic that new technology will improve organizational efficiency where there is greater freedom for employees to take control. Furthermore positive emotions and a sense of ownership among employees are much more likely. The Taylorist vision of assembly lines, including those in car and aircraft manufacturing, which have dominated mass production have not gone away, but recognition of the impact of AMT on the social and psychological features of work has inspired attempts to optimize both the psychosocial needs of the employee as well as the requirements of working with new technology (e.g. Trist and Bamforth, 1951).

We have come a long way since the time when quarrying became mechanized to meet increased demand and the blasting of rocks was introduced. The failure to calculate the human cost of boulders bouncing down hillsides into neighbouring villages in the early twentieth century is not dissimilar to the lack of thought given to human considerations in implementing any technological innovation. The clear route to avoid the failure of new technological implementation is to ensure that an appropriate work design accompanies it (Waterson *et al.*, 1999). Despite this recognition, the attraction of Taylorism remains because it appears to promise management control over production and services to such an extent that the approach which was designed to promote AMT has been imported to manage the human interaction element of many retail and sales functions.

Virtual and impersonal working

The wonder of the new technological workplace has, in theory at least, turned the world of work on its head. It is now possible to be at work without actually being there! The fluidity afforded by remote teleworking, email and the Internet means that increasing numbers of workers can be based away from the physical workplace and/or can work from home. In some occupations this is taken for granted as the waking week takes over from the working week (Parker *et al.*, 2001), but attitudes towards working from home are still mixed in many areas of work and tend to be split between occupational groups. For example, in a university setting, lecturers and researchers can legitimately state they are working at home in order to complete a written piece or fulfil marking obligations, thus avoiding the distractions of daily office life. Yet within university support staff groups there is an expectation by management and employees that they should be in the building every day, despite having to complete a number of functions, particularly computer tasks, which demand just as much concentration and freedom from interruption.

So how is the impact of not physically 'being there' experienced by employees and their colleagues and customers? Within a way of working which encourages physical distance between people, the heat of emotions is no less likely to be felt. The frustration expressed by clients using telephone services for banking or utilities usually results from having to deal with a voice recorded system which directs the caller to where it wants you to go rather than where the customer might choose, whilst giving the impression that should the caller finally get through to a real live operator, the employee will be primed with all the necessary information to deal with the query most speedily: only to find that it is necessary to repeat all the information! Considerable effort is being put into turning such impersonal dealings into user-friendly and responsive ones, as evidenced by the Laboratory for Communication between Humans and Interactive Media at Stanford University. Voice recognition systems are increasingly present in our lives, from obtaining cinema listings to in-car direction software. The level of sophistication now makes it possible to use driving software to help calm angry motorists: in fact the advance in this field is such that subcultures have developed around the assumed personalities of these 'virtual employees'! A best-selling book in Canada charted the biography of 'Emily', whose pre-recorded communications saved her organization over $3 million!

This need to attribute a persona to something which does not actually exist is a curious human trait, almost as if it reduces the emotional distance between person and machine. However, new technology also lends itself to the reverse scenario, whereby the media of email and Internet make it possible for workers to feel more secure in expressing more extreme emotions than if the person with whom they were communicating was standing in front of them. Flame mail represents one end of this spectrum, where the desired impact on the receiver is negative and can be equivalent to being shouted at in person. It is as though the medium affords the sender a false sense of security in behaving in an extreme manner, because by not being there they do not need to take immediate responsibility for the emotional consequences.

There are other unintended outcomes from the habitual use of email and texting which range from difficulty in breaking out of this mode of communication (Cassidy, 2002). Liverpool City Council offices introduced a weekly email-free day in order to promote face-to-face and phone conversations – it had been noted that people were tending to send emails to colleagues working in the same office rather than actually speak to them! Other social consequences on office workers, imposed by our use of new technology, include the gradual disappearance of staff rooms. The need to house photocopiers and computer wiring, the financial premium of office space and the plethora of supposedly compelling emails, mean that there is always work provided by the computer. In order to take a break, those employees who do not smoke and are therefore not wholly motivated to stand outside the building, increasingly find that the photocopy room is the refuge for a more human version of social communication. It is one of the few remaining areas where office workers can feel justified in spending time in the company of others, outside of more formal meetings.

For the teleworker based at home this form of social contact is absent and they may feel that they are excluded from informal and important social contacts. Furthermore the availability of technical support and training provision is reduced, with the threat of computer breakdowns adding to potential strain. The sources of frustration and isolation are likely to be mutually dependent and make emotional release more difficult, with 'tele-rage' the ultimate toll (Cooper, 2000). Whatever the impact on the individual, the changing nature of working in this way also has ramifications for the shape and function of the organizations for which they work.

Exercise 5.1	**Would I make a good teleworker?**

Working from outside the organization requires not only good communications technology and support, but also the ability to deal with competing demands which may not always be relevant to the job. There are attractions to working from home including being able to attend to family demands, and many workers already successfully juggle the domains of work and family. Suppose you had to work from home most of the time – would you be able or want to set up boundaries for carrying out work tasks? Could you get more done by not having to deal with the daily grind of the organization? Would you miss the chit-chat or feel that work had taken over your life?

The scale in Table 5.1 is designed to help you assess your ability to work successfully away from the office. Simply tick the appropriate response and apply the scoring system underneath to assess your answers.

Scoring system: For items 1, 2, 5, 8 and 10: Always scores 1, Frequently 2, Sometimes 3, etc. For items 3, 4, 6, 7 and 9: Always scores 5, Frequently 4, Sometimes, 3, etc. The maximum score is 50, the minimum score is 10.

How did you do?

- 40–50: It sounds like working from home or away from the office would suit your needs very well.
- 30–39: On balance you could do with finding opportunities to work away from the office, which given your personal qualities you could sell very well to your line manager.

Table 5.1

		Always	Frequently	Sometimes	Rarely	Never
1	I need my colleagues around me to help me get things done					
2	I love catching up on the latest gossip at work					
3	I would rather not have to go into the workplace to do my job					
4	I can get by without the company of others					
5	I find it hard to concentrate on work when I'm at home					
6	I am self-disciplined					
7	I prefer to work alone					
8	If the TV is on, I'll watch it					
9	Others describe me as conscientious					
10	The workplace gives me a much-needed change of scene					

- 20–29: Occasionally working away from the office might be useful to you, but too much of it would deprive you of what you value in the workplace.
- 10–19: You certainly need the structure and support provided by the workplace too much to leave it and there's nothing wrong with that if you feel it suits you.

A new organizational culture

The old definition of organizational culture as 'the way we do things around here' (Bower, 1966) may well have been superseded by more sophisticated terms, but it is most apt in depicting the fundamental changes new communications technology have brought to organizational functioning. Schein's (1992) reference to 'a pattern of basic assumptions, invented, discovered or developed by a given group as it learns to cope with its problems of external adaptation and internal integration' also relates well to a virtually oriented working environment which requires a virtual system of management. The freedom for employees which access to email and to the Internet and the ability to diminish and close software windows can facilitate, has grown at a pace which employers have found hard to keep up with. Edicts from the top of large organizations about the illicit and sometimes illegal use of the World Wide Web are increasingly common and represent attempts to rein in the activities of the few. As mentioned earlier in this chapter, electronic performance monitoring enables office organizations to survey what employees are looking at on their computer screens, with a range of outcomes for employees and their employers.

A model of 'remote', technology-driven organizational culture can be drawn from Trice and Beyer's (1984) general approach, which emphasizes four aspects of life at work. It is designed to give a flavour of organizational life where new technology is prevalent, and really hinges on the question: where is the modern organization located? Office-based organizations are recognizing potential savings by encouraging teleworking from employees' homes or by hotdesking (using an office space only for the time one is on the organization's property). The concept of a shop-front was challenged many years ago by the use of catalogue-based retailers and these have become part of the boom which represents Internet shopping. With manufacturing functions it is difficult to move these away from the site of production, but with global communications the trend has been to move premises to countries and regions where labour costs are cheaper. So the heart of an organization may be geographically dispersed or shared across continents or even based in a virtual environment on the Web, but the soul may lie with key employees who carry and share its ideals and perpetuate its representations of culture. Despite the growing distance within organizations there is still a crucial role for emotions and their by-products which resembles those experienced by nomadic civilizations. After all, human survival has traditionally been based on the capacity for mobility rather than being rooted to fixed structures, in order to keep up with food sources or evade the perils of changing seasons. One could argue that new methods of working are having the same beneficial impact on modern organizations.

- Company practices. These are the rites and rituals which contribute to the socialization of employees within the organization. Replacing the ceremonies of traditional organizational life, such as big meetings, are universal emails to all employees welcoming new staff or congratulating individuals on their success. However, these messages may be lost among the many other universal emails detailing the latest change in a product or the next visit of the chief executive to head office.

- Company communications. Trice and Beyer use this aspect of organizational life to emphasize the role of myths and legends in the history of the organization in providing an historical context and examples – which may or may not be true – to current employees. At one time this might have included tales of how much coal one individual was able to hew at the coalface, or how the idea for a best-selling product was drafted on the back of an envelope. Nowadays these are just as likely to depict how an employee got the latest idea while making a mobile phone call overlooking Loch Lomond or how one employee successfully dealt with over 500 emails on returning from a week's holiday.

- Physical cultural forms. In the new technological era, the actual appearance of an organization may matter less as more business is conducted via remote means. However, most organizations have a website which details the services and products on offer and may even include a virtual tour. These days an organization and its status are more likely to be judged by the effectiveness and currency of its website than on the state of the building in which it is housed.

- Common language. Within any job there are jargon and accepted meanings which only the organization or sector's employees are likely to understand and use. In its face-to-face dealings Walt Disney famously refers to its staff as the cast and its customers as guests, while Internet retailing companies will be talking about EDI (electronic data interchange), pixels and megabytes.

The gremlin in the machine

While new technology offers mobility and fluidity to the workplace, it also increases dependence on machine-operated communication systems and networks. The failure of these usually brings the organization to a halt, e.g. 'Our system is down at the moment and so we won't be able to help you – please call back later.' The emotion of the frustrated customer can be easily guessed at and one assumes that the employees are similarly affected at the anticipation of a backlog of work after the problems are fixed. The reason for the occurrence of these difficulties is increasingly to do with the unwelcome interest and efforts of computer hackers and viruses intent on causing mayhem in the system. These modern-day Luddites are likely to be experiencing emotions verging on delight at the problems caused to organizations in this way, but they do help to illustrate the frailties of new technology and the caveat of keeping traditional methods and skills in existence.

The risks associated with using new technology and automated systems have been well-researched in industrial and transport settings, although accidents continue to occur at differing rates depending on the type of industry involved (HSE, 2006). Reason's (1990) framework for understanding the nature and likely cause of accidents divides actions into those which are unintended (slips and lapses) – for example pressing the wrong button on a display – and intended actions (mistakes and violations) – such as carrying out a test programme which contravenes safety guidelines (as happened at Chernobyl nuclear plant in 1986). The role of employees' emotions in accidents has received some attention, although it is hard to isolate this variable from many others present in a given situation. Reason and Mycielska's (1982) diary study of students found that feelings do not seem to be a particular influence where unintentional actions occur, although the response of the individual, which is likely to be motivated by emotion and constitutes deliberate sabotage, is less easy to research.

The study of safety climate in organizations has shown that the key to preventing accidents lies with a range of factors, principally employees' perceptions of managers' commitment to safety and employees' involvement in safety issues and training (Dedobbeleer and Beland, 1991). Furthermore it is possible to harness emotions to help improve safety records by introducing competitiveness between teams of employees and rewarding excellent safety records (e.g. Haynes *et al.*, 1982). Safety is therefore promoted by ensuring that workers have a sense of control in using technological systems, which was not the case for the operators faced with 1600 displays and gauges in the control room at Three Mile Island as the nuclear power plant faced meltdown.

Summary of the chapter

The crux of the impact of new technology and job simplification on employees and organizations rests on where the control is held in the workplace. This chapter has taken as its premise that control underpins effective employee functioning, whether this is control over when and how tasks are carried out, or over the machinery and the relevant employees. At the level of the organization the attraction of new technology has been recognized in lower production and employee costs and increased flexibility, but for employees there can be both positive and negative outcomes. Nevertheless the approaches to introducing and utilizing systems have tended to emphasize the distance between the management and the employee and increase the distance between the organization and the individual employee and customer. One consequence of this is a lack of communication with the relevant workers prior to introduction of new technology, resulting in unrealistic expectations of what a system can deliver, or its operators achieve. Care is needed to ensure that employee control matches the psychological demands placed upon him or her, otherwise there is an increased risk of stress-related problems (Houtman, 1999). Where new technology fails it is not due to the technology but the lack of an accompanying appropriate job design (Parker *et al.*, 2001) as well as a receptive social setting. The resulting changes in organizational culture and the way in which employees and organizations relate to one another have been examined – it may be progress to reassess social traditions, but it is another matter where the threat is over the safety of people at work.

Key terms	
new technology	advanced manufacturing
teleworker	technology
hotdesking	organizational culture
electronic performance	
monitoring	

Questions and answers

1 *Identify the aspects of your work or study which rely on the use of new technology and estimate how much of your time is spent working with it. How much control over the pace or quantity of your work is governed by new technology?* It is sometimes sobering to consider how much you

had to do with designing the hardware and software with which you are obliged to work. Given that the aim of new technology was to save time, how much of this has been true in your experience? Certainly there are ups and downs to this, but if you are given a chance, would you ask to meet with the technology designers?

2 *Now highlight the number of faults/errors/mistakes you have experienced in the last month and how much 'downtime' (wasted time) you have had. How did it make you feel and who or what did you blame?* This is likely to tap into your perceived levels of control, not only over your specific job, but also the processes which impinge upon how well you can perform in your work. And it is not always the new technology which gets the blame! Emotions range from anger and frustration to a kind of learned helplessness where one is left to think 'Here we go again'. If you find your experience is to laugh a lot at what goes wrong, this is probably good for you, but just take care who sees you having too much fun!

3 *In shaping a teleworking job based mainly at home, what would be your main considerations?* The answer to this should relate not only to the physical surroundings and the virtual environment which new technology might afford you, but also your own personality make-up. So in addition to setting up a working space, a protocol for dealing with technological problems and boundaries for when to work and when not to, it is important to consider how much of a balance you need between being in the actual workplace and at home. This includes how easily you can be distracted, not just by other people, but by household tasks, food or television, or simply by an aversion to effort. The absence of work-related social facilitation is likely to be compounded by how others in the home environment react to having you around – how much respect for your work boundaries should you expect? Finally the issue of missing out on organizational decisions or even gossip may leave you feeling disempowered – what strategies might you develop for tackling this?

4 *Using Trice and Beyer's model of organizational culture, produce an analysis of your place of work or study.* Take company practices, company communications, physical cultural forms and common language as subheadings under which you can fill in examples of the relevant characteristics of your organization and the way it functions. Take care to identify the key factors which those outside are able to see. This is not always an easy thing to do, especially if you are feeling

entrenched in or consumed by the organization, but by achieving this you will be in a position to view where you work/study in a similar way to potential clients. You may not always like what you think outsiders see and feel the need to change things.

5 *How 'safe' is the technology you use?* 'Safe' here can mean both in a bodily/emotional sense as well as data-secure. It is worth looking at the reliance on new technology within your job/study role and working out worse case scenarios. If you rely on computers, you have been very fortunate if you have never experienced a corrupt disk or hard drive, or a virus on the Internet, which resulted in valuable time and effort being wasted. How might this translate into threats to your working environment from faulty machines, lift breakdowns, failing air conditioning, overheating electrical equipment, etc.? Are the means to carry on your job safely and effectively still available and what could be done if all the technology you use stopped working?

Suggested further reading

Nik Chmiel's book *Jobs, Technology and People* (1998) is a highly readable introduction to the main psychological issues facing humans in the use of new technology. In order to find out more about the impact of new technology on employees and organizations, *The New Workplace* (2002) by Holman *et al.* represents a good overview and has a companion publication, *The Essentials of the New Workplace* (2004) by the same authors which is aimed at consultants. Janice Langan-Fox's chapter in the *Research Companion to Organizational Health Psychology* (2005) edited by Alexander Antoniou and Cary Cooper provides a view on how advances in the use of technology impact on our functioning and health. For more specific literature on information and communication technologies Gillian Symon's (2000) article provides an informative analysis. There is little doubt that this is an area where literature will continue to rapidly expand and it is worth conducting your own searches too (providing the Internet link is working!). For details on all these texts, please consult the reading list for Chapter 5 at the back of this book.

6　Relationships at work

> It is the individual who is not interested in his fellow men who has the
> greatest difficulties in life and provides the greatest injury to others. It is
> from among such individuals that all human failures spring.
>
> (*Alfred Adler, 1933*)

One of the key determinants of how we feel is our experience of interactions and relationships between ourselves and others. This holds true for life inside and out of the workplace. Naturally there is as wide a range of satisfaction levels with our relationships as there are emotions to express such satisfaction. In our interactions with others, whether in person or by phone, email, fax or letter, it is as though our personal emotional radar is locked on to the other individual(s), constantly checking for nuances of behaviour from which we might draw inferences about how well the interaction is going. Or put another way which is consistent with our evolution as a species, to check whether we are under immediate threat of attack! In the workplace, where survival is the bottom line, our dealings with others can help us to find allies, to spot potential or actual enemies and to get us the resources we need to stay afloat. This chapter examines the emotional dealings which underpin the skills and judgements necessary to ensure our survival.

Emotional intelligence

Emotional intelligence (EI) has been heralded as a predictor of success in a number of life domains, including work (Goleman, 1998a). It has become the new buzz-phrase not only in the study of applied psychology, but management, education, health and in fact anywhere people gather together and need to get on with one another. EI has been variously defined as 'an ability to recognize the meanings of emotions and their relationships, and to reason and problem-solve on the basis of them' (Mayer *et al.*, 1999, p. 267). In other words, 'a person who can easily recognize and regulate his/her emotions, or those of others, is emotionally intelligent' (Ben Ze'ev, 2002, p. 176). Not surprisingly EI has created a wealth of popular and scientific interest in recent years (Mayer, *et al.* 2001) and perhaps most notably through the bestselling books of Daniel Goleman: *Emotional Intelligence* (1995) and *Working with Emotional Intelligence* (1998a). This is not to say that EI is universally acclaimed as a cure for all human shortcomings: in fact there are ethical considerations which are often overlooked in concluding that EI is a workplace commodity in which we should trade (e.g. Fineman, 2000).

EI is concerned with those abilities/skills which have been viewed as quite different to 'pure' academic capability and consequently undervalued. Howard Gardner (1983) was one of the first theorists to distinguish between intellectual and emotional capabilities. He formulated the well-respected theory of 'multiple intelligences' which included not only the traditional academic abilities (e.g. verbal and numerical), but also two emotional factors: the ability to understand oneself and to understand others (intrapersonal and interpersonal respectively). It is argued that EI involves these emotional abilities operating collaboratively with the intellectual ones (Goleman, 1998a). EI by its very nature illuminates the conflict between head and heart, and as such it is relevant to such areas as mental health (Taylor *et al.*, 1999), education (Elias *et al.*, 2000), interpersonal relationships (Flury and Ickes, 2001) and work (Caruso and Wolfe, 2001, Cherniss and Goleman, 2001).

A number of theorists and practitioners have sought to identify the underlying components of EI and a limited consensus on some of these has been reached, but debate continues as to its exact configuration and whether EI constitutes a trait of personality or a cognitive ability. Perhaps the wisest conclusion is that 'the two constructs are not mutually exclusive and may therefore co-exist' (Petrides and Furnham, 2000, p. 427). The key issues which arise from this discussion are how can we assess EI and also can it be developed or enhanced in any way? This section goes on to consider the latter possibility, as it is relevant to potential personal and professional development in the workplace and to those who aspire to join it, but first it is important to examine the likely components of emotional intelligence.

Following on from Salovey and Mayer (1990), Goleman (1998a) suggested five basic emotional and social competencies which make up EI. Subsequently Goleman (2000) has rationalized these to include the following four:

1 Self-awareness – the recognition of one's own emotions and their impact on others, the ability to identify and appraise one's strengths and weaknesses and possessing a sense of self-confidence.
2 Self-management – covers a range of abilities which enable us to keep control over our feelings, to build trust with others and to be conscientious and flexible whilst focusing on attaining our goals and demonstrating initiative.
3 Social awareness – the capacity for sensing and gaining insight into the emotional circumstances of others, supporting them in their own development, identifying and meeting customers' expectations and understanding the prevailing organizational climate.
4 Relationship management – demonstrating successful social skills across settings which require sound two-way communication, persuasiveness, leadership, handling conflict, promoting change and teamworking.

At first glance, these may seem the prerequisites on a person specification for obtaining a fairly demanding job, and whilst differences have appeared in the exact composition of EI as described by different theorists, it comprises a mix of highly useful cognitive and non-cognitive competencies (Mayer, 2001). Scrutiny of the abilities listed above, may cause you to think that at least some of these come naturally to you and without a great deal of conscious thought – 'that's just the kind of person I am'. Indeed researchers recognize that the processing of emotions and rational thought occur at different speeds in different areas of the brain – the amygdala and neocortex respectively – with information from emotions occurring more quickly. This not only means that non-cognitive information is important in helping us reach decisions about what to do next, but that it is physiologically prioritized in order to ensure our survival: for example a successful reaction to fear needs to be quick and require little conscious thought. Similarly our intuition about a colleague can be surprisingly accurate to a high level of success, even when based on a 30-second snapshot of behaviour (Ambady, 1993). However, such a high degree of insight, which appears to have insufficient grounds for perceiving it, is likely to be due to the accumulation of expert knowledge based on experience, rather than on an apparently split-second choice (Ben Ze'ev, 2002). It is not surprising, therefore, that EI is thought to increase as we get older (Goleman, 1998b).

The following sections examine the concepts which underlie EI, drawing on specific examples and illustrations.

Self-awareness and its lack: alexithymia

Alexithymia represents 'difficulty in identifying feelings and describing them to others' (Taylor, 2001, p. 71). It is possible to experience this to a high or low degree, but for those whose approach to life is characterized in this way, limitations are also likely to be present in the ability to empathize with others – this can be partially attributed to problems in identifying emotions from others' facial expressions (Taylor *et al.*, 1999). In terms of self-awareness, high alexithymia can mean a limited inability to experience emotions and to be able to fantasize, as well as a tendency to focus on the specific details of events which are going on around the individual (Nemiah *et al.*, 1976). Alexithymia is more likely to be present in men than women and in those experiencing psychological health problems (Taylor, 2000), including alcohol and drug abuse and eating disorders. In addition it has been found that confusion in recognizing and interpreting our emotions is linked to thoughts of inadequacy about ourselves (Taylor and Bagby, 2000) and maladaptive coping strategies when faced with stress. Alexithymia is a limiting factor and is most damaging where it negatively impacts on our personal relationships, both inside and out of work – perhaps resulting in accusations of bullying – as well as on our health.

Self-management

The Marshmallow Test conducted at Stanford University was designed to assess whether young children of pre-school age would take a marshmallow placed on the table in front of them or wait patiently to be rewarded with this and a second marshmallow after the experimenter had left and then returned to the room. Following up these participants in later school life revealed that those who immediately gratified their needs were more likely to lose their temper and get involved in fights and were less able to focus on achieving their goals. Furthermore these children scored far lower than their more self-controlled colleagues in the American college entrance exam. Goleman (1998a) surmises this disparity is due to the interference of emotions with their ability to pay attention in learning situations: however, he reports how in later life this trend translates into less successful and more distant relationships for those children who initially grabbed the marshmallow. One might surmise that this could relate to colleagues in our own work environments – but be careful not to leave the whole box of goodies in case you are shocked by the outcome!

Case Study 6.1	**You don't have to be 'brainy' to be intelligent: where emotional intelligence makes the difference**

A newly promoted professor was keen to make his mark at a new research unit for which he had been given responsibility. Well known for his publications in his specialist area, he was often called upon by government agencies hungry for up-to-date advice and eager to commission relevant projects. Part of the talent which made this aspect of his job successful was presenting an air of competence to those he considered integral to maintaining this success. In his dealings with research and support staff within the unit, the professor ignored the need for meetings and avoided routine contact with the team. This served to communicate not simply a superior air, but also a lack of regard for them. Whilst he continued to obtain large research grants, he needed to rely on the excellent interpersonal skills of his research staff to gather data for his projects. He had come to construe matters which did not directly affect his research as interference. In a bid to isolate his unit from the annoying distractions of the outside world, the professor authorized the installation of locked doors at either end of the corridor on which the unit was located, thus preventing visitors from entering without a keycode. When a member of staff was experiencing personal problems, he referred her to the personnel department for a disciplinary interview, compounding the individual's misery. ▶

> Failing to recognize the growing discontent in his research team and seemingly impervious to the 100 per cent turnover rate in the small unit, the professor quickly achieved notoriety across the university for all the wrong reasons.

The case study illustrates how a lack of emotional intelligence and consequent failure to act on the warning signs can result in the stagnation of a promising career. As Gibbs (1995) put it: 'IQ gets you hired but EQ gets you promoted' (p. 59). Paraphrasing the words of Goleman, this example also shows how being 'book smart' is less important than being 'people smart' when it comes to making progress in the world of work. In fact the potential of EI to make a positive difference to the functioning of individuals and also organizations is quickly becoming recognized. The rapid growth of academic research and practical workshops on the subject provides strong evidence of this and has manifested itself in settings as diverse as corporate business seminars to primary school dance classes! However, the issue of measuring emotional competencies is less easy to address, as it underpins the question of knowing when an intervention to improve EI has been successful.

The scope for developing EI is evident from studies which show that training and experience can make a positive difference and, as has been suggested, can be due to building up a bank of expert knowledge, i.e. knowing what is required in a particular situation. Whilst there is scarcity of published studies in this area, intervention research has shown an improvement of around 10 per cent in the EI of participants which is sustained three to eighteen months after training (Boyatzis, 2005). Small-scale studies of psychology undergraduates have shown differences in aspects of EI between men and women, as well as those exposed to training courses in emotional competencies (Weinberg and Pearson, 2005). However, there are claims that university Masters programmes which do not aim to alter EI have a similar effect (Boyatzis, 2005). A study of teams assessed for either high or low levels of EI revealed that the more emotionally attuned were able to perform better earlier in a nine-week period – possibly due to a higher degree of cohesiveness – although by the end the various team performances were similar (Jordan *et al.*, 1999). Given the potential impact of developmental factors, such as age and relevant experience (Wong *et al.*, 2006), there is considerable room for further research in this area, particularly relating to workplace settings.

Exercise 6.1	**Measuring emotional intelligence (see also Chapter 9 for a fuller review)**

The development of measures of EI has advanced in recent years, with both performance and self-report instruments on sale. The Mayer-Salovey-Caruso Emotional Intelligence Test (MSCEIT) is a performance test which is a shorter and more reliable version of its forerunner, while the Emotional Quotient Inventory (EQ-i) (Bar-On, 1997) is seen as a 'promising' measure of EI (Dawda and Hart, 2001), with high internal validity and reliability. For UK-based measures, the Emotional Intelligence Questionnaire (Dulewicz and Higgs, 2001) has been designed with business executives in mind, while the Emotional Intelligence Self-Assessment Questionnaire (EISAQ) (Weinberg and Pearson, 2005) aims to assess such competencies among undergraduate students.

This exercise is designed to probe how good you are at managing your emotions. The following scale rates your ability not simply to control your feelings, but also to deal with them in a way which helps you too. The higher your score, the better you are handling the way you feel. If you score below 30, try to note down things you could think or do to make yourself feel more on an even keel, especially when things are not going your way.

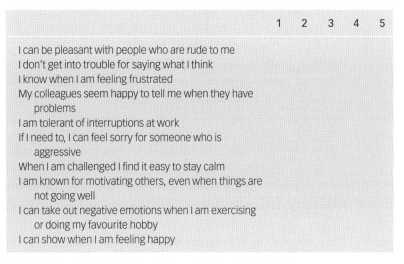

	1	2	3	4	5
I can be pleasant with people who are rude to me					
I don't get into trouble for saying what I think					
I know when I am feeling frustrated					
My colleagues seem happy to tell me when they have problems					
I am tolerant of interruptions at work					
If I need to, I can feel sorry for someone who is aggressive					
When I am challenged I find it easy to stay calm					
I am known for motivating others, even when things are not going well					
I can take out negative emotions when I am exercising or doing my favourite hobby					
I can show when I am feeling happy					

5 = All of the time; 4 = Most of the time; 3 = Some of the time; 2 = Rarely; 1 = Never.

Interpersonal relationships at work

The nature of our relationships at work varies depending on the amount of contact we have, the circumstances which form the background to those relationships and the importance to us of each relationship. One academic worked for ten years at a university without ever possessing a car park permit and so it is logical to conclude that the most important relationship was with the car park attendant who controlled the entrance barrier. This was a relationship based on mutual respect and common cause ('we need each other to keep the organization running'), interpersonal trading of emotions ('Did you watch the football last night?'; 'What do you think of the changes at work?') and most importantly liking ('How's the family?'; 'How is your health these days?'). One day, when the attendant's hut contained a new face, the feelings were those which accompany the end of any fruitful relationship.

Based on the premise that people buy from people they like, training seminars have for many years exhorted sales staff to build relationships with their clients and potential clients. Identifying common ground is seen as the key to success in this endeavour, and the concept of neuro-linguistic programming has been popularized as a technique for demonstrating to customers that sales representatives talk the same language, and may even think the same way. There are many approaches to conducting business – or indeed any work transaction – based on differing expectations and assumptions. At one time salespeople were branded as brash, direct and interested solely in their commission, but in recent times this has been challenged by a shift to take the pressure out of the selling situation and to making the transaction seem as much like a normal conversation as possible. The underlying assumption of this approach is not that a sale is inevitable 'because I am going to force this person to buy from me', but that 'I am going to inform, negotiate and lead the customer to a point where they will want to make the purchase.' However, the continuing emphasis on the need to make that sale has led to something of a backlash against 'soft-sell rubbish' (see the review by Clive Fletcher of *The Hard Truth about Soft Selling* by Dudley and Tanner, 2005 [Fletcher, 2006]). In fact an international study of what motivates sales success found large differences. In Singapore, the Philippines, the US and the UK money was the prime mover, but in Australia and Sweden, the opportunity to use special skills and to 'do new and exciting things' came top of salespeople's lists (Tanner and Dudley, 2003). Our experience is likely to confirm that most workplace negotiations conducted under the banner of reasonableness result in intended outcomes, but how this point is reached may well differ with the culture of the organization and the country in which the transaction takes place.

In his famous 1938 book *How to Win Friends and Influence People*, Dale Carnegie espoused what he observed to be the key to successful negotiations and conversations. A summary of the important concepts would read very similarly to what we now call emotional intelligence. In particular, Carnegie emphasizes the significant impact on others created by our ability to listen and provide positive feedback, verbally or non-verbally. He recounts many anecdotes of people he met or read about which feature the ability to make others feel important by demonstrating an interest in them and appreciation for their work or what they hold dear. The consequence of this is to make others feel important and therefore make them feel good about you – although Carnegie is keen to point out this should be done with genuine feeling and for sound rather than devious motivation. In short, he highlights the importance of arousing positive emotions among others for the common good. Within a work setting, such efforts might contribute to good morale, constructive feedback, empowerment and improved productivity. In the following section, work relationships with colleagues are examined in order to establish the key role of emotions in the way we work. Detailed consideration of the relationship between the individual and their line manager appears in Chapter 7.

The colleague relationship

This is the most common form of work relationship, in which we carry out the same or a similar job role as others within the unit of the organization, perhaps sharing the close proximity of an office, working alongside co-workers on a production line or communicating via more remote means. Whatever the setting, there is little doubt that such relationships are important, as they occupy a considerable amount of our time at work and involve job tasks and performance in common, which ultimately have consequences for us and our co-workers. It is the nature of emotions within such relationships which is the focus for this section.

'The dynamics of organizational relationships are among the most frequently cited sources of intense emotion' (Waldron, 2000, p. 66). Here passions are to be found ranging through trust, jealousy, love, anger, hate and desire. The television phenomenon of *Big Brother* provides viewers with an opportunity to examine in detail the words and actions of volunteers in a confined setting, yet the workplace offers a similar potential, albeit with a reduced audience. The emotions are likely to be the same: envy of another's success, dislike of someone who is seen as different from the rest, lust for an attractive co-worker, admiration for the hard work of another, or betrayal by those who had been previously trusted.

So what are the consequences of emotions experienced in the workplace? In both relevant theory and research, the availability of social support is seen as a positive factor for employee well-being, and possibly a buffer against psychological strain (Stansfeld *et al.*, 1998). However, social support operates differently for men and women: for men the issue is more likely to be the level of support, whereas for women it is the quality of close relationships. The reason for good relationships with colleagues being so integral to our own emotional well-being originates from our development as humans. We are social beings and as such the majority of our species prefer the company of other people to being on our own. This has long been a better guarantee of survival, being protected as part of a group and having access to shared resources. For similar reasons in the work context, we tend to identify more with members of our own work group at a comparable job level. Workplace survival may depend on colleagues covering for us from time to time, or sticking up for us when managers or customers act inappropriately.

However, the quiet pressure to conform to such group norms can result in a reverse of this mutual support. We might come to view a colleague as disloyal should they be promoted to the next level in the organization (e.g. management) or we might object to commonly accepted practices which we regard as offensive. Failure to 'play the game' can lead to rejection by the group, resulting in omission from informal social gatherings or being left out of an important round of communications. The sudden halt to conversations when the 'outsider' enters a room, or the knowing glances between others, are signs that the individual is under scrutiny and no longer seen as trustworthy. When that employee makes an effort to act in the group's interest it is possible for them to be re-admitted, on an emotional level, to the fold. They might share a joke which emphasizes group unity, or speak up on behalf of colleagues, and this will give others a chance to assess their worthiness of group membership. Given that relationships evolve over time, those between colleagues are no different and the likelihood is that the cycle of feeling part of things, and then not part of things, is ongoing. The issue of whether we care what our colleagues think of us will depend on many factors, including the perceived importance of the group to our own identity and happiness and in the longer-term to our working and social existence. Whilst the existence of social support has been highlighted as a predictor of good psychological health, it is not always straightforward.

Relationships with colleagues can exist on several levels, ranging from spending a lot of time in each other's company as members of the same staff group and being friendly, sharing jokes and possibly more, or simply saying hello and goodbye. As individuals it is likely that we will differ in approaches to the job, experience and skill levels as well as sense of humour, yet there are likely to be goals and gripes in common as well as the need to express emotions about these. The canteen or rest room has long been the safe place in which to express such feelings, but in a world where physical space costs money, staff in many organizations find that the photocopy room is fast becoming the only 'haven'. So what happens in environments where there is no obvious safe place to share views with colleagues? The option of keeping things bottled up is open to all, but the potential for the cork on these to pop out is well known. There can be implications for our emotional as well as physical well-being in not having opportunities to express our feelings, such as poor psychological health (e.g. Weinberg and Creed, 2000) and cardiovascular disease (Miguel-Tobal and Gonzalez-Ordi, 2005). Alternatively colleagues may notice that 'emotions find a way out'. It is almost as though an internal reservoir of emotion fills up and has to find a channel through which to release itself. This hydraulic model is used to describe how aggression boils over and the phrase 'going postal' derives from the media coverage of acts of violence by mail carriers in the United States.

The channelling of feelings can produce positive results too. We might use the drive of our emotions in the way we work, perhaps resulting in tasks which we complete quicker or to a higher standard. Anyone who has encountered the fastest supermarket checkout operator in the West (based on the old American Wild West shootouts), may have witnessed the verve with which their household items are propelled past the barcode bleeper and wondered why they are having to pick them up off the floor. Perhaps the testimony of a farm shop assistant is the most illuminating. Such is the rivalry between the two butchers, that each has a tray of freshly cooked sausages on display for customers to sample. 'You can almost smell the testosterone: whilst they appear friendly towards each other on the surface, it is obvious they are trying to outdo each other and see who can make the biggest and best sausage'!

Emotions can act as motivators which lead us to challenge and change what we perceive of as unfair. In this sense they provide a useful survival kit, particularly as there are many challenges to smooth relationships, most of all in the potentially competitive environment of the workplace. As survival often depends on having adequate resources for us to function effectively, gaining access to these can promote a range of responses among colleagues. The pay differential provides an interesting example. Although the UK took legal steps to safeguard equal treatment of men and women at work over thirty years ago, reports of women earning less than men for doing the same job are still widespread. It is suggested that women will be paid around 80 per cent of what their male colleagues will receive, amounting in some cases to a difference of as much as a quarter of a million pounds over the course of a working life. One step to combat this is to allow women, or men, to know what their opposite sex colleagues are being paid. The outcomes of this – one of which should include fairness – are likely to include real consequences for relationships between colleagues. One might guess at the remarks which are likely to be made or at very least the change in feeling towards co-workers, despite the likelihood that this is an example of unethical organizational or industrial policy, rather than skulduggery on the part of an individual. This individual reaction can be understood by likening the organization to the natural environment: in either example there are limited resources and it is arguably easier to blame and compete with others for those resources rather than change one's surroundings.

Looking on the more positive side of colleague relationships, the phenomenon of co-workers beginning short- and long-term relationships in the workplace is under-researched, but has received a lot of anecdotal attention, particularly on television and Internet surveys. The advent of sexual relations between colleagues in workplace settings may well have been the focus of some of the more lurid documentaries, but the incidence of partners working together has been more carefully scrutinized. The positive and negative outcomes of this situation seem to split along gender lines, with the main benefit for the man in terms of job prestige and sense of control, while the woman is more likely to carry heavier non-work roles and experience greater dissatisfaction. The emotional well-being of dual-earner couples where both partners work is examined in more depth in Chapter 8.

Bullying

The organizational climate in which we work also plays a role in how we respond to challenges in our jobs. The example of bullying (introduced in Chapter 2) is pertinent. Accusations that organizations encourage bullying behaviours, by neglecting to recognize they exist or to take necessary action, have cited the problem as 'institutional bullying'. In recent years this has been highlighted in police forces, including London's Metropolitan Police Force, following a number of internal investigations into officers' behaviour towards both colleagues and the public. Indeed this led to the force's then Commissioner, Sir Paul Condon, announcing that 'a significant minority' of police officers were 'intimidating and using violence against fellow officers' (*Guardian*, 1997). Hoel *et al.*'s (2001) study has shown that bullying is widespread among men and women and across many occupations and organizations in the UK, and as such it is certainly deserving of closer scrutiny given its potential to scar relationships in work settings.

Whilst definitions of bullying may vary across countries, there are common themes which have been identified. These include the frequency and duration of the bullying behaviour, the reaction of the target, the intent of the perpetrator and the balance of power between the parties involved (Hoel *et al.*, 2001). However, the three key components which are used to determine the existence of bullying in the light of case law are (Quine, 1999):

1 Impact on the recipient (rather than the bully's intention),
2 Resulting negative experience for the recipient,
3 Persistent nature of the bullying behaviour.

Within the workplace there are many ways in which bullying can take place, and these have been categorized into five aspects of recurring behaviour (Rayner and Hoel, 1997). It is quite likely that most people who have been in the world of work will recognize actions which they have witnessed or experienced. However, it is worth bearing in mind the above criteria.

1 Threat to professional status

This can take the form of undermining or underplaying the work carried out by an individual, criticizing and scrutinizing their performance, intimidatory use of disciplinary or competence procedures and humiliating the person in front of others, including colleagues. These behaviours call into question the ability of the individual to carry out their duties effectively, and are likely to impact on the ongoing confidence of the employee to be able to do it. One might imagine an over-zealous line manager who is keen to ensure peak performance from their subordinates indulging in these or related actions. These are less likely to produce the desired outcome than to generate emotions which will provide an obstacle to future relationships. With quite different motivation, the malicious individual who is intent on inflicting emotional damage on colleagues might behave in this way and actually achieve similar negative results. Naturally there is reluctance in the managerial literature to focus on such similarities (Hoel *et al.*, 2001).

One key issue for the target is their perception of the behaviour. Not only are the repercussions likely to remain with the victim, they are bound to be replayed among colleagues as the word gets around: 'Did you hear what happened to so-and-so?!' Beyond this, the next moves by both parties involved are likely to be scrutinized with much the same curiosity as a television soap story line. 'Viewers' are likely to discuss what so-and-so should or will do next in response, or pass judgement on whether or not the outcome was deserved. 'It is a lingering residue, a buzz, sometimes a contagion, that spreads through an organization in a chain of interaction until it finally fades from public view' (Waldron in Fineman, 2000). Emotional contagion, 'the tendency of individuals to "catch" emotions from others' (Zerbe *et al.*, 2002, p. 278), can spread the negative impact of bullying to others who have not been directly involved. This adds further weight, should any be necessary, to the statistic of 49.4 per cent of UK employees who have either experienced or witnessed bullying at work in the previous five years (Hoel, Faragher and Cooper, 2004).

2 Threat to personal standing

The behaviours in this category are those which are also characteristics of so many playground misdeeds, but which are also an unfortunate

The evidence

One of the largest studies of bullying has included 5288 UK employees in a range of organizations and occupations (Hoel *et al.*, 2001). In attempting to establish how widespread bullying is, the researchers found 10.5 per cent of their sample reported being a target of this behaviour during the last six months, with 24.4 per cent claiming to have been bullied during the last five years. This compares with another UK study recording 18.3 per cent of its sample experiencing bullying in the last five years (Unison, 1997), but differences in measurement tools were noted, which might underpin the variation in recording bullying in a range of studies (Hoel *et al.*, 2001).

In the UK-wide study, the most affected groups included employees in the prison services, postal and telecommunication services, teaching and dance professions, whereas the brewing and IT manufacturing industries and pharmaceutical sales sectors reported the lowest rates of bullying (Hoel *et al.*, 2001). Little differences in the gender and age of targets of bullying were noted, although women were more likely to report experiences in higher education, the fire service and voluntary sector and employees in the under-24 age bracket were considered most at risk. Three-quarters of the perpetrators of bullying in this study were in managerial or supervisory roles compared to one-third of colleagues, although swift addition here reveals the existence of multiple perpetrators in some cases. Men were more likely to be bullied by a manager, whereas women were more likely to face bullying from colleagues. This is a finding borne out by studies in other countries (Vartia and Hyyti, 2002). Within occupations, teachers reported most difficulties with managers (86.4 per cent), while NHS (53.6 per cent) and university employees (51.4 per cent) were the most frequent targets of peer-bullying. The bullying of clients by employees was worse in teaching, retail and hotel sectors, so perhaps it is no coincidence the best-known television caricatures of appalling behaviour emanate from these quarters. More detailed consideration of the interaction between employees and customers is given in Chapters 2 and 4.

Potential causes of bullying

Three possible causes of bullying behaviour have been identified (Einarsen, 1996):

1 'Bullying' personality
2 The nature of human communication in the workplace
3 Aspects of the working environment.

The popularity of the idea of the flawed personality who cannot help themselves but acts like a bully, may lie in its simplicity and also convenience. After all, if one can attribute the whole set of problem behaviours to an internally troubled individual, then the problem can in theory be settled through organizational procedures. The existence in the bully's past of negative experiences in childhood – including problematic relationships with parents or caregivers – can be seen as part of a 'life cycle of violence' (Hoel *et al.*, 2001, p. 64), which is set to continue throughout the individual's adult life (Randall, 1997). However, further scrutiny of this approach also highlights the problems of inappropriately labelling individuals and ignoring the experience of many school age children who have experience of being both perpetrators and targets in various situations (O'Moore and Hillery, 1988). Perhaps the same can be said of adults in the workplace, where there are likely to be workplace factors, rather than simply an individual's personality, such as a manager's, involved (the flaws and fine-tuning of managerial skills are examined in more depth in Chapter 7). Where other explanations have been exhausted there should of course be procedures for dealing with the individual concerned.

Human communication at work is likely to be affected by a host of factors, including the time available and the accessibility of the individuals involved. What may be perceived as aggression by one individual, could be intended as justified assertiveness by another. If you needed to communicate what you considered to be shortcomings in someone's performance, and you had already tried on two or three occasions in clear and reasonable language, what would be the ideal way forward? As the pressures of the situation increased, such as mistakes and increased costs, would it become harder to mask the negative emotions of rising frustration with the poorly performing employee? Would there be time to take into account how that employee might respond to more direct comments about their work? It is entirely possible that the 'disposal of aggression' which is seen as a natural part of working life (Hoel *et al.*, 2001, p. 65), whereby such frustrations spill over, will negatively affect relationships and inflict potentially long-term damage. In the light of such circumstances a supervisor who is widely perceived as supportive can come to be viewed by the employee concerned as someone who always seems to be finding fault and picking on them. The existence of justified need for the manager's behaviour is likely to be the key, but in the complexity of human interaction, how easy would it be for either party to be objective?

By viewing bullying as a social stressor – as has been the case in central European research into bullying – it is possible to classify this behaviour as a function of poor working conditions. Certainly it is in such settings that bullying is more prevalent, e.g in prison environments (Vartia and Hyyti, 2002), and there appear to be differences in the quantity of bullying in different occupational groups (Hoel *et al.*, 2001). Time pressure (Zapf *et al.*, 1996), communication problems and authoritarian management (Vartia, 1996) have been documented as present in bullying scenarios, which is of little comfort to those on the receiving end. Attempts at the classification of causes of bullying can be useful in helping to identify socially toxic factors in the work environment. In this way attempts can be made to change the work climate for the better and eradicate the relevant social stressors. Remembering the beginning of this section, this can be a long, slow process in organizational climates which promote institutionalized bullying, either passively or actively.

Tips on tackling bullying

- Keep a record of negative comments and events, including timing and who was responsible for them, as soon after they occur as possible
- Tell someone you trust, either inside or outside of work, about what is happening and how it is making you feel
- If you feel there is nobody to turn to, try to make use of someone whose job is to listen to problems and protect confidentiality – the workplace may have a counsellor or a confidential phone helpline, or the union office should be happy listen even if you are not yet a member
- If the problem comes from colleagues, sound out your manager's view on their behaviour. This can be done in indirect ways if you feel it is too early to lay your cards on the table
- Remember that bullying is unacceptable and is in breach of employment regulations – you do not have to tolerate what is going on
- If you have done the above and are waiting for the situation to be resolved, try to take some control over your situation, even if these are

small steps which might help minimize the problem or how you feel about it: can you switch your shift, move your desk, take breaks at different times, dress in a way which might convey more 'personal power' or consult with others to see if they have witnessed what is happening.

Summary of the chapter

This chapter has examined the best and the worst of human relationships as they relate to the expression of emotions. It would be great to think that the positive end of the spectrum – such as the concept of emotional intelligence – could be expanded and even trained to ensure that the negative end of things, such as bullying, was consigned to history. Humans are about learning and learning is often about mistakes: some to which we are predisposed and others which we can recognize and from which we can try to move on. Sandwiched in between a consideration of what is involved in both emotional intelligence and bullying and what can be done in relation to each, is a section on the working relationships which most will share: those with colleagues. This is characterized by both ups and downs, as with most relationships, and is subject to the intricacies of everyday social psychology. Again the positives and negatives are evident, but on balance our dealings with co-workers hopefully represent a supportive environment which aids the cause of personal survival at work and where this is not present it is important to locate real allies.

Key terms	
emotional intelligence (EI)	alexithymia
self-awareness	social support
relationship management	bullying

Questions and answers

1 *If someone asked you for a brief description of emotional intelligence, what would you say?* Emotional intelligence is basically about how we conduct our emotional affairs with ourselves and others! EI covers self-awareness, self-management, social awareness and relationship management and is part of a spectrum of multiple intelligences which

is probably linked with the success we have in many aspects of our lives. EI complements the traditional abilities which are valued in schools and can be thought of as a set of skills or traits which enable us to get on with others, as well as ourselves.

2 *Can we improve our emotional intelligence?* It follows logic that the older we become the more likely we are to develop better personal and social skills, simply because we have gained more practice and hopefully learned from our mistakes. Research into the impact of training courses is still relatively new, but there are some indications that improvements can result from attending programmes which focus on improving these types of emotional competencies. The jury is still out on whether or not EI is really a trait, much like aspects of our personality, which can be moulded within certain limits. The attraction of being able to make a difference to the success we have in working with others has always been great (Dale Carnegie's book is an early example) and this is likely to continue to increase the number of courses and trainers in this area!

3 *How important are emotions in the workplace?* Emotions are the life-blood of any organization. How those emotions are utilized or har-nessed can be the key to the success of that enterprise, as they are evi-dent in most interactions and can play a major role in the outcomes of those interactions. Ranging from enthusiasm or passion for one's job to loathing and fear of the organizational machine (or even vice-versa), and featuring the humorous, the caring, the disrespectful and the envious in individual work relationships, emotions are hard to leave behind at the door on our way into the workplace. Depending on your disposition and level of job responsibility, it might be easier if this was the case and there would probably be a lot less to contend with! Yet it is worth considering how interesting or uninteresting the world of work would be without emotions to influence attitudes and behaviour. Would you really want to be without the loyalty and grati-tude of some of your colleagues and customers, in order not to have to put up with the complaints and brickbats from others?

4 *Which factors can account for bullying behaviour?* Whilst being aware that bullying can take many forms, the motivations for using it are also varied. The three main causes are the 'bullying' personality, the manner in which communication takes place and aspects of the work environment. The idea that the bully's personality is the sole reason would make for easy labelling, yet not so easy avoidance. Interest in psychopathic personalities in the workplace is actually growing and

has tended to focus on those at executive level who appear polished and charming on the surface (high in extraversion), but who have little concern for others and are typically untrustworthy (low on agreeableness). 'Mis-communication' seems to be a common feature of bullying situations, where the 'aggressor' may not intend the negative effects which result; however, the perceptions of both parties should be subject to further scrutiny. This may in turn be linked to the working environment, which should ideally permit opportunities for reflection and/or access to an 'honest broker'. In highly intense workplaces the pressure of deadlines can make this extremely difficult, and where a culture of acceptance of bullying behaviour prevails, the situation may remain unaddressed for too long.

5 *How can be bullying be combated?* From breathing exercises to assertiveness techniques, there is a wide range of recommendations for the individual who becomes the target of bullying. The key probably lies in two courses of action: (i) in changing the bully's perception of the target, so they no longer consider their unacceptable behaviour as an option, and (ii) finding someone to confide in and draw support from. Both of these may not easily be achieved and obviously depend on the individuals concerned and the circumstances, however bullying is a breach of employment regulations, regardless of whether the people in the organization have recognized this or not. In addition, an increasing number of organizations have a 'Dignity at Work' policy or an individual whose job is to provide support in these situations. Getting help from either inside or outside of the workplace is highly recommended, and by finding out what support from colleagues can be gathered, it can be reassuring and sometimes surprising to find out that others may feel the same way. If bullying is about the abuse of power, in whatever form, then the careful use of personal power can be an effective tool in breaking the cycle of behaviour and asserting the rights of both the individual and the group.

Suggested further reading

For those wishing to find out more about emotional intelligence, which was discussed in the first part of this chapter, Daniel Goleman's books are highly readable and very widely sold and include *Working with Emotional Intelligence* (1998), as well as the original *Emotional Intelligence*

(1995). For a more academic view, Joseph Ciarrocchi, Joseph Forgas and John Mayer (2001) have gathered together valuable insights from many perspectives including chapters on emotional intelligence in the workplace, as well as using EI to become healthy, wealthy and wise in their book *Emotional Intelligence in Everyday Life* (Psychology Press). For a UK view, Dulewicz and Higgs (1999) write from a tried and tested applied viewpoint, while those wishing to trace a popular history of this intriguing concept, look no further than Dale Carnegie's (1938) classic *How to Win Friends and Influence People*, the title of which has passed into everyday language. Arguably the first well-known text on what we now call emotional intelligence, there have been many guides to follow it, advising us on the best techniques for getting along with others. For a guide which mixes practice and theory well, try John Hayes' (2002) *Interpersonal Skills at Work*, published by Routledge.

The research literature on the causes, consequences and prevalence of workplace bullying is beginning to burgeon. From a relatively under-recognized phenomenon there are studies emanating from many occupations and for a detailed view of these, the key European authors Einarsen *et al.* (2003) have compiled an authoritative text: *Bullying and Emotional Abuse in the Workplace: International Perspectives in Research and Practice*. It is worth looking in journals related to particular areas for more occupationally focused research as there many interesting reviews ranging from organizational to ethical publications.

For an analysis of organizational frameworks which are linked to bullying, see Salin (2003) 'Ways of explaining workplace bullying: A review of enabling, motivating and precipitating structures and processes in the work environment'.

For an ethical viewpoint, why not try: Vega and Comer (2005) 'Stick and stones may break your bones, but words can break your spirit: Bullying in the workplace'.

There are many websites and user-friendly publications devoted to tackling this difficult issue, including www.andreadamstrust.org and C. Rayner, H. Hoel and C.L. Cooper (2002) *Workplace Bullying: What we Know, Who is to Blame and What can we Do?*

How we manage people

Management styles

The availability of management support is seen as a key variable in the psychological well-being of employees. Managers are expected to fulfil a range of obligations, from the giver of helpful advice to the bringer of disciplinary proceedings. For most managers there is a balancing act between the needs of the organization which are often handed down to them – i.e. effectiveness, profit, keeping things legal and healthy – and the needs of the individual – for example reasonable workloads and deadlines, being made to feel valued, opportunities for training. Employees see the manager as espousing the values of the organization and with this comes the unwanted entitlement to be seen as a target for discontent and even aggression. One does not have to look far to find a story about a manager whose behaviour is appalling. Making mistakes with people means those mistakes live as long as the employee, but there is also the possibility that some individuals are just not cut out to be good managers. In addition, it almost goes without saying that what might appear to be sound management to managers can simultaneously be seen quite differently by those who wield less organizational clout. The bottom line is power and how to best utilize it for the benefit of as many as possible.

Given the right conditions, blaming the management can be a staple pastime in the workplace. This is justified in some degree where systems or management style are faulty, but there are also occasions where one could stand back and observe that in a given situation there is little more a manager could do. The employees of a large city hospital in the north of England were faced with horrendous car parking problems, due to urban redevelopment which affected the hospital site. This meant that many often had to park a few miles from the main hospital and make use of a bus service provided by the Trust. Naturally this was a cause for great discontent. Realizing that the difficulties caused by urban traffic congestion were unlikely to be solved in the short-term, the chief executive of the hospital made a point of parking at the commuter site every morning and catching the bus to work, thus taking the opportunity to talk to his staff about this and other problems. This type of action makes a very clear statement about the commitment made by this senior manager to taking his staff's concerns seriously.

One might also marvel (or not) at the loyalty some managers display towards the organization. At a university where the site was split in two by a major traffic route, the head of one of the faculties was run over en route to a meeting on the other side of the road. Despite being catapulted into the air and lucky to be alive, the eager manager assessed her luck at only suffering bruises and pressed ahead to attend the meeting. Unaware of the incident, colleagues at the meeting were stunned to learn of it from a concerned stranger who pursued the individual into her meeting.

So are we really bothered what a manager does? As an employee on the receiving end of their behaviour and direction, the answer is probably, but only as it relates to us. Quite naturally we would want to be assured that our interests were being well-represented and therefore our jobs protected at those important meetings to which our manager is invited, but we are not. In this regard employees often expect their manager to 'care' enough to act on the individual's or team's behalf. In fact it might come as a surprise to some to learn that their manager is not constantly thinking about their own employees' concerns most of the time, but is likely to be preoccupied with feeling as powerless as they do to solve them. Did you know how long it took me to get into the car park today? Have you come up with a solution to the problem I emailed you about last evening? Why are the supplies from overseas taking so long to arrive? Perhaps the best one can hope for is that the manager will listen, seems sympathetic to our concerns and then either says or does something which makes us feel less uncomfortable and as though they are genuinely trying to do their best to remedy or improve things. The key to this, as with many important issues in life, is trust.

The role of a manager, whose duties are to follow the lead of the organization as well as to the staff for whom they are responsible, means that there will be times when they are perceived to transgress the unwritten understanding of one or the other. Despite working in a collaborative and positive manner with everyone in his team, one line manager was shocked to be faced with a verbal tirade from an employee for whom he had promised to find extra resources. The resources had not been forthcoming and to the manager's astonishment, the member of staff accused the manager of stealing away the supplies for his own use! It seems that perceptions of managers are particularly subject to the vagaries of human emotion. Why should this be? The underlying reason in this example may be linked to the exercise of power in the organization. Understandably our line manager is charged with this task in a responsible fashion and any deviation from the outcomes an employee desires can result in frustration or aggression, which one might feel justified in directing at the manager. 'That's what they're paid to deal with', say some: 'I'm only human', comes the reply. The best outcome is one involving tolerance and a faith in each other to do the right thing whenever possible. Trust has already been identified as one of the keys to successful management and indeed positive relationships at work. However, the changing shape and scope of organizations, involving more cross-sections of people, employment conditions and cultures, means that trust does not come easily and can require considerable effort to cultivate. The flip side of this is that betrayal can more readily be perceived and a harvest of discontent accordingly reaped. The intervening variables of distance and handy communication networks can create a new set of expectations and interpersonal experiences, as we have already explored in Chapter 5.

Overall the research literature tends to support the notion that management support is a key variable in the well-being of their staff. Weinberg and Creed (2000) reported on the analysis of interviews with 199 NHS employees about all aspects of their work and non-work lives. The findings showed that the key work factor which predicted psychological distress among employees was the lack of support from management. For every positive story about a manager, it is likely we can all think of several more negative ones. It is hard to tell whether this is due to our tendency to take what goes well for granted, or whether there are actually many more bad managers and management practices. Certainly some of the more memorable television comedy programmes have featured characters with appalling management style. The success of the series *The Office* and its subsequent export to the international media market is attributed to the recognition by many viewers of the behaviours exhibited by the arrogant and insensitive central character David Brent, played by Ricky Gervais. Indeed in one survey 63 per cent of a sample of UK employees blamed David Brent-style management as an obstacle to their careers (*Guardian*, 2005). Long-lasting fame has also been accorded to John Cleese's character Basil Fawlty in the 1970s television series *Fawlty Towers*. Fawlty's sarcasm, mood swings and his bullying of Manuel the waiter often followed failure in his desperate attempts to keep the show on the road, against the backdrop of farce in his relationship with his fellow manager, his wife.

One wonders how either of these characters would have fared in a challenging study by Borrill *et al.* (1998) which invited managers in the UK National Health Service to take part in an 'upward feedback' exercise in which the views of a line manager's impact and style of behaviour were gathered from their employees. Using as supportive an approach as possible, feedback was given to the managers along with suggestions for improvement in their personal approach. However sceptical one might be, the results of the study showed that over the time of the initiative there was a much closer correlation between the managers' own and subordinates' views of the manager's behaviour and an increase in the well-being of both managers and subordinates. From a manager's perspective, participation in such an exercise might cause shudders to go through one's spine, or conversely raise moderate enthusiasm for an opportunity for self-development. Either way, the practice of management coaching has become a growth area, with organizations advocating their use and more and more offering such a service (*Sunday Times*, 2006; Meyer, 2002).

It is worth considering for a moment where managers come from. Surely anyone with reasonable organizational skills and an ability to communicate well with others would be suitable for such a role? This is a good start, but one could be forgiven for dismissing this rather oversimplistic view, until one realizes that many promotions bring with them responsibility for managing others and are actually granted on the basis of being good at one's job, e.g. teacher, sales associate, fire officer, checkout operator, doctor, etc. In fact one could argue that there is nothing in many occupations which inherently requires colleague-management skills. Therefore the basis on which many are promoted to taking on a management role is flawed. The detail embedded in job descriptions and person specifications usually contains reference to 'effective teamworking skills' or 'ability to work with others', but how often is this given prominence over 'being the best practitioner in the organization'? For example ambition and sound management style do not always make easy bedfellows, as the next case study demonstrates.

Case Study 7.1	**The right way to manage a company?**

Tracey's, a successful family owned construction firm, has a reputation for providing exactly what it says to its customers and doing so to high standards. The management team has a hands-on style which is appreciated and means that people have stayed with the organization for many years. However, the owners decide to hand over the firm to a venture capitalist to help it maximize its business potential, and this means Tracey's will become part of a big multinational building corporation. The person leading the change project is a slick and confident young man called Greg who has a reputation for getting results, having turned around a £4m deficit in a previous job.

Tracey's management team has always prided itself on dealing with its employees in a caring but clear manner and with the new project everyone is excited about future prospects. Everyone except for one of the managers, Terry, who heads a specialist department responsible for acquiring new contracts. On a one-to-one level, Terry has learned not to trust Greg. Terry knows from meetings that Greg is capable of spinning the truth and even lying. Terry has also noticed how he and his colleagues are being asked to rush off to other parts of the country at an hour's notice to confirm construction plans which previously would have been approved at the local headquarters. Sensing growing discontent among some of the managers, Terry finds out from another senior colleague that Greg is to be made head of the new organization and almost immediately he realizes he cannot work with a man who seems to have as few principles as Greg. Things come to a head for Terry at the big launch of the new organization which takes place at a local premiership football club. Watching Greg prance around the stage, motivating the assembled crowd with professional zeal and more than a few untruths, Terry's sense of unease turns to dread. He looks about him and sees that he seems to be the only one who has ▶

any reservations, as the faces of his colleagues exude appreciation and excitement. The former managing director appears on stage, half an hour behind schedule, to endorse the new leader, and in this delay Terry reads confirmation that all is not well at the top level either. At the break for the banquet, Terry collects his buffet plate and is standing in a circle with colleagues only for Greg to break in and ask Terry for a 'quick chat'. Terry looks him in the eye: 'Not now, Greg'. As a stunned silence reigns, Greg repeats his request more forcefully and is met with the same response. Terry can no longer control how he feels about the man who is betraying what the organization stood for and he leaves. On the way out, one of the former directors collars Terry and asks 'Why are you going?' A few weeks later an email is circulated thanking Greg for all his work for the new project and wishing him a fond farewell, but it comes too late to change Terry's mind. Retaining control of Tracey's, the big multinational firm continues to run things in the same way and three years down the line, only 2 out of 14 of Terry's colleagues are still working there and the project failed to materialize its venture capital. Terry was right – it was the right time to go and the wrong way to run a company.

So what kind of manager is likely to maintain or even improve the emotional health of the colleagues for whom they are responsible? Arguably this can be summarized as the capacity to get the best from others, but not at the expense of their employees' well-being, or indeed their own. There are no prizes for the manager who works all the hours available and is found dead at their desk! On an emotional level, managers need to be able to handle the negative feelings and displays of others, or their own feelings of failure when a project or work task goes wrong. A common problem in such situations is not seeking support from others. This might be due to a range of factors, for example because this is not available from other colleagues or friends, it would mean a personally unpalatable admission of failure, or because one's coping strategies are those of self-criticism and blame. The longitudinal studies of medical practitioners conducted by Jenny Firth-Cozens (1994) show that this third factor is a major predictor of depression for male doctors. Perhaps what is more surprising is her finding that another predictor of depression among doctors was their experience of negative relationships with a parent of the opposite gender. Could it be that early relationships with a parent or caregiver influence our working relationships with managers in later life?

There is little doubt that the emotional alchemy required to produce a manager with valuable qualities is complex: the next sections will focus on the necessary ingredients.

Managing change

In *The Prince*, Machiavelli points out that 'There is nothing more difficult to execute, nor dubious, nor more dangerous of success, than to introduce, to administer a new order of things' (Machiavelli, 1984, p. 21). Given the relatively new ways we work which have already been highlighted in this book, it is almost inevitable that at some point we will encounter major change. Consequently we may end up working with, or may actually be, an individual who is responsible for taking forward that change. Machiavelli goes on to highlight what a thankless task this can be, when assessed in terms of human relationships, 'for he who introduces it has all those who profit from the old order as his enemies, and he has only lukewarm allies in all those who might profit from the new' (1984, p. 21). As many managers will attest, it is good to take into account everyone's feelings about change, but in the end tough decisions have to be made. How one gets through the process of change is a matter of survival for both managers and their employees.

At this stage, it is worth recalling the common types of change in the world of work. Doubtless there will be new factors which are local to the job we do, such as a new colleague or manager, or perhaps a variation in working conditions, for example moving offices, changes in working times or a new software package. On a larger scale, we might be part of an organization, or indeed sector, which is being re-engineered or 'rationalized' as part of a grand scheme, which may be politically or economically motivated. The withdrawal of British American Tobacco from Burma (under military rule), the relocation of Dyson's manufacturing of vacuum cleaners from the UK to Malaysia (cheaper labour costs), the merger of BMG and Sony and the lay-offs by companies such as BT Cellnet due to the slowing down of the mobile phone revolution are cases in point from 2003–4. Change can also be characterized by an organizational merger or takeover, or indeed by the decommissioning of the company's pension plans. Either way, it is likely that as individual employees we would welcome the opportunity to know what is proposed and how it will affect us. Furthermore, depending on personal motivation and proactivity, we might also want our views to be taken into account and hopefully acted upon. It is interesting to note the number of times people complain they were not told about changes at work, or indeed had their opinions ignored – in fact these are the most reported examples which are cited as bullying in the workplace (Hoel and Cooper, 2000), as discussed in the previous chapter. Not surprisingly such experiences are accompanied by raw emotions. So is it the case that managers are good at misjudging or underestimating their subordinates? Does authority – supervisory and political – mean that it is easier to become complacent about the views of those lower down the hierarchy of the organization? If tough decisions need to be made, is that really an excuse for not listening to the views of those who spend eight or more hours each working day engaged in working with, or for you? Understandably most managers would like to answer 'no' to these questions, but in practice it can be hard to find a compromise between being responsible and accountable for changes at work which recognizes the importance of others' emotions. This is particularly the case where the time available to make a key decision does not permit due consultation. In the manager's defence, timescales are often shaped by a more powerful driver of decision-making which is likely to be out of the manager's control, such as market forces or the chief executive. Increasingly it is recognized that there should be frameworks for consultation. The Health and Safety Executive emphasize the importance of communication within workplaces, especially applicable in times of change. Large organizations, such government departments, are keen to publicize the efforts to which they go to consult with relevant interested parties.

So why are large-scale surveys of employees revealing such dissatisfaction and even distress with communication at work, particularly where their job is affected? The answer is not that opinions alone are being ignored, but that the emotions which accompany them are underestimated or simply not addressed. Part of the reason for this rests with factors such as timescales, overwork and job insecurity, which seem to be beyond anyone's control. Such problems reach every level of the organization, including managers. This is bound to affect their inclination and ability to deal with emotions as they arise. This prepares the way for further difficulties as emotions are likely to simmer and re-emerge later rather than disappear. However, some issues at a more immediate level could be addressed by paying sufficient attention to emotional skills in the workplace (see Chapter 6) and indeed this what managers are increasingly having to do: 76 per cent of UK managers find that they have found that their interpersonal skills are more important than their positional authority alone (Worrall and Cooper, 2001). Furthermore the adaptability to utilize these competencies in a range of contexts is likely to predict managerial success. If managers are promoted to the role on the basis of strong performance in a given job, then they are probably highly skilled in the required technical and cognitive areas. Yet it is the strength in emotional competencies that is evident in cases of excellent practice (Goleman, 1998). In time, the promotion of increasing numbers of individuals who possess greater emotional capabilities, alongside designated job skills, can only contribute to the right climate for shaping those factors such as tight timescales which currently undermine good practice.

So how do the manager and the managed survive the emotional fall-out brought on by change? Part of the answer here rests on not simply reaching common goals, but optimizing the process for reaching these goals. In other words, workers are saying it is no longer sufficient or acceptable to use any means to justify the ends, but instead to behave in a way which goes much further to guaranteeing cooperation and collaboration in future change – change which we all know is inevitable.

As before, the maintenance of good working relationships between the manager and the managed relies heavily on trust. In turn any mutual understanding is characterized by the unwritten psychological contract (see Chapter 4) which requires careful monitoring via regular contact and between the individuals concerned. Quite sensibly any change, proposed or otherwise, to a work situation can be flagged up and concerns anticipated and allayed where possible. On the shop or factory floor the idea of 'walking the talk' has traditionally been the bread and butter of sound communication between different levels of an organization's hierarchy. A manager in a further education college was given responsibility for expanding a new business opportunity, but recognized that resources were tight and more were desperately needed if the enterprise was to succeed and her staff to keep their jobs. At the same time her own family situation was changing and placing considerable strain upon her. The manager informed the staff of her efforts to gain much needed resources from the college management, but also, recognizing the likely impact of the work and non-work pressures upon her, she took the opportunity to indicate that in coming weeks she might be less tolerant and more irritable than usual. By giving advance notice, she was not looking for sympathy, but pre-empting possible consequences and emotional fallout from her behaviour. In time the storms were weathered and importantly were not compounded by unnecessary misunderstandings. Obviously such a strategy needs to be carefully judged against how well a manager knows their team, but does serve to illustrate the potential benefits of honest communication based on emotional awareness.

A primary method for attempting to generate trust during organizational change is to consult with all relevant stakeholders as part of a meaningful process and where possible empower those affected. Through active involvement and genuine attempts to incorporate their views in how the future might be shaped, addressing both hopes and fears, there are gains to be realized in the well-being and job satisfaction of staff. Supporting evidence is to be found in both local and more fundamental organizational change. For example prior consultation with end-users over the design and utility of software packages can prevent the 'firefighting' which is all too often a feature of new computerized processes, such as in the automation of passport offices and air traffic control, as witnessed in the UK at the turn of the century. A large-scale study of 8504 Swedish employees (Karasek and Theorell, 1990) found clear benefits for employee health. Where workers had actively participated in reorganization processes and obtained control over job tasks, the rates of absenteeism and depression, as well as symptoms of coronary heart disease were under half for the comparison group who had not. The introduction of autonomous work groups (see Chapter 3) empowering employees brought particular benefits for the car manufacturers Volvo, where absenteeism dropped from 20 per cent to 8 per cent (Kapstein, 1989).

It is a truism to say that change is stressful, yet it is acknowledged that the stressor lies within the uncertainty which change brings with it – hence Machiavelli's take on the concept of change five centuries ago. One of the key predictors of well-being in uncertain situations is having control and there is no doubt that the Borgias' own brand of poisoning and murder represents a rather extreme approach to dealing with the perceived threats of change by modern standards. If nothing else, it certainly illustrates that the strain caused by unpredictability is not exclusive to those in relatively powerless roles. From a more positive perspective, control is likely to buffer us from the impact of uncertainty. In fact it is the negative impact on control which makes the uncertainty of change such a strain on our psychological resources (Bordia *et al.*, 2004).

One of the ways of developing a sense of control in a changing environment is to make time for an objective analysis of the situation, such that all parties have a clear understanding of what could happen and why. If your next-door neighbour takes down a beautiful old tree which has been an attractive feature of both your gardens, it is much more likely to meet with your approval if you have been informed beforehand that the trunk had rotted and posed a danger to both of your houses – as in organizational life the opportunity to meet and share concerns about impending change is helpful. A popular strategy for achieving a balanced analysis of impending business 're-engineering' is to invite an outside agency to facilitate an 'away day'. This enables all parties to have their say in an impartially led session, thus permitting emotion to be expressed in a relatively safe environment outside of everyday meetings, where feelings which have been bottled up can become too much to bear. In recent decades a plethora of facilitators and advisors have appeared who are keen to offer this role of sounding board.

It is no coincidence that the 1980s, which heralded so much organizational change as global economies shifted, also saw the rise of management consultants, business gurus and troubleshooters. Accompanying this movement has been the evolution of 'management speak' (see the case study on p. 172), a new language which enables all those interested in 're-engineering' (change) to 'sing from the same hymn-sheet' (sound alike). Numerous books appeared on how to manage in a fast changing commercial world and many well-known experts came to the fore. *In Search of Excellence* (Peters and Waterman, 1982), *The Change Masters* (1984) by Rosabeth Moss Kanter, a series of books by Charles Handy such as *The Future of Work* and curious titles such as *The Empty Raincoat* (1995) appeared alongside quick so-called guides to supervisory success such as *The One Minute Manager* (Blanchard and Johnson, 2000). Faced with the challenge of change, large as well as small- and medium-sized organizations were content to pay for expensive management seminars and top rate consultancy fees, in the hope that any knowledge gleaned would translate into a strategy for business survival. One such big name is said to have been earning as much as $115,000 for an afternoon's seminar! If the delegates perceived the payback as a lifeline, perhaps such figures are not surprising, but also illustrate how hungry for answers the organizational managers and business leaders have become. Indeed there is evidence that these 'new' management devices are actually used, with UK managers employing an average 13.7 techniques each year, ahead of both the USA and Japan (Bain and Co, 1995). The lure of consultants is not confined to the commercial sector. Public service organizations are just as likely to utilize their skills and increasingly those who are able and motivated to provide such advice are those who have worked for some time in the services themselves and left to form their own consultancy. Their lead is taken from government, which in the UK and the USA embraced the management gurus, regardless of political leaning – prior to forming the 1997 government the shadow Labour cabinet was sent by Tony Blair to Templeton College at Oxford University to learn about management theory. In the mid-1990s, the Conservative Prime Minister John Major admitted to spending £320 million on management consultants. The bottom line is: do the gurus' ideas work? Despite the vast sums of money changing hands, the answer is remarkably unclear and unsurprisingly cynicism abounds. Gurus have been known to switch their support for ideas, and there remains the inescapable fact that many successful businesses are run by individuals whose strengths include imagination and dedication, rather than a desire to follow management fads.

Renowned organizational theorists from Mintzberg to Drucker have gone further and questioned the need for governments 'to think of people as customers in order to do things that should come naturally' (Micklethwait and Wooldridge, 1996, p. 328). The continued cost-cutting in the long-established UK institutions of the armed forces and the civil service has left many public employees questioning the ethics of change management, especially if it means a reduced service. Another contention is the usefulness of management theory on the workplace front line, where platitudes and management speak are not generally welcome. Either way the 'Witch Doctors' as they have been termed (Micklethwait and Wooldridge, 1996) have been attributed with costing many people their livelihoods, but have retained their attractiveness to big business. This is not say that the friendly facilitator who is hired to run the next workplace away day and helpfully suggests you take time to think about the way you work should be avoided like the plague. It is the ideas of management consultants which should be carefully scrutinized by employees in any organization. There remains one indisputable fact: employees know their workplace best!

Case Study 7.2	**The language of change**

Given the irresistible rise of consultancy and the language which regularly accompanies organizational change, some understanding of the meaning of oft-used terms is likely to be of help, especially to the uninitiated who feel cornered by shifting workplaces which threaten previous ways of working. On the plus side, the use of some of these phrases will demonstrate to others that you are up to speed with the language of the corporate jungle and therefore a force to be reckoned with!

Vocabulary

Corporate jungle – the world of organizations.

Corporate re-engineering – changing the organization.

Outsourcing – giving work currently undertaken by part of the organization to an outside organization, e.g. large organizations often 'outsource' or 'contract out' security work.

Downsizing or delayering – taking out layers of the organization in order to flatten its structure. If one imagines the organization like a tiered wedding cake, it is easier to visualize how this happens, often resulting in job losses.

360-degree appraisal – being assessed on your job performance by a range of different people with whom you have contact via your work, e.g. manager, colleagues, customers.

Hotdesking – not having a permanent desk or workstation, but having to utilize whichever work space is free.

Key phrases

Business process – the way we work

Let's touch base – let's have a meeting

Singing from the same hymn-sheet – making sure we sound like we agree

Let's run it up the flagpole and see who salutes – let's try out this new idea

Rolling out an idea – actually start something

Bottom line – what's this going to cost?

Leadership or management?

Having focused on the concept of management, it is time to step back and see what it takes to be a really good manager in today's world of work. Traditionally, a split has been maintained between what managers and leaders do. Usually the former look after the daily running of tasks or operations of some description and size, while leaders have been viewed as those at the forefront of things, firing off ideas, marshalling resources and investing huge quantities of energy in pursuit of a goal, which with any luck and judgement they have persuaded followers to help them achieve (see Bennis, 1994). If we accept these broad impressions, the essential difference between management and leadership lies not with who really has control, but with who is ready and willing to take that control. After all, one does not have to be at the head of an enterprise to display leadership. Most leaders of industry do not start off with that title, but attain it by demonstrating appropriate leadership qualities throughout their career, until the opportunity to head up an organization appears or is created. In this way, leaders are likely to be around us in all types of roles and guises within the workplace. Some are effective and some are not. Some attempt to shape the way things happen and others go through the motions: it is a bit like any other work activity. The remainder of this section examines relevant leadership theory and real-world examples to establish the good, the bad and the indifferent.

Definitions relevant to the concept of leadership tend to focus on 'the personal qualities, behaviours, styles and decisions adopted by the leader' (Arnold *et al.*, 2005, p. 482), where that individual has been 'appointed, elected, or informally chosen to direct and co-ordinate the work of others in a group' (Fiedler, 1995, p. 7). However, a trawl through the working practices of those recognized by their workforces as excellent leaders reveals that however that person has come to be leader, the fundamental key to positive leadership is 'understanding how to engage people' (Higgs, 2005). This in turn requires a grasp of a range of the emotions, for it is these as we have seen which matter to individuals. Therefore it is not surprising that the concept of transformational leadership (Burns, 1978) is that most cited in the relevant journals (Judge and Bono, 2000) and is the style which is strongly linked with demonstrating emotional intelligence (Gardner and Slough, 2002). The key components of transformational leadership are:

- Recognizing workers' abilities and encouraging their development
- Facilitating others' ownership of actions and the thinking which precedes them
- Shaping and sharing a positive vision which enthuses others
- Charismatic qualities which gain respect, including taking responsibility, showing determination, sharing success and placing the needs of the group above the leader's own.

What has often been presented as an opposing model of leadership, also outlined by Burns (1978), is transactional. Under this approach, the leader administers rewards only if targets are met and intervenes only when problems arise, rather than anticipating such difficulties. However, individuals do vary between the two types of leadership and some of this may relate to just how active they like to be, or indeed how much personal energy is at their disposal. It has been suggested that components of transactional leadership, such as control over rewards for employees, are also linked with strong interpersonal skills (Barling *et al.*, 2000). Allied to transformational leadership style is the concept of charisma which lies with the perceptions of the employees, almost as though leadership is in the eye of the beholder (Arnold *et al.*, 2005). In analysing what it takes to be seen as charismatic, Conger *et al.* (2000) refer to a leader's sensitivity to the needs of others, a willingness to take personal risks, as well as possessing an appreciation of the difficulties of the working environment. This seems to represent a blend of emotional intelligence and strategic awareness. In fact these are the factors which stand out in the *Sunday Times* survey of the 'Best Company to Work For'.

This annual review of UK-based organizations asserts that leadership is the 'most influential factor in an employee's belief that they work for a good company' (*Sunday Times*, 2005, p. 33). Over 20,000 employees were asked to rate both their faith in the leader of their business and their belief that they exercised moral principles in running things. In addition they assessed to what degree the leader inspired them and made them excited about the organization's direction. Top of the charts for the second year running, Mark Adlestone at Beaverbrooks the Jewellers scores 85 per cent or more on faith and inspiration and in line with other top rankers, makes efforts to meet personally with all staff to talk to and listen to his staff: 'I'm not just there to hear the good stuff. We genuinely care about the people who work for us as individuals.' It is the existence of such a dialogue which dominates the top ten companies and for employees who feel they are listened to, the ratings of well-being and satisfaction are much higher. These top-rankers feature a whole range of organizational types, such as manufacturers, retailers and financial, legal, recruitment, computing and charitable services, including a hospice. It is interesting to note that in the *Sunday Times* (2006) number one Best Company to Work For, W. L. Gore, every employee has a 'leader' rather than a manager. Could it be that the skills of sound leadership are those which are needed in today's managers and are the key to their own survival? It would seem that the right kind of leadership is important for performance and well-being throughout the organization, so why should it be limited to those holding the greatest power?

One of the challenges to demonstrating this type of leadership style as a manager is the increasingly remote nature of working, which separates employees via distances and technology. However, as we have seen the successful examples, even among some of the busiest executives, are those who make the effort to close these real or virtual distances. Through personal contact it is more likely that a manager can demonstrate trust and consideration for employees, as well as the structure which helps to steer the organization towards its goals or indeed sort out situations which require improvement (Blake and Mouton, 1964). The nuances of human emotion mean that non-verbal cues such as facial expressions and body posture are easier to pick up and therefore can help a manager address the concerns of their staff (see Ekman, 2003). For example an individual standing with arms crossed, staring at the floor while biting their lip is probably not as enthusiastic about the subject under discussion as their colleague who is smiling, with their head tilted to one side and looking you in the eye – all things which are hard to pick up via email or during a phone conversation. The interpretation of non-verbal behaviour is gaining the reputation of a science in itself, accompanied by popularized versions such as neurolinguistic programming (NLP). However, the increasingly global nature of organizations means that managers require a greater international understanding of behaviour.

Hofstede (1980, 2001) has led the way in analysing what employees want across over 70 countries within the same multinational organization – IBM. In highlighting the assumptions about work made by over 116,000 people across the world, Hofstede has encouraged the development of solutions to gritty problems, such as how an approach valued in one cultural context needs to be modified to work well in another. One of the four key dimensions his research identified was the varying degree to which employees in different cultures would tolerate inequality in the distribution of power. Known as the power-distance dimension, this data showed that in India and France there was acceptance of a large interpersonal (not physical) gap between those in management and their subordinates, whereas in Israel and Austria there was an expectation that consultation would take place in a climate of equality, making disagreements a more acceptable and expected phenomenon. As part of a worldwide study (named GLOBE) of what employees look for in sound leaders, Brodbeck, Brenk, Castel *et al.* (2000) again found cross-cultural differences. Not surprisingly integrity, vision and inspiration were widely demanded, however where western and southern Europe highly valued the characteristic of performance, middle Eastern countries instead placed a strong emphasis on diplomacy (Abdalla and Al-Homoud, 2001).

So what makes for the best manager? The qualities of transformational leadership seem to stand out. While the opportunities to display these can depend on the workplace situation, there should be no real obstacles other than one's own level of motivation for developing them in preparation for what lies ahead or around you. Once again the literature confirms the importance of emotionally intelligent behaviour as illustrated via transformational leadership, which in terms of managing others in the world of work can result in a range of positive outcomes (Antoniou, 2005). The idea that good leaders and managers are born rather than trained is increasingly challenged and it is likely that the mode of learning is the key to the outcome of any programs – including MBAs – in preparing individuals for successful leadership (Boyatzis, 2005; Weinberg, 2000 personal communication; Handy, 1999). 'Bill Gates would have been told he was mad to try and take on IBM' (Handy, 1999), but like so many of us he learnt through trial and error. For those intent on enhancing their management skills the combination of perseverance and determination should apply to learning as well as practice.

Summary of the chapter

This chapter has scrutinized the role and behaviour of managers in an effort to identify a range of styles and to assess the key attributes in times of change. Examples from popular culture which relate to our own experiences are used to help us consider questions about the origin and function of managers and the main challenges which await them in carrying through a process of change. The issue of trust is central to both managers and employees, as is the notion of making sense of the new order of things. The role of gurus and facilitators is examined (although who gets it right is left to you to decide) and the need for leadership qualities in aiding the survival of managers and their staff is highlighted. As managing people has been described as akin to 'herding cats', it is worth bearing in mind that there are likely to be many answers to the question 'How should we manage others?'

Key terms
management support	downsizing
coaching	transactional and transformational
organizational change	leadership
gurus	

Exercise 7.1

Do you have what it takes to be a fine leader or can you get your manager to be one instead?

How good are you or your manager at the following?

Personal qualities	Weak	Able to use	Sometimes puts into practice	Utilizes regularity	Always uses and develops
Keeping staff happy					
Creating enthusiasm for a vision of the future in your workplace					
Building confidence					
Listening to others					
Ensuring things are put right					
Being straightforward and honest					
Showing respect for and valuing staff					
Putting the needs of employees first					
Persistence when things need changing to work better					
Encouraging others to think for themselves					

You can score the above as follows: Weak = 1; Able to use = 2; Sometimes puts into practice = 3; Utilizes regularly = 4; Always uses and develops = 5.

Rate your leadership potential – were you surprised, impressed or can you see room for development?

10–19: There is room for development of these skills or at least serious consideration if they are not seen as important.

20–29: There is a difference between knowing what to do and actually doing it and perhaps there is scope for gaining confidence in using more of these approaches by putting them into practice more often.

30–39: These skills and their effectiveness are well known to you – is there room for even more development, maybe putting oneself to the test by training others?

40–50: You have tried and tested the benefits of these skills and if you are not helping others to develop them, why not?!

If you are considering pursuing training in management or leadership skills, take care to look at how that programme is delivered and whether or not it will appeal to the way you learn. There is a fair range of courses around and you are likely to benefit most from one that already fits with not what you know, but how you come to know it!

Questions and answers

1 *What kind of manager should we trust?* This may depend on the expected role of the manager within the organization, but one rule of thumb for many successful managers in the UK is to be able to 'muck in' and be prepared to do whatever the staff who report directly to them do. This serves to create common ground and breaks down the barriers of 'them and us' which can be an all too frequent theme of employee relations. A manager who treats employees with respect, remembers things which are meaningful to their staff, and shows the ability to listen and then take effective action as appropriate, is likely to gain trust. It is therefore not surprising that the research shows supportive managers are beneficial to their staff's well-being.

2 *How might a management style be changed?* Coaching is rapidly coming to be seen as the concept which can deliver a winning management style for any given organization and situation. However, coaches would be the first to say that there are some myths as to what

coaching can actually do, including providing a socially palatable substitute for counselling in organizations where the words 'psychologist' or 'counsellor' dare only be whispered in discreet corners! Having said that, the use of counselling techniques is not uncommon in a process which involves a working partnership ideally committed to the essential ingredients of support, development, change and feedback. An initial psychometric assessment is a common starting point to create a springboard for focusing on salient issues and can include a 360 degree view of the individual's behaviour. The opportunity to work one-to-one over a period of time with a personal coach is a valuable resource which can create a climate for positive change and progression. The growing emphasis on a positive psychology which aims to bring out the best in individuals is good news for those committed to improving management styles and may take things a step further than the idea of a one-off annual training course on 'How to be a better manager'.

3 *Is all this change really necessary?* The corporate jungle is so described owing to its ever-varying nature and capacity for surprises. If organizations are like creatures which rely to some extent upon their environment, then adaptation is the means by which to survive. There have been many examples of well-established organizations and institutions which failed to do so only to be caught out by changes in their surroundings. This does not mean that change should be self-perpetuating, for example because 'it's time we had one', or because someone feels the need to make their mark. Change should have a purpose and if the reasons for it have been properly shared and employees involved where possible in the developmental stages, then collective ownership and a greater level of trust are more likely to be forthcoming. If after this, the question 'Is all this change really necessary?' continues to be asked, then communication has not been as successful as hoped. In which case, change may be needed . . . (!)

4 *How should change be best managed?* Transitions are worrying times for employees and can appear to pose many threats as well as yielding opportunities. Trust, communication and participation are therefore essential for those affected by any changes. Alterations in the psychological contract are highly probable and it is important for employee well-being and performance that this is not dominated by feelings of insecurity about the future. Effective communication about impending change is likely to become mandatory in the UK and research

studies have already demonstrated the beneficial impact on illness and absenteeism of empowering the workforce during a reorganization (e.g. Karasek and Theorell, 1990).

5   *Which leadership qualities should a manager have?* Among the most successful organizations are those which cherish leadership at all levels within them. A blend of emotional intelligence, strategic awareness and desire for challenge is one way to describe the essential ingredients for successful leadership in the workplace. These are likely to impact positively on the quality of the products and services provided, as well as help to engender an energised team. Labelled as 'transformational' and 'transactional', aspects of these two styles of leadership (Burns, 1978) have been used to highlight what we really want in a leader. The emphasis of the transformational type on charisma and vision and of the transactional leader on rewards provides a persuasive combination, although as Arnold *et al.* note, 'Leadership is . . . in the eye of the beholder' (2005, p. 503).

Suggested further reading

A number of themes arise in this chapter, covering management, organizational change and modern leadership. Given the focus on emotions and the emotional skills which seem to mark out the successful practitioners, it is worth bearing in mind what happens when things go wrong – the impact of betrayal is covered in a sobering chapter by J. L. Pearce and G. R. Henderson in Cooper and Robertson (2001). For those who prefer a more classical and fatalistic view of being in charge of things, the stoicism of Marcus Aurelius's *Meditations* is guaranteed to put things in perspective. However, for those in need of encouragement the rapid advance of coaching psychology is worth examining as reviewed in a chapter by Meyer (2002) (see reference list for this chapter at the end of the book). Indeed the growth of this area is confirmed by the establishment of a Special Group in Coaching Psychology within the British Psychological Society (www.bps.org.uk).

Organizational gurus seem to be the source of so much change that it is worth finding out more about both sides of their story. Pugh and Hickson's *Writers on Organizations* (1996) is clear and readable, as is the critical and sometimes damning analysis offered in *The Witch Doctors* by the *Economist* journalists Micklethwait and Wooldridge (1996).

There have been many writers on the art of leadership, including Yukl's (1998) *Leadership in Organizations,* but for an overview of relevant theory Alexander Antoniou's chapter (2005) 'Emotional intelligence and transformational leadership' is recommended. For those intent on honing their management skills in no time at all, *The One Minute Manager* (2001) by Blanchard attained almost popular cult status at one time.

8   The home–work interface

Sometimes it seems as though there is an unwritten assumption in the world of employment that workers cease to exist outside of their working hours, with the exception of the time they may need at home to complete work-related tasks. This 'myth' of separate worlds (Kanter, 1977) is not an assumption of which anyone is proud and which many would rather deny, but is bound to influence our daily working lives. It is a sort of 'out of sight, out of mind' experience, in which an erroneous climate of living to work, rather than working to live is permitted to flourish. The home–work interface is the boundary at which the domains of work and home meet, though in fact for many 'meet' may just as easily mean 'conflict'.

Home here is used to refer to all life outside of the workplace, such as time spent with partners, family, friends and involved in leisure pursuits and hobbies. It is perhaps the prescription that work should be carried out at specific times which enables that aspect of our lives to be fixed and therefore dictates that the rest should move and accommodate the job. However, there are many realities – both inside and outside of work – which do not respond well to compromise. The ideal of strong personal relationships, the necessity for good (not just adequate) child and elder care, the occurrence of health problems and the surprises of life from punctured tyres and late trains to poorly pets, all dictate that flexibility is the key to managing the home–work interface. Yet all too often the competing reality of working hours and organizational expectations promote the type of role conflict in which we struggle to meet the demands of both home and work. Usually something has to give, and this chapter explores the common conflicts and how these might be resolved, for better or for worse.

The nine-to-five meets the five-to-nine

Until comparatively recently the most widespread working hours were those which began at 9 a.m. and ended at around 5 p.m: the modern reality is that 24 per cent of European employees keep these hours and the advent of a 24-hour society continues to shift this balance (Costa *et al.*, 2004). The reasons for such timing of work in the first place are likely to rest with the occurrence of daylight (with northern hemisphere and seasonal exceptions), the related fact that this coincides with most people being active and the opening times of schools, thus both permitting a biological and social 'freedom' to work. This said, the title of this section is not intended to exclude any permutations of work scheduling, but to include the home–work interface as it is experienced by all workers, whether bound by daylight hours, shift work, telework, commuting, part or full-time job commitments.

The relationship between work and home–life is fluctuating and for the majority a job is a necessity. Work brings with it financial rewards which create desirable choices about life outside work and for the fortunate can also provide a sense of purpose and identity (see Chapter 1), not to mention fulfilment. This is particularly important to those for whom work enables the recharging of emotional resources and is a welcome escape from gruelling home circumstances (see also Hochschild, 1997). This can often be the case for a parent or personal carer and the world of work provides a valuable perspective and outlet which can make the individual feel more able to cope.

In return work demands energy and time, and as we have seen can produce a range of emotions. These can be satisfaction or even elation at things having gone well, but given the physical and/or mental effort required in most jobs, tiredness, frustration and a sense of needing to recharge or relax are never far away. It is at this point you may need to drive a car, prepare a meal, help with homework and housework, hear how bad someone else's day has been and then get ready to do it all again! For some this schedule is enough to define one's choice of job, and certainly there are many for whom flexible working hours are the key to surviving work.

The proliferation of flexible working methods, such as those determined by part-time, casual and short-term contracts, has coincided with – and is probably related to – the changing nature of organizations and work itself. The result has meant that 'flexible working arrangements are undermined by job insecurity' (Lewis and Cooper, 1999, p. 386). It is quite likely that individuals carrying out work in this way are also doing another job role in order keep the home situation financially viable. During the period of arguably the greatest recent global and technological change in the world of work, between 1976 and 1993, men and women employees in the United States increased their average annual working hours by 233 and 100 hours respectively (Bureau of Labor Statistics, 1997), although economic factors meant the impact was not uniformly experienced. The psychological contract between employees and their employers has changed (see Chapter 4) and so has any notion of mutual commitment. It is possible that the insecurity factors highlighted here have also contributed to a new psychological contract between the employee and their family. In the UK there was a 22 per cent drop in the percentage of employees feeling secure in their employment between 1985–1995 and in a Europe-wide survey of job satisfaction the UK came second to last (ISR, 1995). Could it be that the workplace scenario is challenging our attempts to make long-term plans such as the raising of children and obliges individuals instead to focus too much on the short-term problems? (Sennett, 1998.) The concept of the 'spillover' of emotions and difficulties is increasingly being researched and conflict between work and home is explored later in this chapter: however, the legacy of unsatisfactory or even destructive forces at interface between the two major aspects of our lives goes beyond the individual employee. The positive development of stress hotlines for workers to discuss their problems has seen noticeable uptake by family members of the employee (see the *Lancet* 1998) registering their concerns as well as vicarious distress, and this may only be the tip of the iceberg. The perception of job insecurity does not seem to impact on a family's finances, but can produce negative attitudes and beliefs about work among the employees' children.

The key issues in deciding what people want from work and the pay-off they are prepared to accept, even grudgingly, are aspiration and opportunity. How much do people want success and/or satisfaction at work? How highly do people prioritize a home life, whatever that may mean for them? How likely is it that an individual can control the course of their lives to overcome potential obstacles to employment – local economic and social conditions and familial factors – and to balance the demands of work and home? It must be remembered that the spread of employment is not equal across society and contrasts exist between households containing a number of workers, such as dual-earner couples, where both partners work, and households where unemployment dominates. One of Margaret Thatcher's ministers in the UK Conservative governments of the 1980s, Norman Tebbit – portrayed as a political thug in satirical programmes of the time – recommended to the millions of unemployed people to 'get on their bikes' and go in search of jobs as had been the trend in the history of many families over the previous 100 years – although actually often on foot. Such movements in the population were often supported by the existence of extended families, which might look after younger children, enabling parents to go on ahead and secure employment, often in harsh and inhospitable conditions. This cross-generation approach to supporting aspirations to find work has tended to persist in Eastern cultures (Chabot, 1992), whereas this vital resource is less commonplace in Western countries. With so many social, political and global trends affecting employment opportunities, it is not difficult to imagine that among sections of the population a fatalistic and negative attitude towards work has developed, borne out of increasingly long-term difficulties in breaking the trends of unemployment and underemployment.

Viewed in this way the existence of a home–work boundary with its inherent challenges may seem a luxury. In addition media reports of women delaying having children to facilitate their role in the workplace, as well as a decline in the birth rate in many developed economies (Lewis and Cooper, 1999), suggest that work has evolved in such a way as not to suit large swathes of society, whether employed or not. The reaction to this has been varied and has included government-sponsored initiatives such as the Work–Life Balance programme in the UK. In Japan the first shrinkage in the population since the Second World War prompted the government's Health and Welfare Ministry to consider new laws which would oblige employers to instruct employees to take their whole holiday entitlement in the hope that this would facilitate more quality time for couples and families to be together. Despite having a low average number of annual days' leave, workers in Japan tend to take only half of the 18 days available to them (*Guardian*, 2006). However, there remains a nagging suspicion that society is relatively content for people to work too much, but frowns on those who are not able to work at all. It is in striking a balance in prevailing attitudes to the necessities of work and home priorities, that the solution to under- and overemployment is to be found, but for the majority, the responsibility for surviving this quiet revolution is still likely to fall to the individual, as the next case study suggests.

Case Study 8.1	What colour is your parachute?

In the 1980s and 1990s there was an unsurprising increase in the number of guides discussing how to withstand the waves of change. These might include handy similies to help the reader think in terms of survival, such as parachutes to save them as they bailed out of faltering organizations. In finding out how people actually survived periods of such change, it is instructive to focus on separate examples from both public and private sectors, and from the perspective of this chapter it is worth noting that both examples highlight challenges in managing the home–work interface.

Jack worked in a large urban public care organization which was responsible for visiting clients and managing the care they received. David worked as a project manager for a large construction firm, overseeing a range of contracts across the country. Changes in the psychological contracts at work, following on from prevailing shifts in the organization's ideology, led both to confrontations with their managers and to decisions to look around for ways to secure employment. The bitter lessons of putting their 'all' into an organization and perceiving their values as 'betrayed', also convinced David and Jack that they should find employment in a way which would give them personal fulfilment. This had not been a choice open to the fathers of both men, who had left Ireland for mainland Britain in search of employment in the wake of the Second World War. Perhaps drawing confidence from this past, Jack and David resolved to change direction and work for themselves, Jack building on the gift of a creative writing course from his wife and David utilizing the project expertise and skills which had served him so well. Both men were able to draw on a reservoir of personal energy and charm and sheer enthusiasm for making things happen, as well as the devoted support of their spouses.

David set up his own company providing consultancy to the type of well-established clients he had worked with so effectively beforehand. This meant having to move his family to London from the north-west of England for a few years. As his reputation for conscientious and creative output spread internationally, he needed to travel increasingly overseas and realizing access to the airport would be vital, he seized the chance to return to the ▶

north-west which his family, including wife Jane and two school age sons, considered home. David had found his services appealed directly to the governments of countries where regeneration and rebuilding were the order of the day and the daily trip to the office was replaced by plane travel abroad. A typical working week might begin on Sunday with a long journey to Slovakia to meet a government minister, followed by two days spent in the former Yugoslavia and then back to an office in Belfast, returning home in time for the weekend. David was notching up over 220 flights each year as he spent part of almost every working day in the air, travelling to meet clients and oversee projects. From serving the needs of a big corporation and being obliged to espouse its values, David had wrested control of his career. But while the business was an undoubted success, David felt that this relied upon his being able to keep up the frantic pace of the business and continuing to say 'yes' to new work. Jane became increasingly conscious of the full load of family responsibilities, leading a household which included two teenage boys and not having access to her partner to share and solve the natural emotional challenges. The strain resulting from living quite separate lives became a more frequent focus of their weekend conversations. Conscious of not wanting to become a victim of his own success, either in terms of his family or indeed his health, David needed to apply his creativity to a solution which could potentially threaten his business success.

Having resigned in dramatic style from the care organization, Jack enjoyed being at home with his three young children and looking after the home. His wife Gina was successful in her teaching job and was also conscious of the outlet Jack needed for his creativity, which for now was focused on children, to their delight. As their school careers began, Jack had taken on part-time work, but was searching for a vehicle for his talent for entertaining friends and family. Gina bought Jack a creative writing course as a birthday present and this seemed to give him a new direction. Both gregarious and thoughtful, he began to develop confidence in his skills which he had displayed as a playful undergraduate some years before. A visit to the Comedy Store in central London provided the crossroads for Jack. Taking the opportunity to stand up in front of an audience and 'just see how it went' was always going to ▶

be a gamble, so to hedge his bets and as this was only going to be a one-off, he gave a slightly different name from his own. The result was instant success and a feeling of 'being bitten by the bug'. Return visits brought with them invitations to do other gigs, followed by radio appearances. Retaining his concern for welfare issues, Jack got involved in men's health campaigns, which in turn brought contact with high-profile organizations and provided another outlet for his writing. Producing and performing his own material in shows for children and adults at the Edinburgh Festival, he won accolades and was soon touring the country. From warm-up slots at the BBC to student unions and corporate events, he was realizing the potential which he had willingly channelled for so long in other ways. Jack was keen to spend time with his children and would alternate the scheduling of his writing and performing around family life. His success did mean spending time away from home more often, but he would take his eldest son to gigs wherever possible and then to see his beloved Manchester United. Achieving the balance of work and family was possible for Jack in different ways at different stages of his own and Gina's career as well as his children's development.

The issue of sharing home life and its challenges and maintaining meaningful relationships whilst working long hours is not uncommon. What positives and negatives do you foresee in both David and Jack's situations?

Role conflict and family life

If, as Shakespeare once wrote, 'All the world's a stage,/And all the men and women merely players', than as actors in life we would find we had been assigned a variety of roles to play. Role conflict is that outcome experienced when the competing demands of different roles come into direct competition. Much as an actor might find it hard to play two roles simultaneously, so are we bound to struggle, possibly becoming confused and agitated when confronted with such a challenge. Within the workplace these situations are more common than we might realize, occurring where our own views are opposed to those of the organization for whom we work or where we are supposed to act on behalf of conflicting interests. Responsibility for health and safety issues in a department might tempt the same individual to hang on longer than necessary to meet a pressing business deadline whilst the fire drill is taking place. Operating within budgetary constraints might compromise a manager's assurance of obtaining funding for a social occasion. Similarly the role of partner/parent/carer/child is a constant and means that although they are in the workplace, employees are effectively 'on call'. The direction of conflict between work and home roles can flow from work-to-family (WFC) or from family-to-work (FWC).

Three different types of conflict between the domains of work and home are widely acknowledged (Greenhaus and Beutell, 1985):

1 Time-based conflict, i.e. there is a limited amount of time at our disposal
2 Strain-based conflict, i.e. spillover of negative emotions
3 Behaviour-based conflict, i.e. expectations and actions which are incompatible.

In practice, all three categories are likely to lead to unwanted emotions and perhaps unexpected challenges to relationships in the home. The key questions are: is some kind of conflict inevitable and if not what can be done? The latter is addressed later in this chapter.

Time-based conflict certainly seems inevitable in the face of long working hours. Either there is too much work to do, or people feel that by staying in work they are more likely to keep their jobs. Given the drop in perceptions of job security across Europe (ISR, 1995), such presenteeism is perhaps not surprising. For example 71 per cent of UK managers recognize that home is at least as important as work, but they continue to put in long hours, despite also believing that these are having an adverse effect on relationships with their partner (72 per cent) and/or children (77 per cent) (Worrall and Cooper, 2001). These findings are likely to be repeated across all sections of the workplace, where in Europe UK employees are recognized as working the longest average working week. The longest working week in the world has been practised in Pacific Rim economies, where Singaporean and South Korean employees spend 46 hours in the workplace (*Standard*, 2005). However, first steps to invent the weekend, roll back the six-day week and tackle declining birth rates as well as increasing suicide figures have been taken. Pressure from both unions and government have seen the institution of a five-day week in South Korea since 2003 and political moves in Japan to ensure that its employees take their full holiday entitlement to balance the routine of long hours of overtime. In Japan the frequency of *karoshi* (death from overwork) has led to a series of legal cases fought by widows accusing their husband's employers of corporate killing. The benefits of moves to tackle such dire social costs are also economic in countries which have previously relied for success on manufacturing products for export. The leisure and retail industries have burgeoned in some of the IT-dominated cities of southern India and similar outcomes are hoped for in Malaysia where the Saturday morning shift worked by its one million civil servants has been revoked (*Standard*, 2005). Perhaps the most harrowing time-based conflict occurs in rural China, where the common experience of husbands migrating from the villages to take up work in the cities has contributed to one of the world's highest suicide rates among the women left behind (*Guardian*, 2005). Combined with the rising frequency of self-inflicted deaths among city-dwelling 20–35-year-olds, struggling with the pressures of an increasingly competitive society, it is reckoned that suicide is the fifth most common cause of death in China, leading to a quarter of a million fatalities each year. Such tragic consequences may seem a far cry from the resentment which can build up when someone's partner is regularly late home from the workplace, but given the range of life situations in which work is a constant theme, it assumes a significance of its own.

Strain-based conflict is that which is brought on by the spillover of negative emotions from WFC or vice-versa (FWC). This can have a range of outcomes for either the work or home domain. For example a difficult time at work can result in the individual getting home tired, on edge and in an unhappy mood (WFC). The adjustment made on reaching home and facing the family could range from feeling too emotionally drained to do anything but lie down to full-on confrontation and arguments. Alternatively difficult times at home could see the employee underperforming, making mistakes and generally failing to meet expectations (FWC) (Frone, 2003). One might imagine that the experience of conflict in both directions would produce an ever-spiralling emotional discomfort for both the employee and their family and work colleagues. Similarly behaviour-based conflict can arise where actions which are appropriate to the domain of work or home are incompatible with expectations in the other domain. For example a power-driven, no-nonsense and performance monitoring style of behaviour might suit a particular workplace where results mean rewards, but this would not easily translate into a successful approach to relationships at home, where the emphasis is more likely to rest on contributing to a more caring and supportive environment.

The psychological impact of stressors at the home–work interface is well recognized (Brough and O'Driscoll, 2005) such as depression and increased alcohol consumption (Noor, 2002) and coronary heart disease (Haynes *et al.*, 1984). Research has shown that work–family conflict is a contributor to burnout for different working groups, such as nurses and engineers (Bacharach *et al.*, 1991), as well as for poor psychological health among politicians (Weinberg and Cooper, 2003 and see the case study on p. 193). However, in accepting the impact of factors from other domains of life on functioning, it is important to realize that a sometimes complex mixture of stressors from both home and work can contribute to mental health problems. This is not to say that exposure to a certain combination of work and home problems will inevitably lead to personal distress, rather that the presence of such difficulties can increase one's likelihood of experiencing poorer psychological health. It is important to bear in mind (see Chapter 3) that a range of individual factors, such as personality and coping strategies, can also act to moderate the effect of stressors. Put simply, in trying to find out what causes employees strain it is no longer sufficient to focus solely on the workplace, but also the home–work interface and individual predisposing factors. This has been a frequent problem in research studies undertaken until recent years which, despite large financial support, have found that the sources of pressure cannot be isolated, although the evidence of strain is plain to see.

A good example of the more wide-ranging and in-depth approach to highlighting contributors to psychological health problems among employees was undertaken by Phelan *et al.* (1991), who interviewed 1870 employees of Westinghouse Electrical Corporation during a period of organizational change. Of the sample, 27.2 per cent were found to be experiencing an episode of depression, either of a new or long-standing nature, and the key predictors were found to be personal or family history of depression, lack of intrinsic job rewards (e.g. the valuing of individual's contribution at work), conflicting work roles, negative work events, past psychiatric history in the employee's spouse, strain in the marital relationship and a reduced sense of personal control.

Table 8.1	The experience of severe life events and difficulties, comparing those subsequently diagnosed with a mental health disorder and those who were not. The figures show frequency per 100 participants

	Individuals newly diagnosed with mental health disorder	Individuals not diagnosed with a mental health disorder
Severe events	100	27
Major difficulties	65	20

Source: Brown and Harris, 1978

Brown and Harris's (1978) rigorous study of the full range of life events and difficulties of a large sample of women living in Camberwell, south London highlighted the greater likelihood of severe problems during the past year for those who were subsequently diagnosed with a depressive disorder, compared to those who were not (see Table 8.1). Major events and difficulties covered personal and family health, such as heart attacks, terminal diagnoses and death, relationship break-ups or problems with children and other close family, job loss or bullying, financial hardship including unmanageable debt, housing issues – such as threatened eviction or unsuitable accommodation – involvement with the criminal justice and legal system and miscellaneous problems such as the death of a pet. The persistent themes in these types of circumstances are of loss and disappointment, which therefore carry with them a long-term threat to the individual's situation and well-being. This is evident in the separation or anticipation of actual parting when someone is ill or a relationship breaks down, receiving news which causes reappraisal of a close person or relationship, major material disappointment, enforced change of residence and career frustration. In Brown and Harris's (1978) study, 88 per cent of those newly identified with depression had suffered a severe event incorporating at least one loss or disappointment. Almost two-thirds of these individuals developed a depressive disorder within nine weeks and the vast majority within six months.

A smaller study which attempted to build on the work of Phelan *et al.* (1991) and Brown and Harris (1978) focused on the objectively assessed experiences of UK NHS staff. Employees who were experiencing diagnosable anxiety and depressive disorder were compared with same-sex and age-matched colleagues working in the same job role, and were found to have a significantly greater number of objectively stressful situations both inside and outside of work (Weinberg and Creed, 2000). Consistent with the findings of Phelan *et al.* (1991), major contributors to psychological distress were the existence of substantial health difficulty in a close relation, lack of management support, absence of a confidant (with whom one can talk about problems and feelings), family history of psychiatric illness, conflicting work role, having a previous episode of a mental health problem and ongoing marital difficulty (Weinberg and Creed, 2000). The importance of not having someone with whom the employee can talk and confide feelings was a highly significant factor which underlines the importance of having the opportunity to express and deal with emotions, whether the source of the stressor is from home and/or the workplace. The findings from Weinberg and Creed's study were subsequently used by the hospital concerned to justify funding and provision of counselling for its employees. The next section will highlight a range of strategies which can be used to help employees balance the home–work interface and the spillover from one to the other.

Case Study 8.2	**'I must be mad to work here' says MP**

The UK General Election of 1997 saw the creation of the first Labour Government since 1979 and the election of 236 new Members of Parliament (MPs). The vast majority had never before carried out the job of national politician and for many this meant considerable adjustment to their lives. The very long working hours, the need to take work home and an absence of emotional support were significantly more likely to be reported as sources of pressure among MPs who found the adjustment difficult and suffered poor psychological health (Weinberg and Cooper, 2003). Physical symptoms of strain were significantly higher for politicians with school-age children at home and these negative effects were actually characterized by difficulties in the family adjusting to the new situation. Indeed these types of problem were cited by a number of these MPs as reasons for standing down from the job at the following 2001 General Election. Although Parliament began to realize the personal toll of the job on politicians' health and ▶

family life, it was slow to act to address the problems, even refusing to provide a room for women MPs with babies to breast feed. As a seasoned politician commented, 'This is not a job, it's a way of life'.

Juggling the home–work interface

So how do we actually cope with the multiple demands of work and home life? And whose responsibility is it – the employee's or the organization's? The answers lie in a range of strategies which rely on the individual, their partners, families and friends as well as the workplace. The long-standing approach has seen a traditional division of labour between men and women in the home and workplace. This meant that men went to work, while women looked after the home and children. Obviously this has shifted in countries such as the UK with wide-ranging social changes since the Second World War, the almost equal involvement (if not treatment) of women in the workplace and the variety of shapes and sizes of family units. In short it is often asserted that generally in 'traditional' family units men still go to work and are more involved in home and childcare, while women generally also go to work and continue to do most of what they did before at home as well! Alongside these developments, UK government policies have evolved which encourage the uptake and provision of childcare and the greater involvement of fathers with their children through paternal leave. However, such initiatives are more likely to target parents than all employees and may not actually relieve the types of role conflict outlined previously in this chapter. As has been highlighted, the active promotion of a work–life balance has featured in the approaches of advanced economies of both European and Pacific Rim nations, but ultimately the striking of this balance seems to rest with the individuals and their employers, rather than with governments.

Individual approaches

In households where there are two adults, the sharing and division of responsibilities seems an obvious strategy for coping at the home–work interface: however, it has been suggested that the number of working hours (in both home and work-focused tasks) is 2.5 hours a day more for working mothers than for fathers (Noor, 2002). Having said this, there is evidence that ways of coping with the home–work interface are becoming increasingly similar for both men and women (Carr, 2002), although the greater weight of responsibility continues to fall on women, including where they are part of a 'dual-earner couple' (Luk and Shaffer, 2005) The psychological toll of this disparity on working mothers living with male partners may lie in their perception of this division of labour. Thus women who perceive their partner as not carrying a fair share of the household chores are more likely to report symptoms of depression and also of somatic anxiety (physical signs of poor mental health) (Rout *et al.*, 1997). For working mothers who perceive that their partner does not shoulder an equal share of childcare responsibilities, symptoms of somatic anxiety, but not depression, are significantly higher (Rout *et al.*, 1997). These patterns are likely to incorporate attempts by working mothers to try and do too much with the resulting realization that conflicting roles make it difficult to do as well at either home or work as the individual would wish. In such situations, it is not hard to think of the likely emotions attached to a working couple discussing the division of household labour.

There are mixed findings about gender and the direction in which the direction of conflict can operate, but generally it has been thought that work-to-family conflict is greater for women, whereas family-to-work conflict is greater for men (Frone and Yardley, 1996). This might be explained by the significance attached to the work and home domains by the respective sexes (Carlson and Kacmar, 2000). Gender role theory suggests that women are more likely to view their job negatively when it spills over into family life, as this threatens what has been considered the 'central social role' (Grandey *et al.*, 2005, p. 308). Indeed ongoing work–family conflict predicts levels of job satisfaction for women one year later (Grandey *et al.*, 2005). Research into the home–work interface has shown that the prevalence of anxiety and depression among both women and men also seems consistent with the interference experienced in fulfilling the traditional patterns of work and home task allocation (MacEwen and Barling, 1994), i.e. men are more likely to suffer psychological strain if family life spills into the work domain and women experience poorer mental health where work impacts on home life. Alternatively there may not be a gender-specific reason but rather an expectation that people doing certain types of work, in which one gender happens to predominate, find support for prioritizing family life. In the case of an employee whose child is poorly and needs collecting from school early, how easy would it be for the executive whose performance is judged on results to postpone a meeting, compared to the experience of a nurse in a caring role who may need to leave a shift? Many factors would be involved, including the culture of certain working environments and whichever way one answers the question, it is worth bearing in mind that it is just as possible for nursing culture to be as macho as the business world in its view on how employees deal with non-work problems: 'I've coped with situation x, so why can't you!' The cultural characteristics of society obviously underpin the approach taken by employees. For example, in China time for oneself has traditionally been viewed as less of a priority than running the household, and work has not been seen as competing with home life but as contributing to the welfare of the family.

Dividing the labour – What's the deal?

Here are some quotes from partners about their own partner's contributions in the non-work domain. How many apply/have applied to you and at what point did you get to negotiate how things would turn out? It is likely that the amount of control we have over the division of labour in the home plays a significant role in determining our emotional health. Is it time for you to renegotiate as some of the people quoted below did?

'If only he would bring his plate back into the kitchen instead of leaving it on the floor when I've cooked a meal.'

'He's "hooverman", but he still doesn't know how to work the washing machine!'

'She leaves me a list of jobs on the fridge door and expects them to be done by the time she comes home.'

'I can't stand to watch him try and cook – it's much easier to do it myself.'

'I think if I make an appointment to see him, we might be able to sit down and plan our lives outside of work.'

'Work keeps me sane – if I had to spend all day with the children, I would go mad.'

'My mother is wonderful, she does all the cleaning – my husband never would.'

'I just accept there are some things he can't or won't do – just as long as he walks the dog, then that's all I can expect.'

'When our son was three years old, she handed him over to me and said, "There, now it's your turn".'

'He's great – he cooks, cleans and takes the children to school.'

Obviously the households in which two adults are working are only part of the picture when it comes to understanding the home–work interface. Single parents and part-time workers are an ever-larger part of the working population, who may have access to fewer of the non-work social support mechanisms outlined here, although research in this area is still relatively new. Some researchers emphasize that working mothers actually enjoy better mental health (whether full or part-time employees), because they are part of two social networks, rather than one, i.e. work as well as home (Rout *et al.*, 1997). However, the coping strategies employed by working and non-working mothers show no particular differences, with both groups tending to focus on problem-solving or on drawing on social support.

The idea that social support can buffer individuals against the stressors of juggling work and home life is one which has received much attention. Certainly the more back-up from family, friends and colleagues people get, the less the psychological and physical strain likely to be experienced by that individual (Frone, 2003). However, the role of social support is not straightforward and can be affected by the perceived and actual usefulness of the help on offer, as well as the individual's ability to accept it (Brough and O'Driscoll, 2005). Having assessed thousands of patients in his working life, a famous cardiologist noted the importance of having access to social support, not just for psychological but also to long-term physical health: 'Make sure that you also have a best friend who is not your partner!' His message relates to the need to have a safe outlet for emotions in the face of life's challenges, but also serves as confirmation that relationships at home can carry just as many risks to health as those at work. Supportive relationships in the workplace can play a positive role here (Snow *et al.*, 2003). There may not have been definitive research into the best way to cope with the home–work interface, but the idea of being able to take and maintain some control over its multiple demands is likely to be at the centre of any successful coping strategy. Japanese working women have found that redefining their role outside of work was most effective in dealing with the spillover of family pressures into their jobs (Matsui *et al.*, 1995). Even if the reality of circumstances is hard to change, then developing the ability to place different parts of one's life into separate mental compartments – to dwell on at only certain times or places – can help to relieve pressures from more than one domain (Grandey and Cropanzano, 1999). In practice this might involve using the opportunity to use the distractions of the journey home to and from work, such as listening to the car radio or talking on the bus or train, to act as a cut-off after which one tries not to think or talk about the home or work tasks one has left behind. If there is a need for spillover of work or home into the other domain, pre-arranging a time during which to address the left-over issues can help to take the pressure off relationships as well as personal perceptions of overload. The option of avoiding the problem and thereby doing nothing to change things is likely to lead to increased symptoms of psychological strain (Snow *et al.*, 2003).

Organizational approaches

One of the questions posed at the beginning of this section related to whose responsibility is it to juggle often competing demands of work and home life. New government policies across the world have been featured in this chapter as recognition for the consequences of home–work conflict grows. However, employers are also increasingly aware that by helping their employees to address this difficult juggling act, they are likely to gain themselves in a range of ways (Kinnunen *et al.*, 2005), for example by reducing turnover (Thomas and Ganster, 1995). There is evidence to show that flexible working hours reduce employees' experiences of work–family conflicts (Kushner and Harrison, 2002), although it may be the total hours worked which determine their ultimate efficacy (Major *et al.*, 2002). Within some countries the widespread introduction of flexitime, as well as options to work part-time, mean that individuals can with appropriate notice alter their start and finish times and the shape of their working week, to fit better with family and other commitments, as well as vary the number of hours to take account of childcare issues during the course of their working lives.

In principle this sounds the basis of a solution for the type of conflict outlined in this chapter, but such flexible arrangements are only available in some countries and even where they exist, the switch to part-time from full-time employment carries disadvantages if it means taking a cut in pay too (Tausig and Fenwick, 2001). Additionally the effectiveness of schemes designed to help alleviate work–family conflict can depend on how 'right' it feels for employees to utilize them. In Sweden parental leave for both mothers and fathers has been in operation for many years, but there is still stigma attached to men using their allowance and the attitude of the organization will affect individual decisions on whether or not to use the existing policies. Discrimination against pregnant women, including job loss, has also been widespread in many countries (Shellenbarger, 1992). Paid maternity leave has been an entitlement in the UK for many years which has recently been extended to parental rights covering fathers; however, this concept is relatively unusual elsewhere, e.g. parental leave was legislated for in New Zealand in 2002.

In some organizations, such as W. L. Gore and Associates (first in the *Sunday Times* 2005 and 2006 Top Company to Work For), maternity leave is paid for six months with provision for a further six months without pay, during which time holiday entitlement can be accrued. In the United States employers' assistance with their employees' child and elder care has been widespread (Shellenbarger, 1992) and has produced benefits in terms of staff morale and productivity (Thomas and Thomas, 1990). A variety of such arrangements exists from on-site childcare centres to financial subsidies designed to help with meeting the costs of care. Further organizational support can be evident from telecommuting and compressed working weeks which permit the employee increased flexibility in juggling work and home commitments (see Chapter 5 for the ups and downs of working from home).

The success of these provisions will tend to rest on three factors: the approach of the employee's supervisor – either supportive or not – and related to this, the perception of the organization as one which values the personal and family lives of its employees (O'Driscoll *et al.*, 2003) and whether or not the provision will actually work for a given individual. A line manager who permits a reasonable number of phone calls about non-work issues, approves flexible working arrangements and is sensitive to the needs of staff who experience family illness or whose childcare falls through can make a positive difference to how the individual employee perceives the organization (Brough and O'Driscoll, 2005), not just how they view the line manager. In addition the existence of family-friendly organizational policies in themselves is not guaranteed to lead to their use or the perception that it is fine to use them (Thompson *et al.*, 1999). Certainly managers may be more able to exercise discretion when it comes to balancing their own home–work interface (O'Driscoll *et al.*, 2003), but may be wary of utilizing existing policies because of the message this will send out to others in a given organizational context (Allen, 2001), e.g. where the expectation is for staff to work long hours and appear to be totally committed to the company. However, where the culture is more family-friendly and employees' perceptions of the organization recognize this, less work–family conflict and better psychological health are experienced (O'Driscoll *et al.*, 2003). A work–family culture in which 'an organization supports and values the integration of employees' work and family lives' (Thompson *et al.*, 1999, p. 349) is obviously the more desirable situation. This is particularly important as the converse is true: organizational cultures in both the public and private sectors which are seen as unsupportive by their employees can not only result in increased work–family conflict leading to individual strain, but can also directly cause psychological distress to workers (Mauno, Kinnunen and Pyykko, 2005).

The current trend for organizations is to help staff deal with family-to-work conflict, thus preserving optimum functioning in the job, rather than dealing with the work-to-family spillover (Frone and Yardley, 1996). There are exceptions and these seem to focus on bringing working hours into a reasonable set of demands, but it is government rather than organization-led initiatives which are prominent here as this chapter has outlined. Of course there are exceptions: Bacardi-Martini (ninth in the *Sunday Times* 2005 top 100 companies to work for) actually obliges staff to be out by no later than 7 p.m. This may seem late to the many who start work at 9 a.m., but a luxury in some countries where the weekend is a relatively new phenomenon! Whatever the situation, employment has the potential to provide positive economic and personal health benefits which can also cross over from family-to-work and it is the striving for a realistic balance across the whole of our lives 5 p.m. to 9 a.m., not just 9–5, which is a challenge for all.

Summary of the chapter

So it's official! We are human beings who have lives outside of work, or at least we should have. Work serves many useful purposes, not least bringing in money to exchange for a standard of living and increasing the quality of life of the employee by providing access to a range of positive experiences. However the success of our species in some countries is possibly under threat from a culture of long working hours which means that family life is replaced by separate lives for couples. The existence of extended family networks can no longer be relied upon in many Westernized countries to take the strain of managing the home–work interface. Both men and women have increased their job-related hours and this has coincided with more flexible demands on the timing of working. The conflict between work and home life is reflected in time, strain and behaviour, with events in one domain often spilling over into the other and impacting on the well-being of the individual, who is still expected to fulfil their work responsibilities. Nevertheless a combination of governments, organizations and individuals themselves is involved in juggling the demands of the home–work interface, with varying degrees of success. Success stories seem to be characterized by mutual support in which a partnership between the worker and their employer cooperate to make the juggling act an achievable reality.

Key terms	
home–work interface	work-to-family and family-to-work conflict
life–work balance	
flexible working	life events and difficulties
spillover	work–family culture

Questions and answers

1 *How much has work become an obstacle to living, or is it the other way round?* It would be wrong to assume that work is all bad news and that we are better off without it: after all there are many benefits, both financial and psychological. However, talking to employees from a range of occupations reveals a perception that things are busier than they used to be. With the exception of key sectors, it may not be that working hours have increased, but that whatever we put into work is taking a greater toll on our personal resources, hence the rise in stress-related complaints. The home–work interface at which we

try to balance both aspects of our lives has certainly been one point at which difficulties in meeting the demands of work have become apparent and overall the tendency is for the individual to demonstrate flexibility. This kind of power imbalance is felt by some more than others, e.g. part-time employees. Ideally work should facilitate and be part of living rather than get in the way – if it is achieving only the latter then a change is a good idea!

2 *Is conflict at the home–work interface inevitable?* Conflict at the home–work interface is related to time constraints, spillover of emotions and inconsistent expectations, as commitments in one major area of our lives vie with another. It would depend on the circumstances of the job and the employee how often these issues would arise, but if it is hard to foresee a situation without such conflict, then ways of making this fine juggling act less demanding will be a fairly constant concern for the individual involved.

3 *What level of importance should organizations give to the problems of employees which originate outside of the work domain?* The law requires that organizations regard the individual in the light of information which they have about them, which means that if the employee has not declared they have difficulties outside of work, then the employer cannot be expected to know about them. This has been relevant in stress-related complaints, where, in line with the organization's duty of care to the individual, employers should not make unreasonable demands of their workers. In practice individuals may not feel it appropriate to make their private matters known. Also the degree to which non-work problems should be taken into account and commitments like workload reduced is not always clear, but the employer is also entitled within reasonable limits to expect the job to be done. The key word here is 'reasonable', and this is likely to require flexibility on both sides.

4 *Who should take responsibility for solving the societal problems resulting from long working hours cultures – individuals, organizations, or governments?* The drop in birth-rate and the rise in stress-related disorders in some economically developed countries have certainly motivated governments to take action where work–life balance has become a well-publicized concept; however, there has been some variation in national employment laws. At the organizational level, the benefits of working long hours – because that is the way things are usually done – are not necessarily supported by increased productivity

figures and unless workplaces can demonstrate such economic advantages, then there is little reason to maintain the norm of long hours. The role of individual employees in bringing about such a change in attitudes and behaviour within an organization is vital, perhaps by being assertive about finishing times or developing a policy to support healthier working.

5 *How effective are organizational approaches in dealing with the challenges of the home–work interface?* A quick glance through those companies considered the best to work for clearly shows the value placed upon helping the employee juggle the demands of work and home. Whether it is flexible working, child and elder-care entitlement or generous leave arrangements, the key for employees seems to be that the organization demonstrates their commitment to the 'whole' worker. This is likely to generate reciprocal commitment from the workforce and highlights the relevance of such a mutually beneficial arrangement.

Suggested further reading

If you want to read more on this and related topics, research and texts in this area have burgeoned in recent years. Eby *et al.* (2005) provide a comprehensive review of relevant themes gleaned from a trawl of all articles published in industrial and organizational journals between 1980 and 2002 and Brough and O'Driscoll (2005) have produced a concise chapter on relevant research. There are also handy books designed to help with a personal quest for work–life balance, such as *Balancing Your Career, Family and Life* by Cary Cooper and Suzan Lewis (1998).

9 Measuring and assessing emotions in the workplace

One of the fascinating things about people is our curiosity in finding out how we tick. Psychometric measures are those tools, often questionnaires or paper and pencil tests, which are designed to assess a whole range of abilities, attributes and frailties which make up the way we are. This chapter highlights instruments which are often used in gathering information on the key issues covered by this book, i.e. well-being and emotional functioning. The opportunity to buy well-known measures usually requires a qualification in either psychology or in psychometric testing: however you will find examples here which enable you to gauge some of these concepts for yourself. The first section highlights some of the limitations of using questionnaire methods and aims to answer the sceptics among us, like the boss who said, 'Everyone thinks they're stressed – of course they'll answer yes to all your questions so they can get back at the company'!

Apart from choosing the right tools for the job, there is a host of other considerations, such as the likely cost in terms of time and money, but before attempting to calculate these, one should think carefully about the reasons for carrying out this type of study. It is likely that there are ethical issues to be addressed, such as who will have access to the data and what will it be used for? What are the possible repercussions? Will the confidentiality and the welfare of participants be protected? The key is to recognize that information represents power and power can be abused. This is not to say that those wishing to research employees' well-being are likely to act with the naivety of meddling scientists, but it is important to be aware there certainly can be political fallout from this type of exercise. The emotions of those who would not wish to have their organization seen as stress-prone should not be underestimated.

Careful preparation and anticipation of how to handle such defensiveness is required! Hopefully the point of any study of employees' emotional and psychological health is for the benefit of groups of staff and it is essential to bear this in mind in the careful collection of data and feedback of findings.

Survey questionnaires and other methods

Any questionnaire which requires us to fill in answers based on our own experience is only likely to be as effective and reliable as our ability to report faithfully on that experience. For example, how happy have you felt over the last month? Not sure? Or maybe the last couple of days have been particularly good or bad and coloured your view? Either way it certainly isn't easy to recall an average feeling of 'happiness' over the last 30 days or so. We tend not to think of life in that way. This illustrates just one of the difficulties faced by researchers and anyone else interested in finding out about how we are feeling, or at least how we have been feeling lately. The issue is one of self-report. The human being is not necessarily the most exact indicator and is subject to a whole range of potential biases when responding to questions, including those about our health and well-being. It is worth exploring these issues a little more thoroughly in a way which highlights what we should and should not expect from questionnaires and other measures of psychological and emotional functioning.

How important is objectivity?

Any application of science, including in the social sciences such as psychology and sociology, attempts to use methods of data collection which will stand up to scrutiny. In this way it is hoped that the results we obtain are valid and reliable. In other words, we want to be as sure as possible that what we are using to measure something as subjective as emotions and well-being is actually doing just that and that it will also provide a consistent set of findings. This is not just important from a scientific viewpoint, but also from an applied approach such as that adopted in managing and running organizations. After all, if you want to know there is a problem in your workplace, you would also want to make sure that the evidence you mustered was both realistic and meaningful.

Herein lies an interesting philosophical point: should we trust the view of the individual or should we instead use some kind of absolute measure to ensure a scientific way round the individual's biases?

In the area of emotions and well-being, it is important to realize that both perspectives are important. The way we perceive our situation and feelings is vital to us as individuals and is usually less so for the organization, yet we might surmise that the link between how things appear to the rest of the world and how they seem to us is habitually strong. There are obviously occasions where this relationship assumption is challenged, such as the employee who fails to recognize that their 'I don't care' behaviour is totally unacceptable to their conscientious colleagues. Relevant research in this area has also shown some inconsistencies. For example a study of 8838 civil servants found limited support for the idea that 'subjective' ratings by employees and supposedly 'objective' supervisors' ratings of aspects of the employees' jobs would match (Stansfeld et al., 1995). These results may have been affected by the extent of job knowledge among supervisors, but it illustrates the point that perspectives can be hard to measure in an absolutely satisfactory manner. The debate is further fuelled by Stansfeld et al., who emphasize that it is 'employees' perceptions and interpretation of their objective working conditions rather than working conditions per se which directly influence well-being, satisfaction and psychiatric disorder' (1995, p. 53). Lazarus et al. (1985) also argue that it is impossible to consider stressors separately from our reaction to them, which means that our strategies for dealing with challenging situations should be taken into account.

Very quickly one might come to realize that attempting to measure something which is recognized as a problem, such as poor psychological health in a workplace, can give rise to a whole range of considerations – some of which depend on one another and are therefore very difficult to assess at all! Kasl and Amick (1995) suggest a way forward which attempts to tease apart the objective measurement of the environment from the assessment of health and other outcomes. This may be achieved by using instruments which assess the following separately:

- Use self-reports from employees about aspects of the workplace which are independently verifiable, such as the hours worked, the number of colleagues sharing their particular job function, etc.
- Measure factors which take into account individual predispositions and reactions, e.g. personality, coping strategies.

- Assess psychological strain using recognized measures, e.g. the General Health Questionnaire (Goldberg and Williams, 1988) discussed later in this chapter.

In order to combat the reliance on individual's memories of how work factors or well-being may have changed, Kasl and Amick also suggest the use of research designs which monitor situations as they unfold, rather than simply from a retrospective view. In this way they attempt to promote extra credibility to be gained by assessing workplace and health factors both before and after changes or interventions which might impact on employees. This ideal scenario is not necessarily our experience of the workplace, but usually there is some notice of planned change which does lend itself to this type of approach. For example studies of well-being among Members of Parliament have tended to assess the impact of a range of parliamentary events by comparing data from before and after reforms to working hours (Weinberg *et al.*, 1999) and general elections (Weinberg and Cooper, 2003). This type of study design permits comparisons which are likely to be meaningful to the individuals concerned as well as the organizational context, providing data on both the impact on staff and an evaluation of change.

Potential sources of bias

Underpinning the questionnaire approach are a number of assumptions which it is as well to be aware of. Among the many ways in which employee responses to questionnaires can be subject to bias are those linked to the situation and to the personal disposition of the respondent.

- Who will complete the questionnaire? Suppose those who are experiencing severe pressure are the ones who are too ill to fill it in? The way around this is to establish if the sample returning a completed questionnaire are actually representative of the whole group which is under scrutiny. This can be achieved by matching the demographic features of the sample to the population from which it is drawn, i.e. comparing gender, age, etc. Researchers also send out reminder letters to potential participants and compare the profile of these 'late' respondents to the original set of respondents. A good match can permit deductions about the representative nature of the original sample to be made, e.g. the ill ones were just as likely to reply in the first instance.

- Suppose the people who respond are naturally pessimistic and will perceive sources of pressure where others might not? The concept of negative affect was explored in Chapter 3 and refers to the tendency of an individual to perceive aspects of their environment as more threatening and therefore in a negative manner. People who are imbued with high levels of this trait are likely to be anxiety-prone and to focus on pessimistic interpretations of their environment (Spector and O'Connell, 1994) and may actually find that their approach to life leads to more sources of pressure than would be the case if they experienced low negative affect (Magnus et al., 1993). Furthermore such a long-term disposition to negative affectivity is strongly linked with the individual's experience of negative affect at work in a given week (Brief et al., 1988). This is likely to have an impact on how individuals with high negative affectivity respond to questionnaires about aspects of the workplace and indeed their own well-being, as not only is their reporting of work circumstances likely to be influenced, but also their experience of well-being (Warr, 1999). Just as this might seem like a good point at which to give up on ever obtaining a representative idea of people's feelings about their work, it is worth bearing in mind that despite the influence of this pessimistic trait, many researchers have still found strong associations between specific workplace factors and employee mental health (e.g. Cohen and Spector, 1991; Stansfeld et al., 1995). In other words, if there is an effect of some sort, it should be possible to detect it – and don't forget your sample is likely to contain both pessimists and optimists!

- Suppose it suits people to complete the questionnaire to paint a poor picture of the organization? The circumstances under which some stress audits take place can be seen as a handy vent for employees' emotion. Whether this is likely to be expressed and therefore unduly bias the results of a survey is always hard to say, but it should be remembered that questions are likely to be specific and have a structured format in which to provide answers. Furthermore if different aspects of the questionnaire are measuring different things as Kasl and Amick would advocate, then it would be possible to analyse separately the responses about individual well-being and sources of pressure. The collection of data from a number of people, whose strength of emotion about their work situation probably varies, also means that any extreme responses are likely to be averaged out upon analysis.

It is worth bearing in mind that the anonymity which is valued by most who complete such questionnaires is something which employees would not wish to jeopardize. It could therefore be assumed that people will complete them in private and therefore be less subject to group bias. This is not to say however that people cannot fake their responses – they can (Furnham and Henderson, 1983), but whether they will is another question.

● How will I know if the questionnaire is well-designed and fit for purpose? There are aspects to questionnaires which need to be checked during the course of their design and production. Any measure which has been published or designed for a specific purpose should have been subject to checks on its validity and reliability, as well as having been tested on a population to see if it really works. This saves the would-be researcher considerable time and effort. The concept of validity has a range of aspects, but essentially it refers to the capacity of the questionnaire to measure what it is supposed to measure, whereas the concept of reliability refers to the consistency in performance of a questionnaire. Taken in combination, these issues contribute to the usefulness of a measure or set of measures and their construction is known as psychometrics. The marketing material which accompanies questionnaires will often refer to such issues with a positive spin in addition to how to access details of administering and scoring them. An increasing feature is the offer (subject to cost) to score questionnaires electronically and to provide standardized reports. Depending on circumstances this can have the advantage of saving the need for additional training as well as providing some assurances about the accuracy of the final data set. Nevertheless test publishers usually require a minimum level of qualification before selling their materials to the end user, such as a certificate in psychometric testing compliant with national standards in the relevant profession, e.g. Level A with the British Psychological Society.

Questionnaires are not the only route

Determining the prevalence of psychological and emotional distress among any population is largely conducted using available data collection methods. A variety of methods other than questionnaires have been employed, each yielding sufficient results for interpretation in addition to a healthy scepticism about the findings. As well as those described here, qualitative approaches such as structured diaries are gaining in popularity as a way of getting to the heart of the occupational issues under investigation.

1 Interview schedules

These provide the researcher with more control over the data collection process than is possible via questionnaires. In addition, the interview can help to ensure that respondents are 'in tune' with the aims of the various questions and there is also the potential for gleaning greater detail. A notable example of this is provided by Stansfeld and Marmot (1992) whose questionnaire survey found a psychiatric case rate almost double that confirmed by interview (24.8 per cent vs 12.7 per cent). Of course this reduction in symptoms may have been due to a time delay between the completion of the survey and the interview. Equally the level of detail contained in such a clinical interview means that clarification of the frequency, duration, severity and degree of impairment of any indication of strain is much greater.

This technique does introduce the potential for interviewer bias; however, this extra subjectivity may be tempered by the use of standardized measures, as well as via methods of standardizing the interpretation of the data. Compared to questionnaires, the interview is much more time-intensive and may require training for those conducting them.

2 Monitoring absenteeism, turnover and discretionary activities

Figures on absence from work constitute an objective data source in relation to sickness. This can be done in terms of overall time lost or the number of absence periods; it is the former which is considered to reflect involuntary responses to illness whereas the latter represents the role of choice in taking time off work (Warr, 1999). As a measure, self-reported absence is actually quite reliable and is reflected in organizationally recorded absence (Borrill et al., 1998). However, research has shown weaker links between these measures of absenteeism and individuals' views of the workplace. This indicates that a number of factors may influence data on absenteeism. For example information on sick notes may be inaccurate or mask the extent of emotional health problems among workers. Additionally, absences may be controlled or otherwise by organizational factors, such as family-friendly policies permitting leave, an organizational climate of absence, or a system of daily reporting and following up every episode of absence. Outside of the workplace, family pressures may also influence episodes of absence.

Turnover, which is highly correlated with absence (Mitra *et al.*, 1992), can be predicted by overall job satisfaction (George and Jones, 1996) and job-specific anxiety (Spector *et al.*, 1988). However, the availability of alternative work in the locality or within an occupational group should not be overlooked.

Discretionary activities (Warr, 1999) consist of behaviours which are not integral to the performance of a job role, but do indicate the degree of commitment held to that job, i.e. voluntary overtime, prosocial activity (helping colleagues, making suggestions) and adaptive behaviour (attending training courses). Attractive though these factors may be in assessing job satisfaction, their measurement is open to the limitations of subjectivity although objectivity could be achieved by eliciting the frequency of these behaviours.

3 Physiological measures

Physiological indicators of increased arousal of bodily systems and of illness-promoting chemicals provide a mode of measurement which is separate from that used to assess work characteristics and therefore can avoid the types of bias common to self-reports. While large-scale studies have failed to produce consistent links between biological variables and perceived sources of strain (Kasl and Amick, 1995), increased biological risk factors have been associated with an interaction of both objective and subjective sources of strain, e.g. job instability and job insecurity (Siegrist *et al.*, 1988), low promotion prospects and feelings of sustained anger (Siegrist *et al.*, 1991). However, the associated costs of gathering and analysing this type of data and the difficulties in ensuring adequate controls tend to result in small-scale studies which can limit the potential for drawing wider conclusions.

4 Standardized mortality ratios

The comparison of death rates or standardized mortality ratios (SMIs) among occupational and other groups with a population norm is the main method for calculating the relative risk of death due to categories of causes, but can seem a strange way of assessing well-being! However, it is noteworthy as this approach has produced some compelling evidence for the impact of certain jobs, not only on the physical health of job-holders, but also their partners (Fletcher, 1988). Derived from national statistics, findings have curiously shown the elevated risk of death by certain diseases within occupational groups (e.g. coronary heart disease, cancer and respiratory problems), which is almost as high for the spouse as for the employee themselves!

Obviously this method is more likely to be relevant to mental health where this ends with death by suicide, assumed to be occasioned by an episode of severe depression or psychosis. Such figures have been increasingly quoted to highlight the fast rising suicide rate among sections of the population such as young men (Appleby *et al.*, 1996) and the higher than national occurrence among doctors (Lindeman *et al.*, 1996) and farmers (Howton *et al.*, 1998). In the USA suicide is the third most common cause of death for 15–24-year-olds (Jamison, 1999). However, due to the relatively small numbers of individuals included in the calculation of SMIs, the possibility of inaccuracies on death certificates and the acknowledgement that such mortality varies according to social class (Davey Smith *et al.*, 2001; British Medical Association, 1993), measurement of psychological ill-health among the living is likely to provide more insightful data.

So what is good practice?

When faced with the opportunity to carry out a study of people in any setting, there are bound to be a range of questions which spring to mind, not least being 'How am I actually going to do this?' Choosing the right tools for the job is an important part of the picture which will hopefully enable you to collect the right type of data in the right kind of way. Questionnaires have the major advantage of helping the researcher to reach a large number of potential participants at relatively low cost. As such the 'stress audit' retains a level of appeal which tends to outweigh the possible problems in methodological terms which have been highlighted: however, the response rate to a general survey of this nature is often said to be one-third of those distributed. This figure can be increased where one has been able to bring on board all the relevant stakeholder groups, such as managers, union and staff representatives from the groups involved, occupational health and personnel departments. The demonstration of the support of these groups in a covering letter, as well as genuine reassurances about anonymity and confidentiality of any returned questionnaires, can help to overcome the scepticism of a proportion of otherwise unwilling individuals. Carefully publicizing the study in staff newsletters and even on wage packets can also help raise the profile of the project in a credible manner. Personal contact – such as presentations to staff groups and visiting relevant departments – is another way to show your commitment and sincerity about what you are doing and there is also utility in sending a reminder letter with another copy of the questionnaire a few weeks after the original.

Having done all of this and collected what seems like a healthy proportion of the questionnaires which were sent out, it is important to demonstrate that your sample of data is representative of the population (the whole group) from which it is drawn. By showing that your data is drawn from a subsection of employees who resemble the relevant population in demographic profile (e.g. gender, age, ethnicity and occupation), it is more likely the findings can be treated with the potential to say something about the wider organization. On the one hand this presumes that for practical reasons you have not been able to give a questionnaire to everyone who is eligible, but on the other, not everyone will have completed and returned one to you.

A detailed description of how to summarize the information and generate appropriate descriptive statistics from such information lies beyond the scope of this book, but there are many texts on research methods which are useful in this regard, not to mention the many lecturers who spend copious time explaining these issues to under- and postgraduates. As such individuals will tell you, it is essential to exercise caution in extrapolating 'proof' from the findings of any one study and it is therefore important to remind one's potential audience of this, as much as for the benefit of their conclusions as your own. The next section samples a range of the more widely used questionnaires.

Measuring well-being in the workplace

According to Warr (1999) it is possible to distinguish between individual well-being in a 'job-specific' environment as well as outside of work in what he terms 'context-free' circumstances: this encourages us to draw a distinction between the individual's 'feelings about themselves in relation to their job ... (and) feelings without limitation to any particular setting' (Warr, 1999, p. 393). He proposed a model (see Chapter 1) in which psychological well-being can be measured in terms of displeasure–pleasure, anxiety–comfort and depression–enthusiasm. The first of these is commonly measured in terms of job satisfaction and life satisfaction, whereas the other two have traditionally been assessed via more clinical measures. This helps to ensure that the issue of how one interprets scores on such measures in determining 'illness' is left to those with appropriate qualifications, but it is important to be aware that any labelling can carry with it possible risks of stigmatizing or causing unnecessary distress, unless there is clear benefit to the individual concerned in terms of accessing treatment. Obviously no screening test detects illness across the board, however in individual cases it is safer to assume that the total score on a measure above a certain threshold may indicate a *probability* that they have an illness, rather than actual proof.

The rest of this section will focus on the most widely used and best known measures, both job-specific and context-free, for assessing workplace strain, including questionnaires and interview schedules. It should be noted that care should be taken, particularly in relying on the context-free measures as they are more suited to clinical and research purposes.

Context-free measures of mental health

1 The General Health Questionnaire

The General Health Questionnaire (GHQ) (Goldberg and Williams, 1988) is used to detect a range of psychiatric symptoms, including depression and anxiety. It is usually completed by the individual with reference to the previous three months. Derived from the Cornell Medical Inventory (Brodman *et al.*, 1949) among other instruments, the GHQ is based on psychometric analyses of questionnaire items most likely to reflect areas of distress in a community population. These areas are 'felt psychological disturbance', 'unhappiness', 'social inadequacy' and 'lack of identity' (Goldberg and Williams, 1988). The GHQ has been reincarnated in versions of varying length, each of which has been shown to have good validity and reliability. The shortest version, the GHQ-12, has been shown to have high specificity and sensitivity in studies carried out across the world (Goldberg and Williams, 1988) and has been used consistently in major studies of mental health in the workforce (e.g. Wall *et al.*, 1997).

The consistent criticism that has been levelled at the GHQ is related to its limited capacity to detect long-standing disorder by providing the option of responding 'same as usual'. Additionally in terms of the ability of this instrument to accurately detect minor psychiatric disorder, an important point should be made. Numerous validation studies have been undertaken, but some disagreement has emerged. One large-scale NHS study (Wall *et al.*, 1997) incorporated 615 questionnaires and interviews and found a high correlation of 0.7 between measured outcomes on the GHQ-12 and the Clinical Interview Schedule (Revised) (Lewis and Pelosi, 1992). However, the equally large-scale Whitehall study (Stansfeld *et al.*, 1995) involved interviews with the CIS-R and found that only 54 per cent of GHQ-12 high scorers, i.e. four or more, were confirmed as cases at interview. These findings suggest that the GHQ-12 used alone may over-represent the prevalence of minor psychiatric disorder in a given sample.

2 Beck Depression Inventory

The Beck Depression Inventory (BDI) (Beck, Ward, Mendelson, Mock and Erbaugh, 1961) is a widely used instrument for assessing the cognitive rather than physical aspects of depression and like the GHQ may be completed by the individual. It exists in 12 and 21-item versions and is completed with reference to the previous week. Its limitation as a screening measure lies in its original design as a means by which to assess the severity of symptoms of depression following a diagnosis. Thus there is no standard cut-off score.

3 Hospital Anxiety and Depression Scale

The Hospital Anxiety and Depression Scale (HADS) (Zigmond and Snaith, 1983) is a self-rating scale can be used to assess both anxiety and depression by assessing the individual's difficulty in experiencing pleasure. It is more likely to be used within primary healthcare. Like the Beck Depression Inventory, the HADS focuses on the last week, but does have a cut-off score. It has been used in primary care settings and has been widely translated; however, it should not be considered as a screening measure in its own right as it focuses on a limited number of symptoms of depression (Clarkson and Lynch, 1998).

4 Clinical Interview Schedule

The Clinical Interview Schedule (Revised) (CIS-R) (Lewis and Pelosi, 1992) has been successfully standardized for use by lay interviewers and as such has been employed in the Office of Population and Census Survey of psychiatric morbidity in the UK. Studies have shown that lay interviewers can be as reliable as psychiatrists in applying the CIS-R. It comprises 14 sections addressing neurotic symptoms of psychological ill health, e.g. fatigue, sleep problems, irritability, worry, depressive ideas, etc., thus permitting a relatively short interview time of approximately 30 minutes. Each section is preceded by a filter question which if answered affirmatively may be followed up with a more detailed assessment of the symptom in the last week, concentrating on the frequency, duration, severity and degree of impairment to usual functioning. The possible range of scores on each section is mainly 0–4, with an overall maximum of 57. A score of two or more on a symptom indicates high severity and the threshold score for significant psychiatric morbidity is 11/12.

The CISR also permits diagnosis via the use of algorithms. For example, generalized anxiety disorder is determined by a score of two or more on the anxiety section, a duration of at least six months, free-floating anxiety and autonomic overactivity, i.e. resulting in physical reactions.

Job-specific measures of mental health

1 ASSET

ASSET (A Shortened Stress Evaluation Tool [Faragher *et al.*, 2004]) is designed to act as a relatively brief screening instrument which can help to identify 'problem' areas within an organization in relation to employee well-being. The authors recommend that its length aids cost-effectiveness by allowing managers to focus on those sections needing intervention, but also recognize it requires follow-up with a more detailed measure, such as the OSI (see below), to obtain information which will say more about the difficulties experienced by individual staff. Using a Likert rating scale and based on a modernized version of Cooper and Marshall's (1978) model of stress, sections cover employees' perceptions of their job, work relationships, potential sources of stress, overload, control, job security, resources and communication, work–life balance, as well as pay and benefits. In addition employees' attitudes and commitment towards the organization as well as those of the organization towards them are assessed, in addition to symptoms of physical and psychological strain. The authors reported reputable psychometric properties for the ASSET and claim that it takes 10–15 minutes to complete, which is seen as a way to facilitate high response rates (Faragher *et al.*, 2004).

2 The Occupational Stress Indicator

The Occupational Stress Indicator (OSI) was designed by Cooper *et al.* (1988) as a tool for use in organizations to detect and assess stress-related problems, with an emphasis on well-being in groups of employees. It comprises a number of subsections, some or all of which may be used, focusing on potential sources of pressure at work, Type A behaviour, perceived control over one's work environment, job satisfaction, home–work balance, coping mechanisms and emotional and physical symptoms of strain. All items are scored on a Likert scale reflecting the frequency or degree of each response. The subsection on mental health is not diagnostic, but rather an insight into functioning at work and the physical symptoms of stress are more obviously health-related, but are recognizable as psychosomatic or symptoms of depression and anxiety. The OSI can be considered a long and somewhat ambitious instrument to use in its entirety, but it has been used internationally across four continents and has gained a reputation for helping to highlight areas of difficulty in an organization (Jones and Bright, 2001).

3 Maslach Burnout Inventory

The Maslach Burnout Inventory (MBI) (Maslach and Jackson, 1986) has been widely used to assess the well-being of employees in the helping professions, considering the nature of their work and their dealings with recipients of their services. The measure explores three dimensions of burnout which are considered in more detail in Chapter 1: emotional exhaustion, personal accomplishment and depersonalization, i.e. the extent to which workers feel hardened towards the users of their service. The 22 items invite respondents to note the frequency with which they feel fatigued, frustrated, fulfilled, etc. It has been suggested that the assessment of symptoms of exhaustion alone may be the most relevant to measuring well-being, rather than depersonalization and a lack of personal accomplishment, which may say more about the personality make-up of individuals attracted to this kind of intensive work (Garden, 1989).

4 Measurement of job-related well-being

As mentioned earlier Warr's (1990) conceptualization of mental health at work highlights three sets of axes of well-being. The first of these (pleasure-displeasure) is akin to the notion of job satisfaction, however his measures focus instead on the second and third aspects, consisting of the Job-Related Depression–Enthusiasm scale and the Job-Related Anxiety–Contentment scale. Both contain six adjectives, three positive and three negative in relation to which the respondent rates the frequency each is experienced. It is assumed that the higher scores on positive emotional states, the lower those on negative ones and vice-versa. Mullarkey *et al.* (1999) report a number of studies using these measures in different occupational groups and note an interesting pattern in which higher status jobs are associated with more enthusiasm and less depression, but less contentment and greater anxiety, than employment with less status. This outcome is also found among self-employed individuals (Birdi, Warr and Oswald, 1995) and demonstrates a sensitivity to the insecurities likely to be experienced by those whose level of control at work is likely to be high, but whose destiny may well lie with market and other forces beyond their immediate control. However, in attempting to assess the wide range of emotions to which workers are subject, it can be argued that using only two sets of axes may be too simplistic (e.g. Daniels *et al.*, 1997).

Having reviewed a number of well-known measures of well-being, the question facing the researcher (as well as the potential audience for their results) is 'Which one should I use, or should I use all of them?' The answer will depend on whether they are suited to assessing the aspect of well-being in which you are interested and also on the length of the questionnaire. There are resource considerations, such as cost and needing approval for their use by the test publishers. In terms of value for money, this can depend on how well the study is constructed and carried out, as well as factors beyond the researcher's control such as response rate. Either way if advice can be gained in interpreting the findings appropriately and carefully and the overall findings can be used to produce positive change, then it is probably a study worth doing!

Case Study
9.1

Assessing well-being for the common good

Whilst it is important to ensure that any research is carried out well, this can be assured by involving practitioners in the field, particularly where one recognizes limitations in one's own ability. The decision by a hospital working party on stress to consult with a postgraduate research student was born out of this recognition, but also from the need to gather some data on what the members of the group suspected. Namely that in their jobs, whether as occupational physician, counsellor or chaplain, they had each noticed a high level of staff distress and realized that it was hard to meet the increasing demand on their services. The group's preferred option was to expand the counselling service offered within the hospital, but they knew that a sound business case would need to be made. This would mean figures and costs and the key ones would relate to how many staff might actually need help and finding out just how bad things had become for the 6000 employees. A stress audit using established measures and carried out with the cooperation and involvement of all staff groups, as well as backing from senior management, provided the answer. With the data collected and analysed by the experienced researcher, the group was able to access the kind of information which would form the basis for a business case for funding. By meeting the needs of employees, an organizational need was also fulfilled, as senior managers accepted the likelihood of counselling helping to keep people in work and saving the hospital money to cover absenteeism. This example of a successful intervention based on good research is a model which can be applied in any sector and many types of organization.

Assessing emotional intelligence

As emotional intelligence is rapidly acquiring an image as a sexy area of psychology, given its applications and significance, it is also important to know how it can be recognized and even measured (the core components of EI are covered in detail in Chapter 6). The main factors featured in EI models are:

- Self-awareness
- Self-management
- Social awareness
- Relationship management.

Relevant tests of EI tend to reflect the theoretical models on which they have been based, but it is useful to know what to look for when considering the best way to assess it. As has been mentioned already in this chapter, the concepts of validity and reliability are key factors. In addition there are three other issues which deserve attention: first, that any measure of EI should cover a representative set of relevant behaviours. For example the assessment of social skills should take into account a range of things which we do when interacting with others, rather than focusing wholly on one aspect, e.g. listening, non-verbal behaviour, appearing involved with others. Second we would all want a measure of EI to tell us something meaningful, especially where this might have implications for real issues, such as achievements in work or study, the quality of relationships or health (Ciarrochi *et al.*, 2001). The third factor is the distinctiveness of any test of EI from quite different concepts, e.g. memory, whilst retaining similarity with similar concepts, e.g. personality traits. Obviously a measure which stands apart from measures of other constructs is desirable, and helps us to say with confidence that we are assessing EI rather than anything else. However, the issue of overlap has the potential to pose problems in the field of EI, given the modest convergence which exists between certain personality traits and EI: yet there are strong claims that EI is distinguishable from other traits (e.g. Petrides and Furnham, 2001).

Currently there are three varieties of EI measure, one relying on self-report, another on assessed performance and a third on 360-degree appraisal. Some advantages and limitations of self-report measures have been considered previously in this chapter in relation to well-being and some of those caveats also hold for assessing emotional intelligence. Intuitively one can see the appeal in actually assessing those skills in action, however our own and other people's perceptions of how well such skills are used can be just as important (Ciarrochi *et al.*, 2001). It is also possible that individuals may not possess much insight into their abilities, whether emotional or other, or even where they do, they may not wish to appear less than favourably! Examples of each of the three types of EI measures are considered here:

1 The *Bar-On Emotional Quotient Inventory (EQ-i)* is a self-report measure which also takes about 30 minutes to administer. It consists of 133 questions (covering 12 areas) which ask for Likert scale responses indicating the frequency with which the individual will experience a range of emotional states and reactions relating to aspects of emotional intelligence. The scoring and reporting of results is possible by submitting the data direct to the test publishers, who have calculated comparative norms using a sample of almost 4000 individuals. In addition there is the facility to compare EQ scores from this measure with those from a range of other occupational groups, as well as with those who have experienced success in different settings (Bar-On, 2002). The questionnaire also shows promising psychometric properties, although it is important to bear in mind that the subscales are moderately to strongly linked to scores on a range of personality and well-being measures. This can beg the question of how much more does this type of instrument tell us than existing health and personality questionnaires? (Ciarrochi *et al.*, 2001). Another widely used measure is the *Emotional Intelligence Questionnaire (EIQ)* (Dulewicz and Higgs, 2005) which has two versions for use with either managerial or other organizational functions. This incorporates both self-report and 360-degree questionnaires and aims to assess seven qualities, including self-awareness, emotional resilience, intuitiveness, interpersonal sensitivity, influence, motivation and conscientiousness. It takes 20–30 minutes to complete and scores can be reported online.

   Not surprisingly there is an increasing range of self-report measures, which is likely to swell the choice on offer to those interested in assessing emotional intelligence. The *EISAQ (Emotional Intelligence Self-Assessment Questionnaire;* Weinberg and Pearson, 2005) is a short measure (20 items) which incorporates subscales tapping into five aspects of the overall concept. Like other measures it has been developed using student populations and shows promising validity and reliability. It has the advantage of being easily scored and is quicker to complete, although more information is awaited on how it performs compared to the other well-known measures described here.

2 The *Mayer-Salovey-Caruso Emotional Intelligence Test (MSCEIT)* is a performance measure which takes about 30 minutes to administer. The test assesses performance on recognizing moods and the meaning of facial expressions, interpreting and dealing with emotions, as well as relating emotional to other sensory experiences. An overall score is derived by asking the individual to rate their responses on a range of questions which include case study examples and pictorial images – the resulting ratings can be compared with scores from a databank of 5000 individuals to permit a ranking of emotional competence which can range from 'Consider development' to 'Significant strength'. As well as a global score, the MSCEIT can provide component scores on aspects of emotional intelligence. Overall it has also been shown by its authors to be a reliable measure (Mayer *et al.*, 2002).

3 The *Emotional Competence Inventory (ECI)* is a 360-degree instrument (Goleman *et al.*, 2006), which utilizes feedback from others in the work sphere on the emotional intelligence of individuals. Based on Goleman's four cluster model, the questionnaire obtains ratings on self and social awareness, self and relationship management. In this way, our own assessment of emotional competence can be compared with others' views of us in each of those capacities, such as managers, co-workers and those whom the individual manages. Based on research with this measure, it is claimed by the authors that target levels can be set for individuals as part of training and development.

In summary, the assessment of emotional intelligence is likely to remain a popular field for scrutiny, both with academics and practitioners, including managers and employees. As with measures of well-being, the advantages of this lie with the potential to highlight strengths as well as areas for development, which in turn can benefit the individual and the organization. The appeal of emotional intelligence is widespread, especially as it is a concept with which most, if not all, in the workplace can identify. The implications for functioning as individuals and teams can be seen in training and interpersonal dealings. The success of incentives which aim to mould and enhance emotional intelligence remains to be widely explored, but strong EI is becoming recognized as a key component of any work-based survival kit, which according to Goleman counts twice as much as the traditional intelligences in helping us to achieve our goals.

Summary of the chapter

Finding out what makes us tick, as well as the organizations for which we work, is fascinating. The question of how to do this in the realm of employee well-being is addressed in this chapter in a way which is designed to highlight and explain major ethical and practical considerations. In both well-being and emotional intelligence there is a range of methods and with each there are advantages and disadvantages. Such key considerations have been flagged up here, as the information obtained in research can only be as good as the approach taken. Examples of measures of mental health are reviewed – from universal as well as work perspectives – as are a range of tools for assessing emotional intelligence. If this chapter has whetted your appetite for finding out more, then it has been well worth writing!

Key terms	
objectivity	context-free
bias	job-specific
audits	well-being
measures	emotional intelligence

Questions and answers

1 *How scientific is research into people's emotions and can we really be objective?* Scientific procedures help us to know 'real things, whose characteristics are entirely independent of our opinions about them' (Tomas, 1957). As social science involves researching people, who are not renowned for behaving with the predictability of chemicals in a laboratory, a number of things which vary need to be considered. In the light of taking such variables into account, we are in a good position to say something about the usefulness of any results we obtain. It is important to be wary of potential sources of bias, which may be balanced by looking at groups which are similar in their nature, for example, comparing job satisfaction levels of employees from the same occupational group in which one half is exposed to a factor in the workplace and the other half is not. Despite taking care to

eliminate things which may cloud the results, and in recognition of the subjectivity of human emotions, among other things, it is still safer to talk about probability rather than 'proof' – in fact this is exactly the approach taken by scientists who study things which most of us might consider as predictable as rocks! Having said this, there is a growing trend towards incorporating qualitative approaches which actively engage the emotions of participants. The short answer to the question is that it is hard to ensure complete objectivity, and sometimes this may actually lose some of the rich focus we desire in measuring human experience, but there are many types of method and research design which can help control for unusual variation.

2 *What are the main ethical considerations in researching into stress at work?* That nobody should get hurt – emotionally or physically – is the bottom line for considering the potential impact of any research. Indeed it is possible to go further in the case of psychological strain at work and say that research should be designed with a benefit in mind. Obviously confidentiality for participants is crucial as well as the option to withdraw, but it is also necessary to think through what might happen after the study has taken place. Further key questions are how will the findings be communicated and what action might result – these need to be carefully thought out too.

3 *How do I get to find out more about specific measures in which I am interested?* As has been mentioned in the course of the chapter, psychometric tests such as those used to assess psychological health are usually available from publishers at a cost. In order to preserve this commercial viability, details are hard to come by in the appropriate literature, although some more general measures of well-being may be accessible in this way. Additionally some tests require the prospective user to possess the appropriate psychometric training qualification and if this is beyond the scope of the individual or organization to pursue, then it is worth approaching a professionally recognized person, such as a chartered psychologist, for their assistance.

4 *In designing a stress audit for an organization of your choice what are the potential problems?* Having successfully handled all the relevant ethical and political issues raised by proposing this kind of exercise, the methodological considerations of achieving a worthwhile set of data are paramount. You will need to be sure of the validity and reliability of the measures with which your data will be collected and that the sample of participants is sufficiently large and representative that

it will allow you to draw some generalizable conclusions at the end of the process. Appropriate statistical analysis is therefore important, and again it is worth gaining advice if this is not a field of one's own expertise. The writing of an understandable summary of the findings is vital for dissemination, again taking care to account for the readership and any further political implications!

5 *Which do you consider to be the best way to assess someone's level of emotional intelligence?* In the absence of questionnaire measures and potentially the need to assess large numbers of people, the best way to assess EI might be to give them a pet! In this way, it would be possible to gauge the individual's ability to show self-control when it fails to do as it's told, to feel empathy with its needs and wants, to demonstrate social skills in dealing with it and to find out how much that person identifies with the animal as an indication of their own self-awareness. This is not the stuff of usual personnel assessment procedures, but it does tap into the main concepts of EI! Perhaps the questionnaire is less risky and in this chapter a range of measures has been outlined, but do carefully consider the purpose in finding out more about EI as this will inform the choice which you make.

Suggested further reading

For those interested in carrying out their own organizational research there are many, many texts on research methods, particularly in the field of psychology. Given the need to feel comfortable with a guide to such activity, it is recommended that the would-be researcher tries a few taster texts, although for a helpful interactive guide Aron *et al.* (2005) *Statistics for the Behavioural Sciences* is packed with examples. Robson's texts enjoy a good track record and *Real-World Research* (2004), published by Blackwell, promises to continue this trend. For those keen to know how to analyse their findings, any of the books which feature SPSS (Statistical Package for the Social Sciences) and include information on how to interpret the printouts (!) can be worth their weight in gold.

As for finding the appropriate measures to suit your proposed study, Bowling and Ebrahim's (2005) *Handbook of Health Research Methods: Investigation, Measurement and Analysis* provides a valuable one-stop shop for helping to decide on any questionnaires related to health outcomes, while Ciarocchi *et al.* (2001; see reference list for this chapter at end of book) feature a good review of emotional intelligence measures, although this is likely to be a fast-changing menu. Otherwise any of the big psychometric publishing houses are more than keen to provide material about their wares which is why finding the right questionnaire seems so difficult to those who may already have spent a long while trawling the journals and books – the expectation is that you or your organization will be willing to pay and that you have undergone the appropriate training! Rather than a barrier, this should be viewed as an opportunity to gain the necessary qualification to enhance your personal survival skills kit for the workplace of your future.

Part Three

Coping and Survival at Work

Emphasizing the need to recognize and cope with negative emotions and impaired psychological health, this section evaluates the effectiveness of strategies which individual employees and organizations may consider. These are set in the context of potential changes in the future of working.

10 An effective psychological survival kit for the workplace

It is worth betting that more has been written about how to cope with the challenges which life throws at us than about many other subjects, although it remains to be seen how much of this has proved useful or indeed has continued to be utilized by those who have read it! This section of the book does not claim to be able to alter the life of its readers, but does try to encapsulate a range of approaches which the individual and the organization can consider. This means that as one goes through this chapter, there may be ideas which appeal to you or others who might stand to benefit.

In summing up how psychologists, researchers and lifestyle gurus have approached coping some particular themes do emerge. There is general recognition that everyone copes slightly differently and this can be dependent on their personality make-up as well as the type of situation which they are facing. Lazarus, a key author in this field, emphasizes the importance of how one views the problem being faced, highlighting 'primary appraisal' as the initial screening carried out by the individual to identify the level of potential threat posed by a stressor and 'secondary appraisal' as the process of deciding on the best course of action to take in response to that challenge.

Furthermore there is the capacity for humans to vary their strategy between dealing with the problems in hand and handling the emotions which accompany those problems. 'Coping is thus a shifting process' (Lazarus and Folkman, 1984, p. 142) in which the individual can respond to the changing interaction between the person and the environment in a challenging situation. Indeed this variable process of coping may be strongly influenced by how much control we feel we have over a situation (Carver *et al.*, 1989). Studies by both sets of these researchers have indicated that prior to examinations students tend to use coping strategies which are problem-focused, whereas while they await and receive their results, coping is centred on dealing with their emotions. This pattern may be familiar to many employees in the build up to and the aftermath of particular work events, such as interviews, meetings, presentations and key work performances: however, one could argue that the feedback is likely to be speedier. I suspect there are people reading this and thinking, 'Actually the emotions, such as anxiety, are present all the way through stressful events at work' and others are saying to themselves, 'What emotions?'

This illustrates a particular difficulty in reaching definite conclusions and making generalizations about coping, which some believe may be better dealt with on an emotion-by-emotion and problem-by-problem basis (e.g. Lazarus, 1993). Perhaps the difficulty rests with trying to isolate a particular issue, such as coping, and struggling to find absolute answers. After all coping is a normal reaction to, and therefore a part of, daily living (Costa *et al.*, 1996). Whilst 'the management of distressing emotions is the single most important focus of the disciplines of clinical psychology and psychiatry' (Costa *et al.*, 1996, p. 47), there is considerable scope for the flip side which focuses on how we can improve our living experiences. This search for optimizing our lives is the thrust of a developing movement known in some spheres as Positive Psychology (Linley *et al.*, 2006) and which has for many decades been the bread of butter of motivational coaches and lifestyle gurus. Little wonder then at the appeal of techniques which hint at finding the key to happiness and no surprise that so much has been said and written on the topic of coping.

The following sections highlight a range of strategies and the subheadings should not be taken as impermeable, as there is bound to be variation in how we categorize a particular coping technique. The utility of the approach is to provide a framework from which individuals can select options which may or may not be relevant to them.

Physiological coping

The reason why stress-related difficulties are so prevalent in the modern working environment is clear. As an animal, the human species has changed little in biological terms over tens of thousands of years (see also Chapter 12), yet the demands from the environment we inhabit have shifted dramatically, especially in terms of daily activities such as work. We are still physiologically wired to respond to immediate physical danger by fighting or fleeing and to do so on a fairly infrequent basis. The almost constant bombardment of stimuli which require attention and action and which can carry negative – but not life-threatening – consequences means those same biological defences are activated on a very regular basis and create the internal bodily conditions for malfunction (Clow, 2001), yet 'the social rules of our civilised world discourage physical attack or withdrawal' (Looker and Gregson, 1994, p. 23). The brain centre responsible for directing our bodies in readiness for flight or fight is the hypothalamus, which in biological terms is akin to an on–off light switch: however, if we were updating it, it would probably be designed to act as a dial, allowing the regulation of just how much or how little a response is needed. It is the lacking of this sensitivity to our modern daily need which results in frequent bodily readiness for crisis when it is not normally necessary, therefore placing a strain on our physical systems.

The wiring which transmits messages to the parts of the body which need to prepare for action in times of challenge is the bloodstream, into which are secreted three 'stress' chemicals responsible for carrying those messages. Among the actions stimulated by the hormones adrenalin and noradrenalin is an increase in heart rate, the dilation of blood vessels in the lungs, the muscles and the brain, as well as raised sensitivity. The effect of the third chemical, cortisol, is to mobilize necessary resources such as glucose and fats and to prepare the immune system. These outcomes will serve us well when we need to be ready for action. The relationship of these hormones to our emotions is highlighted in Table 10.1 (Looker and Gregson, 1994, p. 19); however, the regular activation of these chemical-led responses has been linked to a range of health problems. The concept of the plaque which lines the arteries breaking away to result in clots, thrombosis and heart attacks is fairly well known and has been ascribed to high levels of noradrenalin during angry outbursts (Looker and Gregson, 1994). The idea of long-term strain compromising our immunity is less well understood, but can be equally devastating. Humans possess two broad types of immune function which normally alternate across a 24-hour day to protect us from problems at the cellular and antiviral levels. Exposure to chronic strain can shift the balance away from monitoring for disease in the cell and towards overactivating responses to infection. In this way the body's capacity for avoiding cancer can remain impaired and yet at the same time it is predisposed to atopic problems, such as asthma (Clow, 2001).

Table 10.1	**Changes in stress hormones related to emotions and behaviours**					
Emotion		Anger	Fear	Depression	Serenity	Elation
Stress hormones	Behaviour	Aggressive 'fight'	Withdrawal 'flight'	Loss of control	Relaxed	Loving, supportive
Adrenalin		↑	↑↑	↔	↓	↓
Noradrenalin		↑↑	↑	↔	↓	↓
Cortisol		↔	↑	↑↑	↔	↓

Source: Looker and Gregson (1994). (http://www.tandf.co.uk/journals). Reproduced with permission.

It is no coincidence that a range of strategies for regaining some balance in our physical systems have become so popular in recent decades. From alternative therapies to aromatic oils, from meditation to mood triangles, there is much which is recommended. However, for simple, practical advice, which is relevant to many in the modern workplace, here are some physiological observations which in turn can inform how we treat our bodies:

● Coffee intake – caffeine stimulates the secretion of adrenalin and noradrenalin and therefore mimics the bodily stress response. This alert reaction has its uses, but moderation is recommended

● High dietary fat intake – in order to facilitate bodily preparedness, fat levels in the blood rise and this can combine with excessive dietary fat intake to produce an excessive increase and undesirable results

● Vitamins and minerals – these are the building blocks for maintaining good physical functioning and are therefore used at a higher rate during long periods of strain, which can leave us vulnerable if intake is not topped up

● Cholesterol reduction – cholesterol consists of beneficial high-density lipoprotein (HDL) as well as less beneficial low-density lipoprotein; regular exercise can increase the levels of HDL by turning this into energy and thereby using up the products of the stress response. In other words it does what would have happened if we had behaved in the flight or fight manner with which our bodies were programmed

● Nicotine intake – smoking while under strain can lead to increases in the levels of the chemicals associated with the stress response, especially noradrenalin, and can therefore exacerbate the body's reaction to strain (Looker and Gregson, 1994, p. 24).

Among the other advice which has been offered by nutritionists and health organizations which may be relevant to the workplace is the emphasis on eating breakfast, rather than missing it, to ensure among other things maintained cognitive performance (Kanarek, 1997). Given the natural variation in bodily rhythms across the course of the day which can result in tiredness and lowered performance in the mid-afternoon, the impact of the 'post-lunch dip' has attracted interest from many professions. However, assessments of the impact of this afternoon deficit in performance have noted only small differences in relation to the content of lunch (Kanarek, 1997).

Having ensured that your body is appropriately stocked up and ready to deal with the necessary challenges, the other key resource which is hard to maintain in busy working and home lives is that of rest. Here again we have slipped into behaving in a way which is actually at odds with how we evolved as a species. A conversation with a group of retired workers provides a clue to this. As they are no longer subject to the time framework imposed by the workplace, it is not uncommon to hear someone say, 'I keep waking up at 4 a.m. or some other unearthly hour.' In some this can be a response to the changing seasons or even preoccupation with some sort of worry, but it can also be a reflection that they are reverting to the sleep patterns which were much more likely to have been those of our ancestors. In exchange for the shackles of clocking on and off, the need to be vigilant against physical attack from wild animals is less warranted in modern times and has helped us to evolve a sleeping pattern which is approximately eight hours during the hours of darkness. This has tended to replace the likely habit of early *Homo Sapiens* of snatching a few hours' sleep here and there which would have aided survival in wilder environmental conditions. It is possible that the 24-hour society (the title of Leon Kreitzman's [1999] book) provides a new danger to our well-being, with an increased demand on workers to function through the night at health costs to themselves (Norgate, 2006). The 24/7 trend is currently more common in North American cities, but is rapidly spreading, as evidenced by a 400 per cent rise over ten years in the UK of phone calls made at 4.30 a.m. (Kreitzman, 1999) and a 7 per cent increase since 1995 in Europe of those working night shifts (Norgate, 2006).

Of course daytime working hours on the warmer European continent have also reflected the need to respond to climatic conditions, and the siesta (long afternoon nap) in hot countries is a traditional coping mechanism when the heat makes work too hard to carry out. In recognition of the almost unnatural demands to work for many hours at a time, the concept of the 'power nap' is one which has become popular in some office-based organizations, where small tent-like structures are made available for employees' use. It is suggested that a short ten- to twenty-minute rest, which can mean sleep, will help to boost the body's energy levels and leave the individual comparatively refreshed for the rest of the day (Hayashi and Hori, 1998). Should the employee fall asleep and the nap continue past the recommended time, it is more likely that they will have entered a deeper state of sleep and therefore feel rather more groggy on waking, with effects opposite to those intended! However, for the majority of employees this may not be a viable option, and the lunch-break represents the only oasis of time to oneself. 'Use it or lose it!' comes the cry from workplace consultants who have observed the growing trend of workers eating at their desks or on the job. Sufficient breaks from the routine of work tasks are necessary for better functioning (Galinsky *et al.*, 2000) and are suggested to have benefits for well-being – if nothing else it can relieve the individual from the pre-lunch emotions which made the morning challenging and bring a much-needed sense of perspective.

In terms of physiological coping, the practical advice (without adding to what we already know about smoking cigarettes) can be summarized as follows:

- Ensure you have access to a safe water source, such as a cooler
- Plan and actually take a break away from your normal work station
- Take some exercise or a rest break
- Limit the amount of coffee you consume and if it is excessive, consider replacing some of your intake with water or juices.

As we shall see, coping physiologically is only one part of the picture.

Emotional coping and cognitive strategies

To express or not to express? – that is the question. Our workplaces have evolved within what we hope is a framework of civilized behaviour, yet the raw emotions we experience do not conform to these. Our emotions often require some tempering in a way which shapes our behaviour to fit in with the expectations and norms of a given situation. The desire to shout or swear loudly when feeling frustrated with the course of a meeting is not one likely to be condoned by colleagues or managers and we might think better of it and decide to channel this emotion into a more acceptable form. This might mean we launch a persuasive argument against the proposal under discussion, which encourages others to our point of view. Such an approach might be a successful use of emotion but may not suit our individual style, instead we might simply voice our concerns in order that we can feel satisfied we have had a fair hearing. Alternatively, if we find it hard to turn the emotional energy created by our frustration into a positive outlet, we might bang something on the table or leave the room. For those who do not wish others to know how they feel, there is the option of keeping the emotion inside and expressing it later in a 'safer' situation, or of feeling helpless and never really addressing how we feel. The key thing to pick up from these examples is that there are no right or wrong answers, but there are outcomes which are likely to be better or worse for our well-being as well as our work situation, which you may judge for yourself.

Those who champion the concept of emotional intelligence highlight self-control as an important component and research does tend to support the idea that venting negative emotion by complaining to others can actually make us feel worse (Brown *et al.*, 2005). Also the concept of habitually expressed emotion has been linked to poor psychological health within families (e.g. Leff and Vaughan, 1981). 'Emotions can be caught by others' (Strazdins, 2002, p. 235) if we identify with those feelings for long enough, either as part of a job or outside of work. This has been termed 'vicarious traumatization' and is the result of exposure to the emotions of others. A workplace parallel could be that of the working group which has developed the habit of complaining negatively about things as a matter of course, rather than in response to specific issues. This type of venting is not always appreciated by colleagues outside of the group indulging in it, and can have the effect of being contagious, spreading negative emotion – in other words, emotional contagion. Furthermore working in this type of atmosphere can also lead to changes in how we process information which in itself would not usually arouse emotion. In this way a prevailing negative approach can encourage individuals to pay more attention to negative rather than positive or neutral information (Cacioppo and Gardner, 1999). In one sense this is different from the idea of social support, wherein we derive comfort from others in a supportive way, but it does use the same mechanism whereby as humans we are at some level likely to be affected by the emotions expressed by others. 'The more individuals engage with and handle negative emotions in others, the more likely they are to experience negative emotions, and this will be where the health costs occur' (Strazdins, 2002, p. 237). This does not mean we should not let others know how we feel: in fact the ability to communicate our emotions to others can be an integral aspect of coping, by actively playing a part and helping to resolve a particular problem. However, an awareness of how others' emotions can affect us, taking into account our own durability, is useful in informing how we cope.

The emotion of anger is one which is perhaps harder to moderate than most. This is especially the case in a work environment where email communication is the norm. So what is the best thing to do with our anger? Should we march right up to so-and-so and let them have know exactly how we feel the moment we feel our frustration boiling over? Should we write an email straight back full of vitriol and hatred? Most would say probably not, for we are all aware that there are likely to be consequences for expressing extreme emotions or even usual ones in an extreme manner. The issue of 'flame mail' is one which is set to become an increasing problem as it is all too convenient to operate in an apparent safety bubble from which we can send a written message to someone in a different location and even time zone. The favoured strategy is to practise our response in such a way that we have a chance to reflect on it and view it without being under the influence of the emotion. In this way writing down a message – which in itself can be helpful in expressing how we feel – or saying it to a friend or even talking at the mirror (best done when alone!) can give us time to look back a few hours or days later and think whether it is fully justified in its original form as well as how our message might be received. By following this approach it is more probable that any communication which results from anger will not give rise to a further escalation of the situation, which could in turn have caused us more aggravation anyway. As for dealing with anger in the meantime, the idea of finding a suitable alternative target, such as participation in a computer game, is becoming more popular – some cars are even being equipped with software to enable drivers to vent their frustration on mock targets rather than real road rivals!

Obviously there may be many other factors involved in a work situation which arouse emotion in us, such as how much influence one can have over changing a situation. Certainly we are more likely to focus on our emotions in circumstances where we have little or no control over events. This means that broad agreement on how best to handle a situation is often hard to reach. It has been suggested that it is best to consider a range of responses in the workplace to different emotions and it is sometimes easy to think that we might be the first person anywhere, ever, to have encountered a particular circumstance. This is where asking trusted friends, family and colleagues can be of great use, i.e. social support (see also Chapter 6). A study of coping strategies in an interesting range of occupations has highlighted that different approaches are favoured depending on the job in question, but that drawing on the emotional support of others, particularly where situations are shared, is an important factor (Dewe and Guest, 1990).

The essential difference between successful and unsuccessful expression can lie in the ability to control the emotion so that when it is communicated it does not seem out of context and it also plays a useful part in prompting desired and appropriate action. This involves incorporating a degree of emotional labour (see Chapter 4) and harnessing emotions to our advantage. A common example is that of sports personalities or teams who have been on the receiving end of negative comments and derive motivation from this to play better. The first victory of the England cricket team for 18 years in the Ashes against Australia in the summer of 2005 demonstrated how undermining remarks from the opposition were turned around into positive energy to perform even better (The England Cricket Team, 2005). This is similar to the 'I'll show them' mentality, but it is not the answer for everybody.

The option to deny our emotions is one which carries certain risks. After all, emotions are integral to how we view our jobs and affective events theory (Weiss and Cropanzano, 1996) is built around this idea (see Chapter 3). In fact those who avoid recognizing the strength or existence of their own emotions may experience increased symptoms of poor health (Snow *et al.*, 2003). A type of avoidance strategy characterized as 'covert' coping has also been linked to increased likelihood of suffering with raised blood pressure (Theorell *et al.*, 2000) and poorer immunity against illness (Jamner and Leigh, 1999). However, the influential and often controversial theories of Sigmund Freud suggest that we might be highly motivated not to recognize our emotions where this would otherwise mean causing ourselves distress. 'Repression' is one of the psychological defence mechanisms identified by Freud as acting to protect our sense of self by pushing negative experience into the unconscious in preference to dealing with it at a conscious and therefore immediate level. The drawback comes in the emergence of this unpleasant information in other ways, such as psychosomatic symptoms of strain (Brown, 1964) and other ill effects highlighted above.

A similar cognitive approach to coping includes passive rationalization. This is highlighted as a strategy employed by church ministers in an eclectic study comparing different occupational groups which also includes teachers, nurses and mail order supervisors! (Dewe and Guest, 1990.) Passive rationalization refers to cognitively reframing how an event can be seen in relation to ourselves, such as 'there is always someone worse off' or 'this situation will pass in time' (there have been a number of heads of department in universities who mark off the days of their tenure on the calendar similar to those characters serving terms of imprisonment!). In Freudian terms, this can be seen as having a similar effect to repression, by helping the individual avoid the negative associations of a particular set of beliefs. In practice the strategy of denial will also shield the individual employee from a rather unpalatable reality, e.g. it isn't that my work is below standard, but it is a better thing for my career that I am being moved to a different department. In addition, the use of prayer should not be underestimated as a method for helping to deal with challenging circumstances – the level of perceived control which can be gained through faith that something will be done is not straightforward, but is certainly powerful. It is left to other texts to advance its concomitant strengths.

A Swedish study of coping strategies has assessed the extent to which managers in different countries use 'open' coping, which involves talking to the person with whom one is unhappy, or covert coping, amounting to an avoidance of dealing with a problem, perhaps taking it home or simply letting things go without comment. Within the study, men and women managers showed no difference in their levels of open coping; however, women managers were far more likely to use covert coping than their male counterparts, a finding which was reflected in a sample drawn from the general working population (Bernin et al., 2003). The authors of this study attribute this variation to the corporate culture or even changes in gender roles in the workplace. It should be noted that the use of covert or avoidance coping is different from that of being able to 'switch off' from a problem. The capacity to take a rest from pondering on a problem or being troubled by it has been found to be a valuable method of coping. Using distraction in between periods of tackling a difficulty is quite different from failing to acknowledge its existence. As a short-term measure, 'switching off mentally' or psychologically detaching from work when away from the job has been linked to feeling in a positive mood and is related to feeling less fatigued at the end of the day (Sonnentag and Bayer, 2005).

Another comparative study has focused on cultural differences in coping (Bernin *et al.*, 2003). Using the relevant scale from the Occupational Stress Indicator it assessed 'control' coping which included 'trying to deal with a situation objectively in an unemotional way', better time management, thinking ahead and prioritizing, as well as 'support' coping which referred to seeking help from others as well as pursuing hobbies and non-work interests. Comparing samples from countries including India, United Kingdom and United States, both types of coping approach were utilized by Bulgarian managers (both men and women) more than the other national groups, with Swedish managers using them least (Bernin *et al.*, 2003).

The range of emotions and the cognitive possibilities for looking at our work circumstances in a more positive light or in a way which will be beneficial to our well-being is undoubtedly broad. It is also unlikely and probably unfavourable that we would use only one approach when presented with a problem. At the end of this chapter (in Table 10.2) are some approaches which workers have used and which they have found work for them, but once again it is important to emphasize that coping as an individual is likely to vary with the circumstances. The type of job and the employee's level of control are influential in how representative these coping strategies are – but there is no doubting the reality of the emotions and the thoughts which accompany them. How coping can influence behaviour is examined in the next part of this chapter.

Case Study 10.1	**Footballers' vibes**
	Whether one is a fan of football or not, the four-yearly climax of the 'Beautiful Game' which is the World Cup tends to focus the minds of the inhabitants of the countries involved. Yet it is not always the players who are centre stage. Sometimes it is the ▶

managers that people recall, and perhaps this is fair as it is always the managers who are held responsible for the outcomes – especially the bad results. The early part of the Millenium stood out in the minds of England supporters as a period of successful qualification for the final stages of major tournaments under the watchful eye of a non-British manager, Sven Goran-Eriksson. This thoughtful Swedish man won many admirers both on and off the field of play, but England supporters noted that Sven nearly always appeared restrained and seemed, to them at least, to lack some of the emotion which they felt might have inspired their team to even greater heights. Such passion was not apparently lacking in the former Brazil manager, Felipe Scolari, who also took his Portugal side to the World Cup finals of 2006. It was here that both men met for the second time in the quarter finals of this tournament and as the whole footballing world looked on, the differences in the ways they each handled their emotions were underlined.

Sven's style	Felipe's form
Sits for most of the match	Always stands
Discusses tactics with his co-manager, who relays the messages	Remonstrates from the side of the pitch with his players
Tends to keep his feelings to himself with relatively few outward displays of extreme emotion	Communicates with anyone who is listening – by shouting, pointing, etc.
Reacts to disappointment by clenching fist and bending forward on the bench	Stands tall and advances on his target – he shouts, waves, points, and threatens
Reacts to success by smiling and jumping to his feet	Reacts to success by running and hugging the nearest colleague

With a tense match between England and Portugal unfolding, Felipe was rebuked and told by officials to retreat from the edge of the pitch. As the game remained at 0–0 and extra time approached, the moment arrived which England fans came to see as pivotal. One of England's most talented and also expressive players, Wayne Rooney, was shown a yellow card for a foul. Just then one of the Portuguese players, Christiano Ronaldo, with whom Rooney played at club level with Manchester United, seemed to ▶

provoke him further and Rooney pushed him away. He was promptly sent off by the referee for his conduct. The contrast in emotions between Rooney and his manager could not have been more distinct, but it seems the similarity with those of Scolari had helped the Portuguese team. Ronaldo turned and winked to his manager as Rooney trudged from the field and despite later denials, one could deduce that those who understood him best may have thought hard to contrive this outcome – this is not to say that how one person expresses emotions works well for all in a working team, in fact quite the opposite. One might wonder what the outcome would have been if the sanguine England manager had anticipated the emotion-focused tactics of his opponents?

Behavioural coping

When facing a situation over which we may have some control, we are more likely to use active coping strategies. These are generally behaviours aimed at relieving the problems in hand and can range from tackling a difficulty head on to gathering the necessary resources to do so. Either way behavioural coping is about action with a positive outcome in mind. Whether or not the desired goal is achieved, many people will say, 'I feel better for having tried to do x or y', because they have tried to exercise their ability to influence a situation.

The success of a particular behaviour strategy begins with the preparation. This is where separating the cognitive and behavioural components of coping seems rather artificial, as it makes intuitive sense to think through the potential outcomes of a course of action before embarking on it, which is what we usually do. At least we like to think that is our habit, but the pressures of the workplace do not always allow us the space or support for considering alternatives or indeed for taking a break to think first. This is where starting to take control of one's time can make this possible, perhaps by rearranging a meeting or even scheduling a short holiday. Too many workers fail to take their full holiday entitlement or end up taking work with them. Where time itself is the problem it is vital to look for opportunities to carve out time for oneself, even if this is taking a walk round the park or shopping centre. The difficulty in making space for ourselves is actually well recognized, but by few more than those whose lives are centred around caring for a family member suffering with a severe and enduring mental health problem. Among the charities who provide support for families in this way is one based in Warrington called 'Making Space'. Such are the full-time demands of ensuring the well-being and welfare of a loved one with a psychological or physical disability, that it is a sobering experience for those who do not face these challenges to view the demands of the workplace with this perspective in mind. The first realization is that most of us have more choice than we are prepared to acknowledge. Making Space does what it says and is a fine example of what can be achieved with support in even the most challenging of circumstances: their existence also says much about how people can benefit from having an advocate who can help people realize their own entitlement to a range of life experiences. In theory this principle could be extended to everybody who faces challenges on a long-term basis, but in practice would mean acting as our own advocate when it comes to thinking about juggling working and living. It amounts to taking responsibility for taking time to look at the things which contribute to our quality of life and where appropriate asking others in our lives for their views too. Why shouldn't this principle apply to all?

If work impinges on our capacity to forge and maintain meaningful relationships, would we really know? Have we asked a partner, friend or family member lately for their view? Sometimes it is too easy to pursue the habit of working in a particular way and not to see the potential consequences because we get used to things. Exercise 10a aims to assess your quality of life and encourages you to highlight those aspects of experience which you miss out on because of your job. It may be that this is how you prefer things to be, and it is not the purpose of this chapter to pass judgement, but simply to act as a facilitator to help you to look at what you *actually* do. By encouraging you to take a few minutes to do this, you may discover something which you would want to change and may even question whether you need to carry on missing out! There is no doubt that work provides a range of positive opportunities, but maybe the job could be even better!

This type of mental preparation is one cognitive-behavioural approach to organizing the necessary mental resources to deal differently and possibly more effectively with life's challenges. However, there are alternatives which can help refresh us by gaining the energy required to play a full role in our work and non-work lives. For many people, hobbies and leisure pursuits are part and parcel of life and are as varied as there are people to enjoy them. From walking to driving, dancing to music, books to television and radio, computer games to talking, working out to helping others, collecting to selling, astronomy to watching sport there are activities which help us gain access to another avenue of expression for ourselves. Each carries its own challenge and embuing a sense of endeavour these can represent passions or simply passing interests. The important factors are that they are voluntary – unlike most work tasks – and are not necessarily subject to the same rigours of judgement passed by others, such as managers. In this way they stand to be more enjoyable because they permit a sense of freedom to be experienced by those engaged in them. Consequently they help to refresh the imagination and the approach we can bring to other aspects of our lives such as relationships and paid work itself. As we have seen, being able to switch off from our jobs is related to feeling in a positive mood during the hours after work (Sonnentag and Bayer, 2005) and allows us to leap from the slippery pole long enough to feel like climbing back up it the following work day. Hobbies also give us access to social networks which can be unrelated to the workplace and supportive relationships have been shown to act as a buffer against psychological strain (Cohen and Wills, 1985; see Chapter 6). It is also more likely that the combination of a favourite pastime and socializing in this positive context will feed back into an individual's feeling of self-worth.

Exercise 10.1	**What have you done for yourself lately?**
	Use this 20-item measure (10 questions on leisure and 10 on your home–work interface) to assess how often you are experiencing a range of aspects of your life outside your job. Whether you are currently working in a paid or unpaid role, these are some of the activities on which you would probably spend time doing if you were not so employed and which are likely to contribute to a positive quality of life. The idea is to encourage you to consider your work–life balance. By giving a score to your responses in each column, i.e. Not at all = 1, up to 2–3 times each week = 5, you should arrive at an overall total. The minimum possible score is 20, so if you score less than 40, think about whether there are things you could ▶

change to ensure you get a wider experience of what life has to offer. Scores of 60–80 indicate that you are well able to weave these into your schedule and perhaps you are thinking about making them more regular or you have reached a balance which is right for you.

In the last month, how frequently have you:

	Not at all	May be once	Once or twice	Every week	2–3 times a week
Leisure-wise					
Played a sport of any sort or exercised					
Gone to the cinema/theatre or a concert/played or listened to music of your choice					
Spent time learning a new skill or done something unusual by your own standards					
Watched a television/listened to a radio programme all the way through					
Taken a walk in the park or countryside					
Visited a museum or place of special interest					
Visited a place of worship					
Spent time on your favourite hobby, e.g. puzzles, models, stamps, painting, etc.					
Bought something for yourself					
Read a newspaper, magazine or book					
Home–work interface					
Made time for yourself to relax – even if it was just for fifteen minutes					
Spent time just chatting with your partner					
Switched off your work mobile phone for a whole evening					

▶

	Not at all	May be once	Once or twice	Every week	2–3 times a week
Spent no time on work tasks outside of work hours					
Gone for a drink or chat with a friend					
Cooked a special meal for you and your partner					
Played a game involving the family					
Visited family members who do not live with you					
Taken friends or family members on a trip					
Spoken to a friend/family member on the phone who lives too far to visit					

Within the workplace, direct action to solve the problems in hand is not everyone's choice: for example, this approach is more popular with nurses than church ministers (Dewe and Guest, 1990). Problem-focused methods of coping cover a wide range of strategies including confrontation, accepting responsibility and forward planning (Lazarus and Folkman, 1984). Each approach requires the ability to:

● Acknowledge the existence of a problem
● Identify the relevant parties who are affected by it
● Communicate effectively with all concerned
● Be aware of the need for damage limitation
● Generate potential solutions
● Negotiate for new reasonable terms where old ones are no longer applicable.

It is a common assumption that all employees are fully skilled in these ways and are happy to be open about their performance, but often these abilities are acquired through experience and/or training. In the meantime this can result in an individual failing to communicate that they are aware of a problem: it only becomes apparent when things come to light via a customer complaint or faulty equipment malfunctioning. Similarly the scale of the problem can draw so much attention that communication with all those involved is given a lesser priority, producing resentment amongst those who have already felt let down by the original error. At the very least some remedial action to put things right is expected and this deserves some follow-up to prevent recurrence of the problem. It is rare for a period to pass without some problem arising in our job and it is worth checking that we have done all we can to ensure higher quality which is to our own advantage, and also to the organization's in an increasingly litigious age. The last quarter of a century has seen many tragedies ranging from the demise of the Challenger space shuttle to the sinking of the ferry The Herald of Free Enterprise, as well as rail and nuclear disasters due to faulty maintenance and faulty procedures. This scale of event is thankfully a rarity, but individuals who have tried their best to tackle rather than ignore problems in their work are more likely to feel they have met their own standards as well as those of their colleagues and clients (which are not always obvious).

The capacity to adopt a problem-solving approach often depends on one's own assertiveness skills. Lack of success in these can affect us in work relationships with people at all levels of an organization, whether up or down the line of management from where we operate. Otherwise the negative outcomes usually amount to taking on extra and possibly inappropriate work tasks. Assertiveness involves being 'open and flexible, genuinely concerned with the rights of others, yet at the same time able to establish very well our own rights' (Alberti and Emmons, 1970). The individual who said, 'I wanted to go on an assertiveness training course, but my spouse wouldn't let me' seems to have made the assumption that their own rights were not as important as at least one other person. Some hope is offered to those lacking in assertiveness by the following set of principles which outlines some key employee rights (Langrish, 1981):

- The right to make mistakes
- The right to set one's own priorities
- The right for one's own needs to be considered as important as the needs of other people
- The right to refuse requests without feeling guilty
- The right to express oneself as long as one doesn't violate the rights of others
- The right to judge one's own behaviour, thoughts and emotions, and to take responsibility for the consequences.

The key to these rights is the emphasis on the individual's freedom to feel good about themselves and be able to act in a confident but not over-bearing manner. A variety of behavioural assertiveness skills exist and are applicable depending on circumstances (e.g. Table 10.2); however, the potential for conflict can underlie such encounters and it is equally important to know how to respond where things are simply not going according to plan. Having said that, conflict is not always destructive and can actually help to promote reasonable questioning of the way things are done as well as releasing tension by bringing it to the surface. The type of conflict which leads to improvements in working methods, acting as a catalyst for creativity and self-evaluation, can be beneficial, provided of course it does not result in long-term divisions and rancour. Thomas's (1992) model of conflict management styles highlights five approaches which could result in a range of outcomes, but are doubtless ones we all recognize in people we know both inside and out of the workplace:

1 'Competition' represents the 'win–lose' use of power which strident managers are prone to employ.
2 'Collaboration' ('win–win') tries to utilize the knowledge and skills of all involved to produce a workable solution and emphasizes the spirit of cooperation.
3 'Avoidance' reflects a lack of assertiveness and amounts to withdraw-ing from a situation to prevent overt discussion of the source of the problem.
4 'Accommodation' prioritizes the wishes of the other party, often reflecting altruism.
5 'Compromise' requires both parties to give up some of what they want in order to create a fruitful way forward.

There is at least one further strategy for handling conflict which often goes unrecognized and that is humour. Provided it is used in a non-offensive manner, improvised humour is likely to defuse most situations where tension has arisen and can serve as a plateau from which a more positive interaction can be constructed. At the very least a smile or friendly gesture can have the same effect as in the natural world, where animals wishing to avoid fighting will signal this intent. Certainly differ-ent situations demand specific solutions, but there can be little doubt that the bottom line to problem-solving in the workplace, whether with tasks or people, is emotional flexibility. Those who survive the chal-lenges posed by difficulties in jobs and relationships are individuals who have responded to changing circumstances. As in the natural world, adaptability is the key to survival!

| Case Study 10.2 | **Tips on increasing assertiveness (after Langrish, 1981)** |

In order to break through some of the smoke-screens found in organizational hierarchies, or even when faced with persistent salespeople, the 'broken record' technique can prove very helpful. By calmly repeating what you want (or don't want) in the face of numerous attempts to deflect or distract you, the persistence you have demonstrated will send a clear message that you are not going to put off. This can also be done in such a way that it shows you are still human too!

Manager: 'Please could you submit the report requested from you last month.'

Employee: 'I've had terrible trouble with my teeth for weeks now.'

Manager: 'I'm sorry to hear that, but I still need that report from you.'

Employee: 'I'm still getting terrible twinges in my gums.'

Manager: 'This does sound serious – perhaps we can arrange for you to see the occupational nurse (so you can finish that report in comfort).'

Furthermore a 'negative assertion' allows you to recognize that criticisms made about your own performance have some substance, but that you have a view on these and you realize where changes need to be made, e.g. 'I am prepared to accept that there are some things which could have been done differently and it would be helpful to talk about ways forward for the future.'

Of course there is the old truism that 'it's not what you say, but the way that you say it' and this applies to an extent to being assertive with others. It is important to establish meaningful eye contact and sit or stand in such a way as to appear comfortable (i.e. not fidgeting), whilst maintaining a strong and steady voice. Statements including 'I feel' and 'I believe' as well as suggestions including 'we' and 'let's' help to convey your personal strength as well as an interest in working collaboratively with someone to achieve a common goal.

Table 10.2	How do we cope? Examples of physiological, emotional/cognitive and behavioural approaches to coping at work						
Job	Level of control within organization	Negative thoughts	Negative emotions	Possible negative outcome	Positive physiological action	Positive emotional/ cognitive response	Positive behavioural action
Builder	Owner (self-employed)	This employee is not trying hard enough	Frustration with lazy individual	Shouts at employee	Works harder on the job to ensure the business is not affected	Makes note not to re-employ this individual on the next job	Takes employee to one side and shares expectations
Signwriter	Works alone	I feel over-whelmed by the amount of work	Anxiety over completing work on time	Fails to meet deadline	Avoids alcohol	Expresses concerns to a trusted friend	Seeks help to get the work done or renegotiates the deadline
Teacher	One of many in a large organization	I do not like the lack of respect shown by some students	Anger at the way some students speak	Shows a mutual level of disrespect to students resulting in a formal complaint	Walks away from what seems likely to be a confrontation with the students concerned and takes time to calm down	Realizes the shortcomings of the students concerned and that they would benefit from a role model on how to talk to others	Involves the students, their parent and/or line manager in helping to change behaviour or negotiates not to teach them

Job	Level of control within organization	Negative thoughts	Negative emotions	Possible negative outcome	Positive physiological action	Positive emotional/ cognitive response	Positive behavioural action
Caterer	Works for the owner in small outlet	I am uncomfortable working in this heat and small space	Tiredness and irritation	Has an accident resulting in injury to others	Keeps cool drink at hand and takes breaks when possible	Considers that the job is not worth getting hurt for and resolves to inform authorities or to find work elsewhere	Shows the manager what might happen/ seeks a safer workplace
Nurse	Works shifts on a busy hospital ward	I am too snowed under with paperwork to spend time with patients	Unhappiness with job	Feels helpless to change things and cries openly at work	Avoids the overuse of alcohol which can be associated with high strain health service jobs	Focuses on the positive things that doing the job achieves rather than what cannot be done	Shares views with trusted colleague and decides what can be done to change things, even if it is only small step

Summary of the chapter

This chapter has endeavoured to provide the reader with an analysis of personal coping strategies at our disposal. Whilst it is not intended to be an exhaustive review, it does focus on the relationships between emotions and our bodily responses, our thoughts and our behaviour. Like all relationships, these are changing, but there are also habits into which we can become entrenched and which we need to think about carefully if they are only making things worse! The role of our physiology in our well-being is something we are exhorted to review regularly according to the media, government and possibly also our friends and family, so why not also take the opportunity to look at our emotions and what we do with those too? The reader is encouraged to consider ways of thinking and behaving – from problem- to emotion-focused – which have been subject to research and which offer hope to those who would benefit from reflection on what can be done to help oneself, particularly when it comes to being assertive, handling conflict or learning from others' mistakes.

Key terms	
coping	channelling emotions
stress hormones	open and covert coping
sleeping patterns	assertiveness
emotional contagion	handling conflict

Questions and answers

1   *What does coping really mean?* Coping is the process by which we deal with problems, emotional and practical, and which therefore requires a range of skills and a certain degree of flexibility. As Lazarus points out, coping can be determined by two stages, the first of which prioritizes the seriousness of the challenge, and the second which leads to decisions on how to deal with that challenge. The role of emotions in this can be helpful and/or a hindrance, by focusing our efforts on a particular course of action. Whether coping is successful or not may

be best judged by ourselves a little way down the line after the situation has arisen. Not surprisingly this is why coping is not always easy!

2 *What changes from a busy working routine might help us cope better on a physiological level?* Getting away from the workplace or workstation for at least a short while part way through the working day or shift can help to refresh us emotionally as well as physically: this can be in mind or body – through a power nap or a walk. By ensuring that we try to drink and eat in tune with our body's requirements, we may find that we stay alert longer without artificial aid, avoid that dragging sensation when tasks seem too much effort to complete, as well as benefit our physical health. The benefits of a good breakfast, a digestible lunch away from the desk or machine and replacing high caffeine intakes with water are the simplest aids to coping physiologically.

3 *Is it better for our emotional health to express emotions or keep them in?* The answer, as you may already have been thinking, is likely to depend on the specific circumstances. When a really strong emotion is being experienced, it is easier said than done to keep it in, but if we can consider the longer-term impact of what might happen if it is expressed, then we could save ourselves a lot of trouble. On the positive side, there is the chance to cool down and look again at things when we are not as 'uptight', as well as the advantages of helping not to escalate the situation. Against this is the temptation to demand emotional justice, by getting back at the other person – we might think this is going to make ourselves feel better, but how easy is it to get away with such an 'on the spot' retort. After all, it is when we walk away we usually think of 'what I really should have said or done'! As far as our emotional health is concerned, research (e.g. Brown *et al.*, 2005) suggests this will make us feel worse – almost as though reliving the emotions is likely to have a negative effect. The notion of 'catharsis' suggests it can be helpful to wallow in emotions from time to time, and this can feel right provided we can return feeling purged and ready to fight again. For others, denial is the best strategy, but again, this only works for as long as it benefits the individual and this may need rethinking when it becomes a barrier to emotional well-being.

4 *How might we start to deal with others' emotions in the aftermath of our own mistake?* Everybody makes mistakes. Some are easier to rectify than others, but they are invariable accompanied by feelings – often negative ones from those on the receiving end. Usually some

acknowledgement of a work-based error and how they have made the other person feel makes it possible for the two parties to 'tune in' to each other's emotions. By denying the wronged party the opportunity to express how they feel, there is a likelihood that this will come to the surface at some point, particularly where colleagues need to work alongside each other. Therefore it is often better to recognize the emotion first in order to work constructively to resolve the problems arising. It is helpful to have some potential solutions ready, but care is needed in implementing these before even consulting with the other party!

5 *Having read this chapter, can you identify three things you will definitely do differently to help you cope better with pressure?*

Suggested further reading

What many consider the seminal text on coping is *Stress, Appraisal and Coping* by Lazarus and Folkman (1984). *Living with Stress* by Cooper, Cooper and Eaker (1988) has been a favourite for some time, and there are now many self-help books on the topic of coping, from a range of coaches and lifestyle gurus: if this is what you are after it is worth shopping around for one which suits you as an individual.

For those struggling to cope, there are many helpful websites with useful tips, including the Royal College of Psychiatrists (www.recpsych.ac.uk/). The field of Positive Psychology is a major growth area and this emphasizes optimum functioning in humans, which can be seen as a way of proactively coping with the challenges put before us, even before they arise.

For a further helpful academic overview, the relevant sections in Jones and Bright's (2001) *Stress: Myth, Theory and Research* are worth consulting.

A survival kit for the organization

There is an important question to ask when it comes to working out the best way forward for the emotional health of the workplace and its employees. Who is responsible? The previous chapter highlighted strategies which the individual might employ, but surely this should not mean that the employee is solely responsible for their well-being when they are exposed to an environment which they did not design? In fact the law in the UK and many other countries stipulates minimum standards of health and safety in the workplace as well as enshrining the responsibilities of the employer to the worker. Yet given the broad brush approach of a whole organization to any given circumstance and the need for individuals to safeguard their health, perhaps the best answer is to say that both the employee and the employer should share the responsibility of ensuring well-being – after all the benefits are to be felt by both.

This section highlights the range of strategies which can be used within the organization to realize its potential to survive. The approaches to improving well-being within organizations fall into three broad categories (Schmidt, 1994), but these should not be viewed as exclusive of each other, as a combination of strategies may yield the best outcomes. Furthermore these interventions can be at the level of the individual and/or the organization (Giga *et al.*, 2003a):

- Primary interventions which focus on the prevention of problems, e.g. job redesign, organizational change
- Secondary interventions aim to manage the symptoms of strain and target the individual/organization interface, e.g. stress management programmes such as fitness training, relaxation techniques and time management

- Tertiary interventions are designed to help the individual or organization who may need more specialized help to deal with the strain, e.g. employee assistance programmes offering counselling or referral for medical help via an occupational health department.

The sections of this chapter deal with each of these in turn.

Preventing strain in the workplace

Organizational or primary level interventions which prevent strain among the workforce seem at first sight a highly attractive option to those who wish to improve the well-being of all employees. The reality of trying to introduce and evaluate such initiatives has meant that they tend to be the least favoured of the three approaches discussed in this chapter (Giga *et al.*, 2003b). In fact the majority of interventions are focused on the individual and tend to respond to difficulties which have already arisen, which means this remains an emerging area of psychology at work with great potential to be explored.

At the organizational level a range of strategies may be employed (Elkin and Rosch, 1990, Giga *et al.*, 2003a) and these are highlighted with reference to published examples drawn from the literature.

1 Appropriate selection and placement

The appointment of employees with the necessary skill mix to perform and survive in the job can be smoothed by providing support for them as they move into a new work environment, as well as job previews which aim to ensure a good match of mutual expectations and help reduce uncertainty (Schweiger and DeNisi, 1991). This seems a fairly standard and 'taken for granted' approach, but the cost of employing the wrong individual is likely to be significant to the organization, i.e. higher error rates, poorer productivity, cost of replacement, as well as to the worker, e.g. low job satisfaction, absenteeism. The legal rulings on stress make it clear that the employer should take the individual as they find them, so it is doubly important to get this stage right.

2 Job redesign

Jackson and Wall (1991) revealed improved job satisfaction and productivity among machine tool operators when they had been empowered to maintain rather than to simply monitor equipment (see Chapter 3), while Miller (1994) found positive outcomes from a staff-led job redesign trial among till operators at Marks and Spencer. The latter provided shopfloor employees with an opportunity to schedule their own work rotas and rotate job tasks, ensuring a maximum as well as equal time working on the tills. The leadership of the initiative rested with the workers and meant they could promote the scheme with their colleagues. The successful intervention resulted in increased job satisfaction among the staff, based on feeling valued and being involved in a way which could influence their own jobs, as well as developing an increased appreciation of staff needs and confidence in employees' abilities to self-organize among managers.

3 Redesign the work environment

Some working environments naturally present more natural risks than others, whether related to the physical environment, such as that faced by firefighters or the client group, e.g. prison officers (Sutherland and Cooper, 1990). Realistic steps to reduce the likelihood of harm to employees should be legally accessible in these occupations; however, there are also less obvious risks for workers in supposedly safe environments, e.g. 'techno-stress' in computer-filled offices (Arnetz 1996). Campaigns which promote healthier working by raising awareness of potential stressors have been shown to have a positive impact and entitlement to the assessment of office workstations is widespread in the UK. An analysis of 'health circles' in Germany found that regular employee meetings as part of a long-term organizational commitment to health promotion has led to positive impacts on well-being and sickness absence (Aust and Ducki, 2004).

4 Establish flexible work schedules

The benefits of flexibility in scheduling work were discussed in Chapter 8, as this can help employees to achieve a balance at the home–work interface. The scheduling of shiftwork requires particular care in order to keep negative impacts to a minimum and can be achieved by identifying optimal shift patterns and appropriate start times, as well as raising awareness of possible side-effects among employees (Sutherland, 2005).

5 Encourage participative management through communication

Initiatives which increase workers' perceived control within their jobs are likely to lead to improvements in well-being (e.g. Perrewe and Ganster, 1989). The opportunity for control, particularly in change situations, requires effective channels of communication to dampen insecurity and will contribute to improved organizational functioning (Adkins *et al.*, 2000). Workers who feel involved are also more likely to feel empowered which is vital when it comes to programmes for tackling stressors in the workplace.

6 Employee training and career development

Training and education initiatives, particularly in relation to new working methods, help to control strain and increase innovation among employees (Bunce and West, 1996). Such opportunities can be further identified through effective appraisal systems within organizations, where it is important to keep them separate from pay-related discussions (Sutherland, 2005). Staff development also has an important role to play where redundancies are likely, as job-seeking skills and retraining can help to cushion the impact of career change on the individual (Sutherland, 2005).

The use of coaching represents a growing trend in more hands-on training for managers. An interesting variant of this featured in a tranche of interventions utilized among NHS staff in the UK (Borrill *et al.*, 1998). The 'upward feedback' intervention took place over an 18-month period and evaluated whether 'staff feedback to managers about their managerial styles improved the way managers and staff worked together' (Borrill *et al.*, 1998, p. 65). One group attended a management skills workshop and the other did not. Amongst those managed by the attending group, staff ratings of their managers improved on ten behavioural dimensions (e.g. creating a team environment, providing feedback, communication) and perceptions of work demands and role conflict were reduced. Interestingly benefits in improved mental health were noted among both these managers and their staff, who recorded statistically significant decreases in symptoms of depression and anxiety (Borrill *et al.*, 1998).

7 Analyse work roles and establish goals

The clarification of job roles can help to tackle both role ambiguity and role conflict (see Chapter 3), wherein the employee is either not sure what is required of them or faces two sets of expectations which are in opposition to one another. Unsurprisingly, both of these have great potential for damaging an employee's well-being. The establishment of goals is a useful mechanism for rectifying the situation and was utilized to good effect in an insurance organization where supervisors and their immediate staff received training in setting and meeting goals as well as providing feedback (Quick, 1979). Along with significant reductions in both role ambiguity and role conflict, a decrease in absenteeism was noted five months later.

8 Establish fair employment policies

The communication via clear messages from senior level management about acceptable behaviour in the workplace is integral to encouraging a culture in which mental and emotional well-being is prioritized. As well as a commitment from the top of the organization, the implementation of processes which involve all employees will encourage ownership of interventions and provide the means for tackling serious issues on an ongoing basis (Nytro *et al.*, 2000). Fingret (1994) outlines a method for introducing a new mental health policy within an organization which emphasizes the inclusion of all relevant stakeholders and good communication loops to ensure that all groups and subgroups are fully involved and therefore more likely to be committed.

9 Build cohesive teams

There is a general acceptance that working in teams provides strength to the position of the individual employee and encourages productive co-working. As this book has examined there can be both advantages and pitfalls to working with others, but how does this compare to working in isolation or with less close-knit groups? As part of a large NHS study, Borrill *et al.* (1998) found that the psychological health of employees who worked in a recognized team with clear objectives, different roles and frequent contact was significantly better than those who did not and than workers who were part of a 'quasi-team' which only featured some of these characteristics. Furthermore, the development of cooperative and close working was shown to predict improved well-being within six months and increased job satisfaction within one year (Borrill *et al.*, 1998). The use of quality circles in industry to improve performance through collaborative teamworking to improve products and services has been long-established and is very much alive today. Toyota UK featured such team success on the front page of their members magazine, where the quality circle approach saved one team of six employees production costs of £381,000 over one year (Tmag, 2006).

The impact of interventions

Despite the wide range of potential interventions, progress in preventing strain at work has been described thus far as 'disappointing' and therefore 'a significant barrier to ... reducing work-related stress' (Kompier *et al.*, 2000, p. 375), although this is set to change. There are a number of reasons for the current situation and it is worth contemplating these, not for the purposes of turning away from this approach but to inform and energize interested parties to rise to the challenge. The first reason is that interventions of this sort may be under-reported (Giga *et al.*, 2003a) and could be seen by managers as part and parcel of everyday work, but there are more complex possibilities. 'Organizational stress is different from coping with individual stress. Organizations are not simply mechanistic, they are subject to important psychological processes that influence the ways people manage their work relations' (Health Education Authority, 1997). Often these involve organizational politics and can result in a lack of motivation to change working practices, because it is more convenient and less problematic to retain the status quo. This can be reflected in the failure of senior level management to take responsibility for implementing relevant change, tending instead to attribute difficulties to employee-related factors such as lifestyle (Giga *et al.*, 2003a). Changing an organization can also be costly and in justifying such human and financial outlay, those holding power will want to be convinced that an intervention will work and is likely to be of lasting benefit. Furthermore it is difficult to maintain the beneficial aspects of an intervention in modern organizations where constant change is an obvious reality (Giga *et al.*, 2003a). Certainly the structure and climate of an organization can determine the amount of strain endured by employees (O'Driscoll and Cooper, 1995), bearing in mind employers' statutory duty of care to ensure the health, safety and welfare at work of their employees.

Primary level interventions most usefully incorporate an audit of well-being among employees to establish a baseline assessment and provide a point of comparison after any subsequent action. However, from a researcher's viewpoint there are also other methodological reasons why organizational interventions are tricky to evaluate. These include the rarity of studies which actually randomly allocate conditions in the way a laboratory experiment might. This lack has been seen as undermining the reliability of any findings, although support for alternative approaches such as the case study is gaining, whereby organizational projects are necessarily recognized as bespoke and therefore specific in the mould of a case study (e.g. Kompier *et al.*, 2000). In addition the potential of 'looking back' to compare groups depending on how much they were or were not exposed to an intervention has been highlighted (Randall *et al.*, 2005). Such approaches are likely to be welcomed by researchers, especially as one comprehensive review of the published literature from 1970 to 1996 identified only four studies which met the authors' criteria, including the use of a control group with which to compare the impact of an intervention (van der Klink *et al.*, 2001). Kompier *et al.* (2000) have contributed to broadening the literature in this area by attempting to gather data on an organizational intervention from each of 14 European Union member countries at that time. Eleven nations submitted data and nine of these were included in the final analysis, ranging from policy changes to training and even wholesale redesign of work. Three studies (from The Netherlands, Belgium and Sweden) resulted in significant decreases in absenteeism and with the addition of the Danish data, four projects indicated financial benefits (Kompier *et al.*, 2000). Seven interventions demonstrated positive self-reported effects, such as fewer health complaints. Only the Dutch intervention featured a valid control group, with the others relying on appropriate evaluation measures, but overall the authors accepted that 'it is at least plausible that the positive outcomes can largely be attributed to the intervention programmes' (Kompier *et al.*, 2000, p. 385).

So how close are we to deciding that primary level interventions actually work? Having stated that there is a lack of evidence, there have been published attempts at a wide range of approaches, as well as many more unpublicized initiatives. This creates difficulties for wide-ranging academic evaluation, but in an emerging area for research this does not mean we should not draw some initial conclusions. After all, there is a widespread view that fixing the organization will solve most problems. Studies attempting to measure such effects have tended to focus only on the individual, or absenteeism rates at best, and it is likely that changes take time to work, meaning a longer-term evaluation is necessary. It also makes sense to assess the perceptions and coping strategies adopted by employees, as these are likely to impact on the effectiveness of organizational change (van der Klink *et al.*, 2001). This has led some to conclude that when looking to reform jobs where employees have low levels of control, organizational interventions which increase autonomy are recommended and they should be accompanied by cognitive-behavioural measures which modify how the individuals view the work (see p. 265; van der Klink *et al.*, 2001).

A more comprehensive stress prevention and management package which has the support of top level management and which fully involves the relevant parties seems to represent the ideal, provided this is directed at both the person and their work environment (Giga *et al.*, 2003a). In this way a 'bespoke' intervention is likely to have the greatest value (Giga *et al.*, 2003a). Certainly a participative approach which engages workers in its design, implementation and evaluation is more likely to yield positive results (Elo *et al.*, 1998) and can utilize the services of objective facilitators, often from outside the department or organization, to good effect (Parkes and Sparkes, 1998). Where possible the impact of factors at the home–work interface should also be taken into account (Weinberg and Creed, 2000). Where both the change and the manner of its introduction are important (Kompier *et al.*, 2000), one main difficulty is accurately evaluating the impact of an organizational intervention enabling us to decide which of the changing factors is actually affecting psychological and emotional health. In a competitive environment where the performance of employees is affected by their well-being, researchers are finding ways around this (e.g. Randall *et al.*, 2005; Weinberg and Cooper, 2003) and these are surely steps worth taking! Put simply, great ideas need to be implemented properly and will not succeed in isolation. Just ask any government minister!

The OPHICE approach to improving employee well-being

1 One step at a time
2 Proper risk assessment and diagnosis
3 Highlight potential interventions which are suited to the employees and environment
4 Involve employees and managers
5 Commitment from top level management
6 Evaluate individual and organizational outcomes for the best chance to detect improvements (based on Kompier *et al.*, 2000).

Case Study 11.1

Changing the workplace for the better: two examples

At a time when some local government offices and postal services in the UK complain of high levels of absenteeism among their workers – to the extent that good attendance itself may be rewarded by financial incentives – it is interesting to note an example which employs the OPHICE principles outlined above. One borough council in Greater Manchester, UK, decided to see how they could improve the quality of the working lives of their employees, by capitalizing on their work–life balance. They surveyed their workers and decided upon a flexible 'working-from-home' policy which would remove the need from many to travel three hours each day and enable those with family responsibilities to juggle these more easily. This also had the potential to suit the perspective of senior management goals such as quality, performance and productivity. The first five ingredients of the OPHICE approach were in place and by following up the impact on employees, the success of the initiative was clearly demonstrated: absenteeism rates decreased and productivity improved. Employee responses indicated increased satisfaction with the job as well as the home–work interface – individuals claimed this was more important than a pay rise!

The Ruby Take-Away is owned and run by Mohammed, a 39-year-old entrepreneur who juggles the non-stop responsibilities ▶

of his family, his neighbourhood and his business. Mohammed's commitments mean that he travels (one and half hours each day) to open and run the shop every evening before returning home after 1 a.m. As a key figure in his local Bangladeshi community, he is often coordinating fund-raising and commercial activities to support others and to improve opportunities in his area. The take-away is proof of his philosophy and he provides work for a number of his friends and also family members. The success of the business is obvious and its growth has owed more than a little to the owner's personal charm and awareness of cultivating strong relationships with his clientele. However, the nature of self-employment means that Mohammed takes responsibility for the successes and challenges of the service his shop provides, whilst continually striving to stay ahead of competitors who are numerous. Should things go badly, his family, as well as those who work for him, are the ones who would suffer. The strain of working non-stop in hot temperatures and ensuring a friendly face for all used to be evident and in private he would confide that lack of sleep and palpitations bothered him frequently. The decision to take a step back and hand over to his trusted staff one night a week was a big one, but the benefits became readily apparent. Not only did Mohammed have time to spend with his wife and young family after school, his employees began to blossom in the role of sharing some of the responsibility which he carried. The pressure of maintaining relationships with all his customers was partially relieved as confidence among the employees grew. Before too long, Mohammed was able to take a second night away from the business each week, still with the mobile phone handy, but more secure and a lot healthier in the knowledge that things would not fall apart.

Emotional management at work

By far the most popular approach to tackling psychological and emotional strain in the workplace has been via stress management: in other words the identification of symptoms of strain and the introduction of methods to help individual workers deal with them. The widespread use of this approach fits with the idea that the onus for improving well-being does not rest with the organization, but with the individual. This is undoubtedly easier for the organization and is generally less likely to cause political fallout, but runs the risk of conveying the message that the responsibility for both generating and experiencing strain lies with the employee, or put more starkly: 'situations that get out of control are a direct consequence of human incompetence or weakness' (Giga *et al.*, 2003a, p. 288). Whilst this impression may be unintended, it is important that top level management is aware of it.

Since the 1980s the stress management industry has boomed amid promises that the tide of emotional strain can be stemmed by investing often large amounts of money in the products on offer. This is not to undermine the efficacy of these techniques, which will be examined in more detail shortly, but to establish a context in which managers and front-line employees are frequently introduced to such interventions. Their focus can be preventative, aiming to increase awareness and recognition of psychological and emotional strain as an issue for employees, teaching them skills designed to reduce physiological and psychological arousal levels (Murphy, 1996). Examples of stress management include exercise programmes, relaxation workshops, cognitive coping strategies, time management and biofeedback (Cooper and Cartwright, 1994). Overall this approach is sponsored by the organization and is designed to enhance the coping strategies of the individual in the context of the workplace. This differs from the section in the last chapter on coping strategies in that these relate to actual services provided by the workplace, e.g. on-site keep-fit facilities, lunchtime seminars, etc.

One-third of stress management interventions involve either relaxation or cognitive-behavioural therapy, and these are the most popular forms to be found (Giga *et al.*, 2003a). Relaxation techniques encourage the individual to focus on breathing and muscle relaxation, which can be used in times when acute pressure is experienced. There are many variants:

- Progressive muscle relaxation (Jacobsen, 1938) – this involves learning to recognize tension in groups of muscles, for example in the neck region, and practicing 'letting go' so as to release it.
- Biofeedback – this technique provides the individual with feedback on a particular aspect of functioning, for example conveying heart rate via the sound of an audible tone. This makes it possible for the

person to learn to consciously manipulate their heart rate and thereby learn associations which could prevent their heart rate from becoming unduly raised when facing a pressure situation.

- Meditation – this has been modified from transcendental meditation for use in work settings (e.g. Benson, 1976, 1993) and has become a popular technique. It requires the individual to sit comfortably in a quiet place with eyes closed and to quietly repeat a word, such as 'one', each time they breathe out, which can focus the mind and help induce a relaxation response. Benson has shown that this technique can be learned quickly and can reduce bodily and emotional symptoms of strain (Murphy, 1996). Employees have utilized this method in their own office or in a nearby green space.

As detailed in the previous chapter, cognitive-behavioural methods aim to modify the way in which we think about situations and there are two types of this technique which have been used with a number of occupational groups, including teachers, nurses and police officers (Freedy and Hobfoll, 1994). Both are designed to aid the employee's capacity for accepting negative events, without attempting to control them (Bond and Bunce, 2000):

- Rational-emotive therapy (Ellis, 1977) – this A-B-C-D-E approach enables the individual to challenge the irrational aspect of thoughts by interrupting and replacing them with more rational ones. This traces the person's appraisal of threat in a situation from their origin in a negative event ('activation'), to the 'beliefs' which this gives rise to, and the resulting 'consequences', e.g. emotions and behaviours. The next stage 'disputes' the irrational beliefs and has the 'effect' of restructuring the beliefs, so they do not recur. This can change the irrational attitude that 'all my colleagues hate me' (one has to go far to achieve this in reality!), to a view that 'there are one or two people at work whom I just don't get on with, but there are plenty whom I do'.
- Stress inoculation (Meichenbaum, 1977) – this is designed to help the individual realize how they have responded to negative events in the past. Based on this insight it sets out to equip the individual with a set of improved coping skills prior to the occurrence of another such event. These responses are rehearsed under the supervision of the therapist and aim to replace the negative self-talk which has led to dysfunctional coping previously, e.g. 'This deadline will give me a test

for which I am prepared', rather than, 'I will be sacked if I don't meet this deadline'!

A large-scale review of both 17 relaxation and 18 cognitive-behavioural therapies focused on treating individuals found that overall the latter were more effective in reducing symptoms of strain, in particular where levels of control were inferred to be high (van der Klink *et al.*, 2001). The authors conclude that this may mean employees with more autonomy in their work situation have greater opportunities to utilize such strategies, although more research needs to be carried out on this factor. Despite this both relaxation initiatives and interventions which employed more than one stress management technique (multimodal) both showed success in reducing complaints of symptoms experienced (van der Klink *et al.*, 2001). Support for the multimodal approach is strong (see also Murphy, 1996) and as mentioned in the previous section proves a powerful addition to any organizational intervention, however in evaluating the range of secondary level interventions there are reservations too. There has been a tendency to offer this opportunity in white-collar jobs and in a way that is not necessarily tailored to the workplace. Therefore strain management techniques tend to be generalized rather than situation-specific, giving rise to unconvincing findings about their effectiveness. Concerns include a lack of maintaining the trained skills over time and difficulty in evaluating the effectiveness of interventions with self-selected groups of attendees (Murphy, 1996).

An example of a bespoke intervention of the sort recommended earlier in this chapter was provided to medical students at the Royal Free Hospital in London (Michie and Sandhu, 1994). Seventeen per cent of the students in the first year enrolled on a course of three weekly two-hour sessions which addressed a range of sources of pressure relevant to their work, including learning problems, dealing with 'difficult' consultants and non-work issues. Participants were required to develop personal action plans and to use the sessions to discuss pertinent issues, during which they also received training of the type outlined above. Evaluation by questionnaire revealed improvements in work functioning which were maintained over the ensuing year and which proved to be significantly better than among a control group who had been placed on a waiting list. It is interesting to note that a positive aspect of the course had been the 'opportunity to discuss their problems and getting collective support' (Michie and Sandhu, 1994, p. 530), which is an unintended aspect of such interventions, but nonetheless a particularly valuable one.

In addition to the cognitive-behavioural and relaxation methods approach, workplace health programmes have achieved some popularity among organizations, particularly in North America, where they provide 'vigorous cardiovascular exercise, activities which promote muscle tone and flexibility, life style counselling and fun and fellowship' (Dishman, 1988). Such programmes claim to cut illness costs, improve productivity and maintain good health, but evaluation is again infrequent (Schreurs *et al.*, 1996). Where this has occurred, benefits have been found for both the physical and mental health of the employee, as well as the functioning of the organization (Voit, 2001). Members of a UK corporate health and fitness club were found to be significantly more positive in their mood and emotional state than both non-members and those on the scheme's waiting list in terms of levels of energy, elation, clear-headedness and confidence (Daley and Parfitt, 1996). An evaluation of the employee fitness programme at the ING bank in the Netherlands demonstrated a significant decrease in absenteeism for both regular and irregular participants and indications of an overall improvement in scores on a general measure of tension, agitation and anxiety compared to non-participating employees (Kerr and Vos, 1993). A study of automobile manufacturing plants in Michigan, USA, went further and established the cost-effectiveness and clear benefits to well-being of employee health and fitness schemes which provide a range of exercise options and regular outreach and follow-up counselling (Erfurt *et al.*, 1992).

These examples show that strain management initiatives to improve or safeguard psychological and physical well-being can be activated within an organization, although the focus may remain on the individual's needs and problems. Striking a balance between the role of the individual and the organization in coping with stress-related problems has proved elusive, although the need for employers to assume responsibility is now widely acknowledged (Williams, 1994). Interestingly, Sallis *et al.* (1987) evaluated three types of scheme and found improvements among all three groups of participants, but it was their conclusions which stood out more than their promising results. They surmised that the specific skills taught in workshops and therapies may be less relevant than the opportunity provided by the sessions for obtaining colleagues' support and airing work difficulties. Once again this illustrates the human desire for social contact in a way which aids survival in the workplace. Yet surely the ideal way in which to manage emotions at work is not simply to channel employees into special schemes for a small proportion of their working time, but to ensure that their emotional well-being is part of the very framework in which the job is done. This aspect of the evolving workplace is explored in the next chapter. The following section examines the benefits of the one-to-one approach, which unfortunately often comes only after a problem situation has arisen.

Treating the walking wounded

One of the first advertisements for a UK privatized telecommunications company declared 'It's good to talk' and there is a publicly held view that psychological help for any problem requires simply talking about how we feel. Not surprisingly discussing one's feelings and motivations requires a little more than just talking, but this is not the only misconception. There is a general assumption that we all have the opportunity to talk about problems, perhaps with family, friends or colleagues, and that workers make use of such emotional outlets. However, the capacity for obtaining emotional support as and when we need it is not always available, and this can lead to a build up of negative feelings which become difficult to deal with. This situation need not be confined to the individual who knows nobody and feels they have nobody to talk to, but can equally apply to the individual who is surrounded with family, friends and good colleagues who are all too busy to listen or with whom the individual does not wish to share their feelings. Talking about private thoughts and challenges is not always easy and may be something we are simply unused to, and possibly opposed to doing. There are the questions, 'What good will it do?', 'Who is really interested?' and 'Shouldn't I be able to deal with this myself?' but it is almost inevitable that at some point in our lives, quite possibly during our working lives, multiple challenges will contrive to arise in such a way to test our coping strategies to the limit and sometimes beyond. The efficacy of 'talking cures' in a work context will be explored, but first it is useful to identify the nature of structured schemes designed to help employees cope in times of personal crisis.

The first port of call for any employee feeling unwell is likely to be their GP or the occupational health facility in their workplace. Similarly a manager who feels that an employee is poorly is likely to talk with them and to refer them as necessary to the medical help available in the organization or facilitate them going home and contacting the doctor or hospital. In the case of physical health problems this process is fairly straightforward, but where emotional problems are involved, the expectations of the individual and/or the manager are not always clear. Certainly the same process can be followed, but it will depend on the ability of the employee to recognize their own distress and their desire to seek help, as well as the appropriateness of sharing their distress with their line manager.

The concept of Employee Assistance Programmes (EAPs), featuring counselling as the main component, has gained popularity over a number of decades along with the realization that it is important for workers to have opportunities to discuss their emotions and psychological well-being with a third party who is not part of their organization's management and provides a confidential source of help. For those unclear as to the exact nature of counselling, this has been defined as 'the skilled and principled use of relationships to facilitate self-knowledge, emotional acceptance and growth and the optimal development of personal resources' (more professional body information is provided by the British Association for Counselling and Psychotherapy). In line with this, the EAP has been defined as a 'mechanism for making counseling and other forms of assistance available to a designated workforce on a systematic and uniform basis and to recognized standards' (Reddy, 1993). EAPs are provided in-house or by a specialist provider and can take the form of a freephone telephone service or face-to-face counseling and are likely to branch into Internet-based services. Taken overall the EAP seeks to provide emotional support not only to employees, but also to family members, such that they can feel respected and hopefully realistic in relation to their specific circumstances. The emphasis lies in 'breaking down interpersonal and inter-group barriers, reflective listening, non-directive counselling and encouragement of the individual to "own the problem and empower them to take action"' (Berridge and Cooper, 1993). In this way, EAPs seek to offer a 'safe' psychological environment for exploring, clarifying and potentially modifying emotions and beliefs. The number of sessions on offer to employees as part of an EAP can vary, but access to between four and eight 50-minute time slots is common (Arthur, 2000).

The beginnings of EAPs are to be found in attempts by organizations in the United States to tackle alcohol abuse among employees: the success of these led to the creation of over 50 schemes by the mid-1950s (Trice and Schonbrunn, 1981). The first clear use of employee counselling was at the Western Electric Company in the 1920s and 1930s. The Hawthorne Studies conducted within the organization led to the conclusion that 'companies should manage workers' irrational emotions by paying more attention to their feelings and concerns' (Lee and Gray, 1994, p. 218). Interviews with 20,000 employees at Western Electric as part of research into productivity highlighted the link between the opportunity to express emotions about work and subsequently improved functioning as well as a decrease in tension (Arthur, 2000).

EAPs have burgeoned in recent years, and in the UK over 1.75 million employees across 775 organizations have access to such a service, which represents a growth of 40 per cent since 1994 (Arthur, 2000). Four-fifths of large and over one-third of medium-sized US employers utilize EAPs (Lee and Gray, 1994), where the emphasis is less on self-referral than in the UK (Cuthell, 2004). It is estimated that the UK alone has at least 14 main EAP providers (Arthur, 1999). The reasons for such growth may be related to an increased willingness among the population to admit and discuss mental health problems, as well as a recognition among organizations that they need to be seen to be in place, at the very least to avoid litigation (Arthur, 2000). The first EAP to support doctors – a group which traditionally has been reluctant to seek help because of entrenched self-perceptions of their role as 'helpers' – was established in 1987 in Canada and their example was followed by the British Medical Association in 1996, with a 24-hour stress hotline which received 6000 calls during its first two years of operation, including from doctors, medical students and family members (*Lancet*, 1998). The majority of calls were concerned with experiences of anxiety, depression and psychological strain (*Lancet*, 1998).

As the need for EAP provision has been recognized and increasingly implemented, research has begun to turn to the nature of services offered under the umbrella of an EAP, their effectiveness and the well-being of those individuals making use of them. There is no magic mix of components for constructing such a scheme, although as with any intervention sponsored by the organization – as seen earlier in this chapter – commitment from the highest level, involvement of relevant stakeholders (such as unions), clear policies and procedures, protection of employee confidentiality, proper publicity of the services on offer and provision for follow-up of the service users are integral to a successful and well-used EAP (Arthur, 2000). Furthermore the evaluation of the scheme helps to estimate the potential costs and benefits in a financially resource-conscious economy – over ten years ago UK employers were spending £6m annually on EAPs, yet only one-third of EAPs were objectively evaluated and only half of these used comparison group data (Highley and Cooper, 1993). Expense, lack of time, an emphasis on treatment rather than research and an organizational desire not to discover if a 'failsafe' system is itself failing can all contribute to a lack of knowledge about the effectiveness of EAPs. In other words the political considerations are ever-present when it comes to the laudable aim of helping those in distress. EAPs can be seen as a public relations exercise, but also one which can save an organization from getting sued by unhappy employees, as the Court of Appeal (*Daily Telegraph*, 2002) has advised ruling in favour of companies which provide access to such schemes (see Chapter 2). The prospect of evaluation can itself raise doubts for the organization and the provider: about who will have access to the data, should the research be carried out by the provider of the service, how might the results affect the company's image and what should be done if the EAP is to found to be ineffective? However, it is common practice for a provider to give anonymized figures on the use of its services to the organization (Arthur, 2000). Further data comparing the emotional well-being of employees before and after their use of the EAP is less common, but makes eminent sense for the purposes of effective evaluation.

It may come as no surprise to learn that objective evaluation studies of EAPs are rather thin on the ground and to date there is little sound research into their efficacy. Of the existing examples the headline grabber has been the American McDonnell Douglas cost–benefit study (Alexander Consulting Group, 1989). This piece of independent research assessed the impact of an EAP over four years, gathering data before and after the intervention, as well as comparing findings with a matched control group: the consultants reported four dollars savings for each dollar invested in the scheme. The only possible fly in the ointment was the reliance on data from users of alcohol abuse EAPs (Masi, 1997), which may well have yielded different benefits from those relating to the experiences of employees with other psychological health difficulties. Elsewhere the evidence has been mixed. The study of an EAP used by Australian government employees demonstrated the capacity of the scheme to break even, ie. be cost-neutral (Blaze-Temple and Howat,

1997), while use of the State of Ohio's EAP did not yield benefits in terms of staff absence and turnover (McClellan, 1989). However, compelling the need for financial satisfaction, there is little to be gained in underestimating the psychological outcomes for employees who begin to function for the better after using an EAP. The reduction from 84.5 per cent to 27.6 per cent of UK NHS employees reporting high levels of distress following counselling is a case in point (Borrill *et al.*, 1998). Another is an American study of human services employees who reported significant improvements in work performance, attendance, workplace relationships and levels of stress following their use of an EAP supplied to 30 per cent of Fortune 100 companies (Masi and Jacobson, 2003).

A review of UK EAPs highlighted the beneficial impact of counselling on individual well-being and a decrease in sickness absence (Berridge *et al.*, 1997) and these findings were further borne out by a well-designed evaluation over three years of the UK Post Office's counselling provision. Using standardized measures to compare the well-being of 250 users of the counselling service before and after treatment with a control group of 100 employees, the study revealed statistically significant reductions in reported symptoms of depression among 60 per cent of service-users and of anxiety among 62 per cent of service-users (Cooper and Sadri, 1991). Among this 'improving' group of employees, there was a 22 per cent drop in the number of days' sick leave. Not unexpectedly the control group showed no change in well-being and was also found to have significantly better health than the counselled even after the intervention (Cooper and Sadri, 1991). This aspect of the findings was consistent with those from the evaluation of an EAP in a Canadian transportation organization, where those receiving help also had significantly more problems before, during and after treatment than members of the control group (MacDonald *et al.*, 1997). Rather than suggest a failure in these evaluation studies, such findings indicate the seriously high level of distress experienced by employees who turn to the EAP for help, such that 'If they received a psychiatric assessment they would probably be considered to be suffering from a psychiatric disorder' (Arthur, 2002, p. 73). Of the respondents to a survey of employees utilizing EAPs, 42.3 per cent scored either the maximum score or one short of the maximum of 12 on the General Health Questionnaire (see also Chapter 9) and 92 per cent admitted their problem was moderate/serious with 76.6 per cent recognizing their work performance was affected by it (Arthur, 2002). Around two-thirds of participants believed that in the absence of counselling provision, they would have felt it necessary to take time off from work (Arthur, 2002).

Overall the mixed findings suggest that the tertiary level approach alone is not the answer for employees. Indeed there is evidence to suggest that for some people the experience of revisiting old feelings can be counterproductive by interfering with the mental processing of highly stressful or traumatic events (Sijbrandji *et al.*, 2006). Care should therefore be exercised by organizations, as well as in the cases of individuals, to ensure that where they do so, they buy into a reputable EAP/counselling service. Notwithstanding such considerations, as indicated earlier in this chapter, it is the combination of organizationally and individually tailored solutions which is most likely to yield the best outcomes for all concerned. Whilst it may be expedient to think that 'Sick companies produce sick employees' (Carroll, 1996) and there are probably situations where this is true, the way to move forward from experiences of suffering and distress in the workplace is most commonly via a partnership whereby employers recognize the benefits of well-being to both the worker and the organization and play their part in collaborating to create opportunities to ensure these benefits are realized.

Summary of the chapter

This chapter has reviewed a range of organizationally sponsored approaches to facilitating emotional and psychological well-being among employees. The onus for organizing and participating in the various approaches may fall to either the individual and/or the organization, but can be broadly summarized as preventing, managing and treating stress – known as primary, secondary and tertiary level interventions. A variety of organizational reforms have been highlighted with examples, although these are less widespread for both political and methodological reasons. Emotional and stress management interventions have proved more popular as they demand less fundamental change for an organization, although the efficacy of these relies more upon individual practice and use within work settings. The provision of treatment for those who are already experiencing poor psychological health has grown in recent years as EAPs have spread in their number and nature. Again evaluation of this approach has been subject to organizational politics and where found, it has generally benefited those who have used EAPs. Taken overall, there remains considerable scope to improve well-being at work and it is suggested that this may be successfully achieved through combining aspects of different levels of intervention, based on guidelines for careful introduction and implementation. The potential for partnership between employees and their workplaces is the key to creating the right kind of emotional momentum and the benefits are for all.

Key terms	
interventions (primary, secondary and tertiary)	stress management
	cognitive-behavioural therapies
prevention	relaxation techniques
management and treatment	Employee Assistance Programmes
management commitment	(EAPs)

Questions and answers

1 *How much can the organization realistically do to improve employee well-being at work?* The short answer is that lots can be done, as this chapter has outlined, in relation to many aspects of the work environment, as well as provision for individual employees. There are different levels at which interventions can take place in preventing, managing or even treating psychological and emotional strain. It is important that prior to adopting a particular strategy, or set of strategies, steps are taken to ensure it can meet a specified need and therefore have the potential for success, e.g. a job redesign where job dissatisfaction is high, or buying into an Employee Assistance Programme (EAP) when psychological strain is a significant factor among the workforce.

2 *Which organizational factors impede primary level interventions to tackle emotional and psychological strain at work?* The realities of organizational politics dictate that for institutional change to take place there need to be arguments which convince on both economic as well as moral grounds. Only by ensuring the commitment and involvement of top level management, as well as other relevant

stakeholders, can primary level interventions have a realistic chance of success. In implementing such change, the way in which this is communicated to the staff affected is also an important predictor of success – having won the political arguments, it would be unfortunate if employees felt this was being done 'to' them instead of 'in the genuine interests of all'.

3 *Across the whole range of interventions, which are most likely to yield positive results?* This is obviously dependent on organizational circumstances, but there is little doubt that stress management training and EAPs are commonly utilized and are seen as the least disruptive strategy in dealing with psychological and emotional strain. Specific provision within an organization, e.g. gym and recreational facilities, also help to create an ethos of interest in staff welfare. However, this is only likely to deal with situations on an individual and awareness-raising basis, rather than alter aspects of the workplace which may benefit from change. Approaches which attempt to do all of these could yield optimal results. Given the importance of suitable levels of control, reasonable workloads, positive social support and perceptions of justice, appropriately managed organizational initiatives which aim to ensure these as part of an overall strategy have a good chance of producing the right kind of outcomes.

4 *Are EAPs as effective as we might like to think?* From a situation in recent years in which EAPs received little methodical scrutiny, evaluation of their impact is now more widely considered and therefore can yield the type of data with which this question can be answered. In order to assess their effectiveness, it is important to have an overview of the uptake of the EAP and where this is part of an in-house service, it may be possible to negotiate with the providers to undertake an evaluation of client outcomes using some of the standardized measures featured earlier in this book. Larger cost–benefit analyses may require a wider remit, but again the data collected can play a useful role in attempts to secure further funding.

5 *Isn't it easiest to buy into an EAP and hope that it 'fixes' the psychological health of organizations?* Whilst this has been cited as one possible motivation for utilizing an EAP, political expediency is hopefully not top of the list, although action which can be seen to offer some protection from possible future litigation has been known to promote change! The idea of fixing the psychological health of the organization is an ambitious one and can only be meaningful in the context of

the workplace in question – that said, most employers are aware that more can be done and again it is worth reflecting on the examples of so many of the top-rated companies which effectively promote partnerships between employees and employers in order to produce fine services and healthy workplaces.

Suggested further reading

To find out more about organizational interventions, helpful reviews are also to be found in Giga *et al.* (2003a) as well as Schabracq, Cooper and Winnubst's (2002) *Handbook of Work and Health Psychology*, published by Wiley, which also includes Lawrence Murphy's detailed critique of stress management approaches. Jac van der Klink *et al.* (2001) in the *American Journal of Public Health* provide a useful research-based review of these secondary level interventions. Andrew Arthur is a leading UK publisher on the real state of EAPs and for a review of the direction of EAPs, *Emerging Trends for EAPs in the 21st Century* (edited by Nan Van Den Burgh, 2001) provides a useful summary. For further information on the various modes of counselling and some of the approaches used in occupational and other contexts can be found in texts such as Egan's (1986) *The Skilled Helper*, published by Brooks/Cole.

12 The future of emotions at work

The disciplines of psychology and philosophy, and indeed possibly most of the other hard and social sciences, have underestimated the role of emotion in everyday life in terms of understanding actual behaviour as well as the thoughts and beliefs which shape that behaviour. This may be due in part to the objectivity and detached approach which science has traditionally relied upon as its guiding principle. Therefore science has steered away from those things, such as subjectivity and feelings, which have been perceived as likely to get in the way of serious investigation and advancement of knowledge, because they are seen as variable facets of daily human functioning. This is not to say we know nothing about emotions or how they work, otherwise it would have been difficult to write this book, but there is much which remains to be explained. As our species has reached a point where improvements in physical functioning and achievement are likely to be minimal – without radical genetic intervention – it is in the realm of psychological factors that greater advances can be made. For example, the positive attitude of Lance Armstrong has helped him to overcome cancer and go on to become world cycling champion on seven occasions. Similarly in the heavily commercialized world of football, who would have predicted the storming progress of a village football team to its national cup final, as happened to Scotland's Gretna Green in 2006? It would be hard to argue that emotions have played little role in these types of success. Within the world of work, the winning stories are often those which have determination, adversity and positive energy as their hallmarks, whether inventors such as Richard Dyson (vacuum cleaning and automatic washing technology) or innovators like Anita Roddick (Body Shop), Richard Branson (Virgin companies), Nighat Awan (Shere Khan foods) and Sir Alan Sugar (Amstrad computers). Obviously it is not everyone's desire to achieve at this level, but if we can harness a winning combination of emotions, with which we are all imbued to some degree, then who is to say that our working lives will not be improved? This chapter sets out to explore the future of our emotions in the workplace.

Emotional evolution in the workplace

Relationships

There can be little doubt that emotions are important. As individuals we experience them, possibly value them and have the potential to control them. Sometimes they are useful and give us the drive to achieve what we want, while at other times they may present insurmountable barriers. And we might like to think that all this is happening before anyone else knows how we are feeling! Yet we are able to tune into the wavelengths of others and pick up with varying degrees of success the signals of underlying emotions from their posture and expressions and use of language. In turn the emotions of those around us have the ability to cause us to feel differently: frustration, happiness, disappointment, satisfaction. All of these experiences feed directly and rather powerfully into how we deal with those people in the short-term, even if not the longer term. It is not easy to forgive the colleague who without apparent justification calls your integrity into question, yet there remains an organizational requirement to work with them. Similarly the first impressions given off by a new and pleasant co-worker are more likely to increase your capacity to cooperate with them and make a success of any collaborative projects. So how easy is it to change our emotions about specific individuals and objects and just how good will we need to become at this kind of emotional sensitivity and management?

The concept of emotional intelligence (EI) is receiving increasing coverage (see Chapter 6) and its relevance to the workplace continues to grow (e.g. Cherniss and Goleman, 2001). The components of EI have an obvious relevance to optimal functioning at work, as well as other aspects of our lives: self-awareness, self-management, social awareness and relationship management. Indeed these have been linked with increased chances of success for those who have strengths in these areas.

For over a century the traditional intelligences such as literacy and numeracy have been emphasized in schooling systems the world over, yet those emotion-based skills which enable us to get on with our fellow humans have received relatively scant formal attention, outside of the headteacher's room after playtime at school or in the boss's office in later life, invariably when things have already gone wrong! Given the advances in communication, which have effectively caused the world to shrink, and the changes which have increased the access to work of so many groups within the population, the significance of being able to work well with all people regardless of personality type, gender, ethnicity, religious affiliation, nationality, sexuality, age, etc. is even greater. Those who can learn to employ appropriate social skills will stand a better chance of succeeding in a globally competitive environment, and the continuing popularity of studying disciplines such as psychology and counselling is evidence of widespread recognition of a need to find out more about our fellow humans, what makes them tick and what can be done when things go wrong. In other words, emotional evolution is one of the keys to workplace and lifestyle survival.

Self-awareness

Learning to work effectively with others at the interpersonal level is only one part of the jigsaw. As Gardner's (1983, 1993) theory of multiple intelligences points out and Goleman's (1995) approach elaborates, there are also intrapersonal considerations in our emotional survival. After all, learning to live with ourselves is just as, if not, more important a factor for emotional and psychological well-being. Affective events theory (see Chapter 3) suggests that in order to try and understand people's performance in their work, managers and researchers should not be looking at job satisfaction (loosely defined as an attitude toward a set of tasks), but instead at employees' emotions, which are 'evaluations of oneself; they are appraisals of one's own well-being' (Ashkanasy et al., 2002, p. 6). The key to understanding workers' emotions is therefore to be found in recognizing the importance of daily 'hassles and uplifts' (Basch and Fisher, 2000). It comes as no surprise to most that one working day can bring extremes of emotion depending on the success or otherwise of conversations with customers, meetings with colleagues, or progress on a particular task, and we are told that a week is a long time in politics!

Chapter 10 looked at ways in which we might cope with such variation in our feelings and the bottom line for individuals is learning to live with oneself. It may sound reminiscent of those business and lifestyle guru-led seminars which implore you to 'Like yourself' and to 'Make time for you', but our positive well-being does require the need to recognize our own emotions and to have at least some understanding of why we feel the way we do. If we can stake our claim for time to reflect on these at some point during a day or a week, then there is a better likelihood of identifying problem and/or prospect areas of our lives which we can use as stepping stones to solve difficulties and make the most of our opportunities. The importance of claiming some time to oneself to do this cannot be underestimated, whether it is the grabbing of a few minutes to write in a diary or taking more leisurely time to think out loud by talking over feelings with a trusted and listening friend. The pace and intensity to which the modern workplace is geared does not make this easy to do, and it is therefore essential not to fall into the trap of 'living to work'.

Handling challenge and change

The theme of change and understanding its impact has been a consistent theme throughout the middle part of this book (see Chapter 4–9). Very much like the breaking of waves on the shore, the tides of change are constant: some are larger than others and have differing impacts on the way things were before. One could compare organizations to human creations built on or near the shoreline, some made of rocks, some of sand and others with carefully crafted shapes such as sandcastles adorned with pebbles and the occasional feather! OK, he's getting carried away now, you may be thinking, but it is worth remembering that the principles of organizational life are not that different from natural realities and have just as much to do with survival. Each new wave brings a challenge to the structure and parts, or all of it may be affected by the advance of a gradually incoming tide. Preparation for a rough environment may have included a moat and ramparts, but depending on the size and materials used in the construction, these can only delay the inevitable. The history of organizations (and sandcastles) is littered with examples of grand enterprises which once towered over whole countries or the world, such as the East India Company (shipping), Metro-Goldwyn-Mayer (films) and Enron (energy) and which have long since been eroded or over-taken, and whose place at the front has been replaced by other ambitious structures. Viewed in this light the meaning of starting anything new may seem unclear, even a waste of time, but the nature of our species is to enquire and create because our survival depends on such activity. It is important not to rely on structures to last forever, but to recognize the need to evolve by changing direction or the shape of our enterprise – the alternative is to find oneself marooned and cut off from help. Rela-tionships are the lifeblood of organizations and working life, so learning to cope with change demands that we constantly update our skills to ensure that we see the advancing tide and are as prepared as possible to deal with its likely consequences.

Many professions expect continuing training and development from their members to ensure that skills are kept relevant, and we all need to check up on how we get along with others and whether our approach to emotions is still the best one for our circumstances. The happier and more contented workers (as well as their organizations) are likely to be those who have moulded themselves in tune with the long seasons of their career and learned to avoid the potentially costly risks of relying on past successes to determine their continued survival. This is not to say that the equivalent of market forces at a given time should dictate our actions – survival is about the longer term and at some point very soon the pressing issues of the moment will be past and no longer important. This may seem a little too stoical for some, but a perspective which helps us to deal with raw emotions and seemingly overwhelming situations has been helpful to many. Not the least of such philosophical Stoics (as they became known) was the Roman general, Marcus Aurelius, whose personal suffering while on a long military campaign motivated him to commit to writing his philosophical work *Meditations* on how we might view adversity and best ensure the survival of our ideals, even if not ourselves.

Exercising emotions

It would be wrong to prescribe the best way to manage emotions, but we also come to realize that there are ways which work better or worse in given situations. Emotional labour (see Chapter 4) requires that we project an emotional 'image' to the outside world which may or may not reflect how we feel, but is the version of our emotions which employers and line managers would like us to show to our customers, clients and co-workers. In practice this can mean behaving in a way which is often at odds with what we think or feel. In his play *The Misanthrope*, Molière – France's leading seventeenth-century playwright in the court of King Louis XIV – featured the comic consequences of talking to others in a way which reflects what is actually on our minds. It is a theme often repeated since, not least in the 1980s film *9 till 5* which featured three women working for a chauvinist boss: they first imagine and then carry out their revenge for his unreasonable and prejudiced behaviour, with hilarious results. Such a coup remains the stuff of dreams for most of us who know that if you want to stay in employment it is hard to say what you think the whole time. Yet to feel true to our emotions is important for well-being. Whether it is happiness or frustration, these will build up and find their own outlet, but not always in the appropriate way. It is not surprising that the giggling undertaker or the unempathic counsellor may not remain in their jobs for long. The ability to channel emotional energy in an acceptable manner is therefore important for the individual employee as well as the organization. Appropriate opportunities to uncork bottled up emotions are a possible answer and these already exist in a range of guises from 'clearing the air'-type meetings to paint-balling and raft-building! In an increasingly service-oriented world, more organizations will need to take responsibility for recognizing, and attempting to reduce, the emotional price being paid by employees while carrying out their duties. This can be achieved by highlighting such issues to candidates at the selection stage and subsequently reviewing the design of service-oriented jobs. It is better for all concerned that these job opportunities exist, but there is no reason to forget the lessons of the workplace in times when manufacturing was the main work activity.

It took from the beginning of the twentieth century to the 1950s to establish the principle of designing work and people in harmony with each other, and it has taken another fifty years or so for some workplaces to turn the clock back again! The breed of conveyor belt factories of the ilk which produced Ford's motor cars by specifying the nature and pace of employees' work have evolved to promote employee control and teamworking (see Chapter 5), yet in the service industries which rely so heavily on call centres we see once again the same kind of prescription of what the operator should say and how much time they should spend with customers. The adage that 'people buy from people they like' is widely recognized, but is hardly served by stilted and superficial interactions. For employees, the psychological contract (see Chapter 4) which incorporates feelings of justice and equity in relation to our treatment by an organization can clearly influence our emotions and behaviour at work. Therefore a clear link is likely to exist between emotional labour and the psychological contract, where our willingness to use the former is informed by our feelings about the latter. Presenting the organization's preferred image is bound to be harder when we are feeling at odds with how it has treated us, and one would suspect it is easier when our expectations as employees are being met.

Survival mode

So in the changing, faster-paced and more immediately competitive world of work, what are our emotional priorities and is there a need for us to evolve? The continuing prevalence of high levels of psychological strain and mental health problems across the workforce (see Chapter 2) suggest that we need to make a more conscious effort to prioritize our well-being, both as individuals and agents of the organizations we serve. Recognizing the symptoms of strain (see Chapter 1) as well as the sources of these emotional challenges is particularly important (see Chapter 2 for a selection of likely culprits, such as bullying and emotional labour). Work which demands as much effort from our emotions as physical tasks have traditionally asked of our bodies, takes a particular toll. There are boundaries to how much information – emotional or otherwise – we can digest in a given period and there may well be a genetic legacy for future generations in working so hard that it makes us psychologically and/or physically ill. Will the hard-wiring of our brains begin to adapt in unthought of ways to the constant bombardment from work-related challenges, such as e-stimuli and new technology? The answer is likely to be 'yes'! Certainly the bodies of some IT operators have already posted warning at remaining seated at the computer screen for hours on end without a break: the result is 'e-thrombosis', a work-induced deep vein clot (*Guardian*, 2006). However within the brain, semi-permanent changes have been found in the amount of grey matter in adults who have acquired a new skill, such as juggling (Draganski *et al.*, 2004). This kind of 'plasticity' of the brain – to be moulded in a way which shows adaptation to the demands of the environment – may also have negative effects on emotion, such as the potential to programme fear in response to certain signals (Monk *et al.*, 2004).

The time we have to devote to relationships outside of work can also be threatened with negative consequences, therefore it is important to plan for family/non-work time as much as, if not more, for our working hours. Awareness of what our limits are and the distress signals in ourselves and others are the first steps towards being able to do something about them. Similarly knowing when things are going well and trying to replicate the ingredients of those experiences are equally important for positive working too. Using tools which can help us to understand our workplaces and therefore identify which aspects are good and which require development (see Chapters 3 and 9) can provide employees and employers with an insight into their particular piece of the world of work. Indeed such an approach may confirm what we already suspect, but by borrowing a more objective set of criteria from outside of the organization, the unsatisfactory aspects are less easy to ignore and may justify future plans to change things for the better.

We know that we need to evolve to survive and as a species we know this is what we are good at. Across one's own lifetime, the lessons of emotional experience are a valuable commodity and it might be logical to assume that emotional intelligence therefore increases with age. It is probable that we have varying levels of confidence in engaging with such a change in approach, or at least in being seen to be part of it. The growing acceptance of the role for 'soft' skills in working alongside others and feeling at ease with ourselves is gaining and is the main evolutionary change which is unfolding. But whether we do it quietly or shout it from the rooftops, we should recognize that work does not have to be about losing through violence – to the body or the spirit – as Studs Terkel wrote in 1972. It needs to be about winning through learning – this is the key to survival.

Organizational guidelines for the use of emotions in the workplace

- Keep communication channels open and acknowledge expressed emotions
- Develop and enhance emotional intelligence among the workforce

- Foster 'positive emotional climates'
- Design work with emotions in mind
- Recognize the role of emotions in decision-making
- Pay attention to emotion-laden events
- Show sensitivity and regret for the impact of actions, including mistakes
- Provide training on recognizing and dealing with emotions
- Monitor the demands of emotional labour on employees
- Make it possible for workers to recharge their emotional resources
- Provide a forum for the safe expression of emotions
- Provide interventions to support individuals and groups to deal with challenges (based on Ashkanasy *et al.*, 2002).

Case Study 12.1 | **How emotional investment can produce positive change**

Pengwern Hall in North Wales is part of the national charity for young people with learning difficulties (MENCAP) which was acquired from the Manchester and Salford City Councils in the mid-1960s. Set in its own grounds, the home built by Lord Mostyn in the 1770s had seen many changes since the days of French Revolution and American independence from Britain. The challenge identified by Pengwern's new director, taking up his post during a time of great social change of the 1960s, was how to create opportunities for and shift attitudes towards young people with learning difficulties away from the isolating realities of the past towards a more 'normal' way of life, which was more integrated within society. Whilst this was not to be easily achieved from such a location, the director, aided by his young family and a band of loyal staff, set about building this vision.

Beginning literally with the bricks and mortar to refurbish the old buildings which had once housed horse-drawn coaches, and harnessing the skills of experienced and new staff recruits, volunteers and students, as well as the 'trainees' (the young people with learning difficulties), the transformation began. The trainees were of school-leaving age, often having been bypassed by the education system, who now had the opportunity to learn new skills and to be encouraged in how to interact with others successfully. Funded by their local authorities, they kept coming from all over the UK ▶

and sometimes abroad and so did increased demands for the innovative service being offered by Pengwern. New initiatives sprung up as houses and shops in local villages and towns became part of the project where young residents would graduate from the main site to develop further social and living skills to enhance their chances of success when they returned to their localities. Over 20 years, attitudes and opportunities certainly did shift and government policies were informed by the work at Pengwern. A group of highly talented people worked long hours to help to bring this to fruition – but how does such an enterprise flourish?

The guidelines for harnessing emotions in the workplace were obviously central, as they are for most successful organizations. The style of leadership provided the key via open communication. Ensuring a positive emotional climate and helping colleagues to hone those behaviours which would facilitate this was a major component of the success at Pengwern Hall. Recognizing and handling emotions had to be a priority for working with the young people, but also importantly for the staff who worked together in this setting with the often challenging nature of the work. A failure to integrate these priorities would have spelt the failure of the whole initiative! This type of change required a huge emotional investment and its success is a testament to the ideals, capabilities and emotional reserves of those involved – my parents, Martin and Risha Weinberg, and their colleagues!

Surviving the future of work

What will work be like in the future? Those black and white films of the last century which foresaw humans after the year 2020 dressed in space-suit-like outfits, travelling on machines through the air and communicating via thoughts alone make us laugh – for the sake of the wobbly background sets made of wood if nothing else! However, the brave new world of advanced technology has seen us using hand-held devices to talk to people on the other side of the planet and carrying the equivalent of a small library of information in thumb-size gadgets. Opportunities for accessing communication and information abound, but not the spacesuits. Of course these advances rely on energy sources which we continue to exploit in an increasingly changing and unpredictable environment. Nevertheless as people we have not changed very much at all. In fact it is suggested that studies of human genetic material reveal little that is different now from 5000–10,000 years ago. So the world we live in is fundamentally altering and fast, but as humans we are not. For most species this is a recipe for extinction.

Naturally the answer to this is that it is our behaviour as well as our biology which determines survival and in this way, humans have evolved most successfully, by having brains which are receptive to environmental stimuli. Yet the costs of using so much of the planet's natural resources in a comparatively short evolutionary time are clearly apparent. In other words there are challenges which humans have faced before, but with a frequency which we are less prepared for. Larger populations, decreased living space, disproportionate demands on existing resources and global climate change are key examples. However, the study of epi-genetics suggests that such challenges on a grand scale can have consequences for the human genetic blueprint, determining which characteristics are expressed and which are not. Findings have been presented which show that the experience of a particularly stressful environmental event, such as famine, can leave a genetic marker which is passed on to future generations and may only begin to express itself in the grandchildren of those exposed to the event! (Kaati *et al.*, 2002.) Furthermore it has been proposed that the timing of this type of challenge can impact on men and women differently and is linked to reproductive development (Pembrey *et al.*, 2005).

As this strand of theory unfolds, it would fit with a notion that evolution is continuous and can reflect strong experiences, perhaps even those in the workplace. It has been demonstrated that pregnant women exposed to mentally, but not physically, demanding jobs for 40 hours a week are more likely to experience premature birth (di Renzo, 1998), so one can wonder at the potential impact of emotional labour, bullying and psychological strain on future generations. Furthermore the decline of the birth rate in some economically developed nations has also been linked to the prioritizing of careers over home life. Ways in which a better balance at the home–work interface can be achieved are being considered and have resulted in a range of governmental and organizational initiatives across the globe (see Chapter 8). In relation to the longer-term impact, much more research needs to be carried out, but there are indications that the quality and quantity of work may have more to do with the survival of the species than we might initially think.

Some of these ideas present challenges which are hard to comprehend, particularly when it comes to generating solutions. There is an acceptance that it is better to have work than not: for personal and economic necessities as well as those reasons related to self-esteem and fulfilment. Yet the way we work certainly conjures up difficulties with which we daily contend. One of the problems in working and much else besides that the future may bring is the rethinking of how we use the wonderful new technology which recent decades have brought. Reliance on fossil fuels remains heavy despite its finite limit and gloomy predictions abound of great reductions in its availability by 2050, as well as those foretelling a rise in sea level due to global warming and accompanying threats to sea level conurbations. The challenge of maintaining the energy supplies which power offices and factories, including the huge computerized networks which govern so many of our utilities, is not so far away. Alternative energy sources are being explored, but there is a possibility that these will not be 'on tap' in a way which could make access to functioning computers a serious problem. On the one hand we might consider this the domain of a government's emergency plan for times of peril, or on the other we may need to think what we would do differently to ensure working in the ways which we have come to accept as 'modern'.

Try thinking about that for a moment and see how much might change in an economically developed nation: being obliged to walk to work or use public transport as there is not enough fuels for cars, only being able to use the computer, Internet and emails at specified 'log-on' times in the week, trying to find information in books (just like the good old days), not being able to use mobile phones as the recharging of batteries is centralized and has a waiting list, etc. Except for the committed Luddite, the frustration of a 'slow' computer system would pale into insignificance! (Luddites protested against the price changes in the weaving industry in the early 1800s by sabotaging machines, and came to be seen as opponents of technological advances.)

The experience of older workers is also invaluable here, as they often have a more detailed knowledge of the history of doing things within occupations and organizations. The postponing of the early retirement threshold in the UK and the discussion of its abolition altogether are responses to keeping enough people in the workplace to avoid overloading the welfare system and to the increasing age profile across the EU. For many this will come as a disappointment and for others a relief: such is the two-edged nature of stopping doing something one has done for years and decades. As Sartre recognized, what we do defines who we are and without this, we may become lost. From an objective viewpoint, if we consider the tasks of our paid work are integral to our self-concept then this is a reason, provided we are able, for continuing to work past whatever is deemed to be the retirement age; whereas if we value more the roles enjoyed outside of work, then after many years of service, that is where our efforts deserve to be focused. The ideal may lie somewhere in between, which should make it possible to spread work differently across time and make routine a gradual switch from full- to part-time employment in the years up to the point at which we decide to stop working – trailblazing practitioners include my own father, Martin Weinberg.

Whatever the changes in the future, one will still be able to rely on the undiminished presence and strength of human emotions. History shows that a lack of resources can have a range of effects on a population. The oppression which adverse global conditions can bring, such as war as well as hostile climates, can also serve to bring peoples closer together and help to foster a sense of camaraderie within the boundaries of a community or nation. A new understanding of what is and is not possible will undoubtedly bring fresh ingenuity to the fore, as humans once again adapt to survive. The search for viable robot technologies for everyday use may yet reach undreamt of heights. The use of microchips compatible with human tissue and even our natural electrical activity could find us with implants which interact with our surroundings. Radio frequency identification chips have already been used in pets and manufacturers are keen to sell them for health and security purposes. A UK hospital doctor volunteered to have such a pre-programmed device inserted under his skin and was able to get the hospital doors to open on his arrival and to switch on his palm-held computer to announce his itinerary for the working day!

However, competition for limited resources can also have a negative emotional impact upon those affected. The genuine drive to provide for loved ones could spawn a different level of motivation to compete for those jobs which are currently commonplace in an economically developed nation. The label of economic migrants could apply to so many more than it does today and as greed and selfishness are unlikely to disappear, the 'gangmasters' who have had a legal entitlement to provide workforces to a variety of industries in the UK, may include more of those unscrupulous individuals who care little for the physical or emotional well-being of their employees. Such dereliction of duty led to the tragic drowning of 23 cockle-pickers in Morecombe Bay, Lancashire in 2004 and the subsequent gaoling of their employer. Fortunately such incidents are rare, but this is set against the backdrop of a UK recruitment industry booming from a value of £3bn in 1993 to £23bn in 2005 and it is estimated that between 2–5 per cent (approximately 500) of such companies are rogue operators (www.Supplymanagement.com). The health and safety of workers in any capacity is a concern for all and whilst the legal and moral imperatives are well-served by vigilance, it is the willingness to act on such information – as whistle-blowers have increasingly demonstrated (see Chapter 2) – which produces real change for the better and makes unofficial as well as recognized workplaces a priority for scrutiny.

The desire to give credence to emotions which can facilitate much-needed job reform is within all of us, although the UK must not lose sight of what has already been achieved in improving working conditions in recent years: e.g. maximum working hours, minimum wage thresholds, parental rights and duties of care. The scope for designing and implementing interventions within organizations remains considerable (see Chapter 11) and is the next major challenge for applying psychology in the workplace. However, the mantra of making things better should not simply apply to those situations which need urgent change, but also to all jobs which would benefit from continued and further enhancement. A role for Positive Psychology which seeks to optimize well-being and to build on what we are capable of achieving is developing. We hope that learning to harness our emotions in some of the ways outlined in this book will define the way ahead and in due course give us more than simply survival in the workplace.

Summary of the chapter

So the answer to surviving the workplace is as simple or as complex as we might like to make it – harness emotions and our environment in a way which optimizes the outcome. In other words, we already have the potential to change, not only in our behaviour but also inside our brains, and we need to recognize that the world of work can be shaped in a way which encourages positive adaptation. We not only owe this to ourselves but also to future generations!

Key terms	
evolution	epi-genetics
survival	retirement
brain plasticity	gangmasters
global climate change	

Questions with no answers – except your own!

1 How important are emotions in turning adversity into a platform for future success?
2 Why can't everyone say what they really think?
3 How well can you handle your emotions in times of change – do you deal equally well or otherwise with changes at work or at home?
4 How much do you rely on your employing organization to guide your emotions in relation to new developments?
5 Should work be so enjoyable that we might want to abolish retirement altogether?

Suggested further reading

The Emotionally Intelligent Workplace, edited by Cary Cherniss and Daniel Goleman (2001), provides an insight into the assessment, selection and development of EI skills in the workplace. *Managing Emotions in the Workplace* (eds Neal Ashkanasy, Wilfred Zerbe and Charmine Hartel, 2002) contains a valuable range of chapters on the role of emotions in both theory and practice and of particular relevance here is the applied chapter by the editors entitled 'Management tools that come out of this'. In paperback, *The Essentials of the New Workplace* (edited by David Holman, Toby Wall and Chris Clegg, Paul Sparrow and Ann Howard; 2004) provides an up-to-date business-oriented view of the modern world of work, emphasizing the impact of technology and working trends. However, any trend which captures your imagination is worth finding out more about in a world of work which is guaranteed to keep changing and encourage us to strive to balance human needs, efficiency, technology and ethics.

References

Introduction and Chapter 1

Birdi, K.S., Gardner, C.R. and Warr, P.B. (1998) 'Correlates and perceived outcomes of four types of employee development activity', *Journal of Applied Psychology*, 82, 845–857.

CBI (Confederation of British Industry)/AXA (2006) 'Cost of UK workplace absence tops £13bn'. New CBI survey, accessed at http//:www.cbi.org.uk/ndbs/press.nsf on 15 May 2006.

Clare, A. (1980) *Psychiatry in Dissent*, 2nd edition, London: Tavistock.

Clow, A. (2001) 'The physiology of stress', in F. Jones and J. Bright, *Stress: Myth, Theory and Research*, Harlow: Pearson Education Limited.

Cooper, C.L. and Bramwell, R. (1992) 'A comparative analysis of occupational stress in managerial and shopfloor workers in the brewing industry: mental health, job satisfaction and sickness', *Work and Stress*, 6, 127–138.

Cooper, C.L., Sloan, S. and Williams, S. (1988) *The Occupational Stress Indicator*, Berkshire: NFER-Nelson.

Davidson, R.J. (1994) 'On emotion, mood, and related affective constructs', in P. Ekman and R.J. Davidson (eds) *The Nature of Emotion: Fundamental Questions*, pp. 51–55, New York: Oxford University Press.

Department of Social Security (1993) *Social Security Statistics*, London: HMSO.

Di Renzo, G-D. (1998) 'Premature births among full-time working women', paper presented at Tommy's Campaign Conference, 7 September.

Elkin, A. and Rosch, P. (1990) 'Promoting mental health in the workplace: the prevention side of stress management', *Occupational Medicine: State of the Art Review*, 5, 739–754.

French, J.R.P. Jr, Caplan, R.D. and Harrison, R. (1982) *The Mechanisms of Job Stress and Strain*, Chichester: Wiley and Sons.

Friedman, M. and Rosenman, R.H. (1974) *Type A Behaviour and Your Heart*, New York: Knopf.

George, J.M. and Jones, G.R. (1996) 'The experience of work and turnover intentions: interactive effects of value attainment, job satisfaction and positive mood', *Journal of Applied Psychology*, 81, 318–325.

Goleman, D. (1998) *Working with Emotional Intelligence*, London: Bloomsbury.

Hackett, R.D. (1989) 'Work attitudes and employee absenteeism: a synthesis of the literature', *Journal of Occupational Psychology*, 62, 235–248.

Guardian (1997) £739bn – the hidden earning power in your home that gets swept under the carpet, 7 October.

Higgs, M. and Dulewicz, V. (1999) *Making Sense of Emotional Intelligence*, Windsor: NFER-Nelson.

Hoel, H., Faragher, B. and Cooper, C.L. (2004) 'Bullying is detrimental to health, but all bullying behaviours are not necessarily equally damaging', *British Journal of Guidance and Counselling*, 32, 367–387.

Iaffaldino, M.T. and Muchinsky, P.M. (1985) 'Job satisfaction and job performance: a meta-analysis', *Psychological Bulletin*, 97, 251–273.

Johnson, S. (1999) *Who Moved My Cheese?* Ohio: Vermillion.

Jones, F. and Bright, J. (2001) *Stress: Myth, Theory and Research*, Harlow: Pearson Education Limited.

Judge, T.A., Thoreson, C.J., Bono, J.E. and Patton, G.K. (2001) 'The job satisfaction–job performance relationship: a qualitative and quantitative review', *Psychological Bulletin*, 127, 376–407.

Judge, T.A. and Watanabe, S. (1993) 'Another look at the job satisfaction–life satisfaction relationship', *Journal of Applied Psychology*, 78, 475–490.

Kasl, S. and Amick, B. (1995) 'Work stress', in S. Kasl (ed.) *Research Methods in Stress and Health Psychology*, pp. 239–266, Chichester: Wiley.

Kessler, R.C. and Frank, R.G. (1997) 'The impact of psychiatric disorders on work loss days', *Psychological Medicine*, 27, 179–190.

Kinman, G. and Jones, F. (2004) *Working to the Limit*, London: AUT.

Lazarus, R. and Folkman, S. (1984) *Stress, Appraisal and Coping*, New York: Springer Publications.

Lee, R.T. and Ashforth, B.E. (1996) 'A meta-analytic examination of the correlates of the three dimensions of job burnout', *Journal of Applied Psychology*, 81, 123–133.

Lewis, A.J. (1963) 'Medicine and the affections of the mind', *British Medical Journal*, 2, 1549–1557.

Locke, E.A. (1976) 'The nature and causes of job satisfaction', in M.D. Dunnette (ed.) *Handbook of Industrial and Organizational Psychology*, pp. 1297–1349, Chicago, IL: Rand McNally.

Martocchio, J.J. (1994) 'The effects of absence culture on individual absence', *Human Relations*, 47, 243–262.

Maslach, C. (1982) *The Cost of Caring*, New York: Prentice Hall.

Maslach, C. and Jackson, S. (1986) *The Maslach Burnout Inventory*, Palo Alto, CA: Consulting Psychologists Press.

Maslach, C. and Leiter, M.P. (1997) *The Truth About Burnout*, San Francisco, CA: Jossey Bass.

McKenna, E. (2000) *Business Psychology and Organizational Behaviour*, 3rd edition, Hove: Psychology Press.

McNeely, B.L. and Megliano, B.M. (1994) 'The role of dispositional and situational antecedents in prosocial organizational behaviour: an examination of the intended beneficiaries of prosocial behaviour', *Journal of Applied Psychology*, 79, 836–844.

Netterstrom, B. and Juel, K. (1988) 'Impact of work-related and psychosocial factors on the development of ischaemic heart disease among urban bus drivers in Denmark', *Scandinavian Journal of Work and Environmental Health*, 14, 231–238.

O'Driscoll, M.P. and Cooper, C.L. (2002) 'Sources and management of excessive job stress and burnout', in P.B. Warr (ed.) *Psychology at Work*, 4th edition, pp. 188–223, London: Penguin.

Ostler, W. (1910) Quoted in M.P. O'Driscoll and C.L. Cooper, 'Sources and management of excessive job stress and burnout', in P.B. Warr (ed.) *Psychology at Work*, 4th edition, 2002, pp. 188–223, London: Penguin.

Ostroff, C. (1992) 'The relationship between satisfaction, attitudes and performance: an organizational level analysis', *Journal of Applied Psychology*, 77, 963–974.

Reeve, J. (2005) *Understanding Motivation and Emotion*, Hoboken, NJ: John Wiley and Sons.

Rosenman, R., Friedman, M., Straus, R., Wurm, M., Kositchek, R., Hahn, W. and Werthessen, N. (1964) 'A predictive study of coronary heart disease', *Journal of the American Medical Association*, 232, 872–877.

Salovey, P., Woolery, A. and Mayer, J.D. (2000) 'Emotional intelligence: conceptualization and measurement', in G. Fletcher and M. Clark (eds) *The Blackwell Handbook of Social Psychology: Interpersonal Processes* (pp. 279–307), London: Blackwell.

Sanderman, R. (1998) 'New insights into the onset of heart disease and cancer', paper given at the 22nd European Conference on Psychosomatic Research, Manchester: University of Manchester.

Selye, H. (1956) *The Stress of Life*, New York: McGraw-Hill.

Stansfeld, S., Fuhrer, R. and Shipley, M.J. (1998) 'Types of social support as predictors of psychiatric morbidity in a cohort of British Civil Servants (Whitehall II Study)', *Psychological Medicine*, 28, 881–892.

Steiner, D.D. and Truxillo, D.M. (1989) 'An improved test of the disaggregation hypothesis of job and life satisfaction', *Journal of Occupational Psychology*, 62, 33–39.

Sunday Times (2001) *50 Best Companies to Work For*, Supplement.

Tait, M., Padgett, M.Y. and Baldwin, T.T. (1989) 'Job and life satisfaction: a re-evaluation of the strength of the relationship and gender effects as a function of the date of the study', *Journal of Applied Psychology*, 74, 502–507.

Warr, P.B. (1987) *Psychology at Work*, 3rd edition, London: Penguin.

Warr, P.B. (1999) 'Well-being in the workplace', in D. Kahneman, E. Diener and N. Schwartz (eds), *Well-being: The Foundations of Hedonic Psychology*, 392–412, New York: Russell Sage.

Weinberg, R.S. (1995) *Foundations of Sport and Exercise Psychology*, 4th edition, Champaign, IL: Human Kinetics.

Williams, S., Dale, J., Glucksman, E. and Wellesley, A (1997) 'Senior house officers' work related stressors, psychological distress, and confidence in performing clinical tasks in accident emergency: a questionnaire study', *British Medical Journal*, 314, 713–718.

Wootton, B. (1959) *Social Science and Social Pathology*, London: Allen and Unwin.

Wright, T.A and Staw, B.M. (1999) 'Affect and favourable work outcomes; two longitudinal tests of the happy-productive worker thesis', *Journal of Organizational Behaviour*, 20, 1–23.

Chapter 2

Arulampalam, W., Booth, A.L. and Bryan, M.L. (2005-6) 'Is there a glass ceiling over Europe? Exploring the gender pay gap across the wages distribution', Institute of Social and Economic Research Working Paper, University of Essex: ISER.

Barling, J. and Sorenson, D. (1997) 'Work and family: in search of a relevant research agenda', in S.E. Jackson and C.L. Cooper, *Creating Tomorrow's Organizations: A Handbook for Future Research in Organizational Behaviour*, 157–169, Chichester: Wiley.

Brown, G.W. and Harris, T. (1978) *Social Origins of Depression – A Study of Psychiatric Disorder in Women*, London: Routledge.

Cabinet Office (2004) *Findings from the Whitehall II Study, London*, Cabinet Office, accessed at http//:www.pcs.org.uk/shared_asp_files/uploadedfiles/{137355E7-73D3-42B3-AA94_2782F72F9943}Whitehall%20booklet.

Caplan, R.P. (1994) 'Stress, anxiety and depression in hospital consultants, general practitioners and senior health service managers', *British Medical Journal*, 309, 1261–1263.

Chartered Institute of Personnel and Development (2006) 'Working hours in the UK', accessed at http//:www.cipd.co.uk/subjects/wrkgtime/general/ukworkers.htm, accessed 10 August 2006.

Cooper, C.L. and Sadri, G. (1991) 'The impact of stress counselling at work', in P.L. Perrewe (ed.) Handbook of Job Stress (special issue), *Journal of Social Behaviour and Personality*, 6, 411–423.

Cooper, C.L. and Robertson, I. (eds) (2001) *Well-being in Organization*, Chichester: Wiley and Sons.

Cooper, C.L. and Sutherland, V.J. (1992) 'Job stress, satisfaction, and mental health among general practitioners before and after introduction of new contract', *British Medical Journal*, 304, 1545–1548.

Daily Telegraph (2002) 'Judges tighten rules on stress payouts', 6 February, pp 1–2.

Davidson, M. and Cooper, C.L. (1992) *Shattering the Glass Ceiling – The Woman Manager*, London: Paul Chapman Publishing.

Eaves *v* Blaenclydach Co. (1909) 2 K. B. (Eng.) 73.

Federation of European Employers (2005a) *The History of Working Time Regulation 1784-2002*, accessed at www.fedee.com/histwt.html, 11 August 2006.

Federation of European Employers (2005b) *Untangling the Myths of Working Time*, accessed at www.fedee.com/workinghours.shtml, 11 August 2006.

Gillespie, N.A., Walsh, M., Winefield, A.H. and Stough, C. (2001) 'Occupational stress in universities: staff perceptions of the causes, consequences and moderators of stress', *Work and Stress*, 15, 53–72.

Guardian (2004) 'We remain almost invisible', 14 December.

Guardian (2005) 'Women in private sector paid 45 per cent less than men, says equality watchdog', 20 December.

Hoel, H., Cooper, C.L. and Faragher, B. (2001) 'The experience of bullying in the UK, the impact of organizational status', *European Journal of Work and Organizational Psychology*, 10, 443–465.

Hoel, H., Faragher, B. and Cooper, C.L. (2004) 'Bullying is detrimental to health, but all bullying behaviours are not necessarily equally damaging', *British Journal of Guidance and Counselling*, 32, 367–387.

Howton, K., Fagg, J., Simkin, S., Harriss, L. and Malmberg, A. (1998) 'Methods used for suicide by farmers in England and Wales: the contribution of availability and its relevance to prevention', *British Journal of Psychiatry*, 173, 320–324.

Huxley, P., Evans, S., Gately, C., Webber, M., Mears, A., Pajak, S., Kendall, T., Medina, J. and Katona, C. (2005) 'Stress and pressures in mental health social work: the worker speaks', *British Journal of Social Work*, 35, 1063–1079.

Johnstone *v* Bloomsbury Area Health Authority (1991) ICR 269.

Kinman, G. and Jones, F. (2004) *Working to the Limit*. London: AUT.

Lewis, G. Pelosi, A.J., Araya, R. and Dunn, G. (1992) 'Measuring psychiatric disorder in the community: a standardized assessment for use by lay interviewers', *Psychological Medicine*, 22, 465–486.

Lindeman, S., Laura, E., Hakko, H. and Lonnqvist, J. (1996) 'A systematic review on gender-specific suicide mortality in medical doctors', *British Journal of Psychiatry*, 168, 274–279.

Littlewood, S., Case, R., Gater, R. and Lindsey, C. (2003) 'Recruitment, retention, satisfaction and stress in child and adolescent psychiatrists', *Psychiatric Bulletin*, 27, 61–67.

Nadaoka, T. Kashiwakura, M., Oija, A., Morioka, Y. and Totsuka, S. (1997) 'Stress and psychiatric disorders in local government officials in Japan, in relation to their employment level', *Acta Psychiatrica Scandinavica*, 96, 176–183.

Office of Population Census and Surveys (1995) *British Household Psychiatric Survey*, London: HMSO.

Office of Population Census and Surveys (2002) *British Household Psychiatric Survey*, London: HMSO.

Phelan, J., Schwartz, J.E., Bromet, E.J., Dew, M.A., Parkinson, D.K., Schulberg, H.C., Dunn, L.O., Blane, H. and Curtis, E.C. (1991) 'Work stress, family stress and depression in professional and managerial employees', *Psychological Medicine*, 21, 999–1012.

Piotrkowski, C.S. (1978) *Work and the Family System*, New York: The Free Press.

Royal College of Psychiatrists (1995) *Defeating Depression – Depression in the Workplace Conference*, 19th April, London: Royal College of Psychiatrists.

Royal College of Psychiatrists (1995) *Defeat Depression Campaign*, London: Royal College of Psychiatrists.

Schlotz, W., Hellhammer, J., Schulz, P. and Stone, A.A. (2002) 'Perceived work-overload and chronic worrying predict weekend-weekday differences in the cortisol awakening response', *Stress*, 5 (supplement), 68.

Scott, H. (2002) 'Nursing profession is finding it harder to retain nurses', *British Journal of Nursing*, 11, 1052.

Staniforth, M. (1964) *Marcus Aurelius – Meditation* (translation), Harmondsworth: Penguin.

Vartia, M. and Hyyti, J. (2002) 'Gender differences in workplace bullying among prison officers', *European Journal of Work and Organizational Psychology*, 11, 113–127.

Walker *v* Northumberland County Council, High Court (Queen's Bench Division) (1995) *Industrial Relations Law Reports* 35.

Wall, T.D., Bolden, R.I., Borrill, C.S., Golya, D.A., Hardy, G.E., Haynes, G., Rick, J.W., Shapiro, D.A. and West, M.A. (1997) 'Minor psychiatric disorder in NHS Trust staff: occupational and gender differences', *British Journal of Psychiatry*, 171, 519–523.

Weinberg, A. and Cooper, C.L. (2003) 'Stress among national politicians elected to Parliament for the first time', *Stress and Health*, 19, 111–117.

Weinberg, A. and Creed, F. (2000) 'Stress and psychiatric disorder in healthcare professionals and hospital staff', *Lancet*, 355, 533–537.

Weinberg, A. and Huxley, P. (2000) 'An evaluation of the impact of voluntary sector family support workers on the quality of life of carers of schizophrenia sufferers', *Journal of Mental Health*, 9, 495–503.

Weinberg, A., Williamson, J., Challis, D. and Hughes, J. (2003) 'What do care managers do? A study of working practice in older people's services', *British Journal of Social Work*, 33, 901–919.

Winefeld, A.H, Gillespie, N., Stough, C., Dua, J., Hapuarachchi, J. and Boyd, C. (2003) 'Occupational stress in Australian university staff', *International Journal of Stress Management*, 10, 51–63.

Zapf, D., Isic, A., Bechtoldt, M. and Blau, P. (2003) 'What is typical for call centre jobs? Job characteristics, and service interactions in different call centres', *European Journal of Work and Organizational Psychology*, 12, 311–341.

Chapter 3

Agho, A.O., Mueller, C.W. and Price, J.L. (1993) 'Determinants of employee job satisfaction: an empirical test of a causal model', *Human Relations*, 46, 1007–1027.

Aiello, J.R. and Kolb, K.J. (1995) 'Electronic performance monitoring and social context: impact on productivity and stress', *Journal of Applied Psychology*, 80, 339–353.

Arnetz, B.B. (1996) 'Techno-stress: a prospective psychophysiological study of the impact of a controlled stress-reduction program in advanced telecommunication systems design work', *Journal of Occupational Environmental Medicine*, 38, 53–65.

Ashkanasy, N.M., Zerbe, W.J. and Hartel, C.E.J. (2002) *Managing Emotions in the Workplace*, New York: Sharpe.

Barsky, A., Thoresen, C.J., Warren, C.R. and Kaplan, S.A. (2004) 'Modelling negative affectivity and job stress: a contingency-based approach', *Journal of Organizational Behaviour*, 25, 915–937.

Bass, B.M. (1985) *Leadership and Performance: Beyond Expectations*, New York: Free Press.

Borrill, C.S., Wall, T.D., West, M.A., Hardy, G.E., Shapiro, D.A., Haynes, C.E., Stride, C.B., Woods, D. and Carter, A.J. (1998) *Stress among Staff in NHS Trusts: Final Report*, Institute of Work Psychology, University of Sheffield and Psychological Therapies Research Centre, University of Leeds.

Caplan, R., Cobb, S., French, J., Harrision, R. and Pinneau, S. (1975) *Job Demands and Worker Health*, pp. 75–160, Washington, DC: HEW Publication, NIOSH.

Cohen, S. and Williamson, G.M. (1991) 'Stress and infectious disease in humans', *Psychological Bulletin*, 109, 5–24.

Conger, J. and Kanungo, R. (1988) 'The empowerment process: integrating theory and practice', *Academy of Management Review*, 13, 471–482.

Cooper, C.L. and Bramwell, R. (1992) 'A comparative analysis of occupational stress in managerial and shopfloor workers in the brewing industry: mental health, job satisfaction and sickness', *Work and Stress*, 6, 127–138.

Cooper, C.L., Sloan, S.J. and Williams, S. (1988) *Occupational Stress Indicator*, Windsor: NFER-Nelson.

Cooper, C.L. and Robertson, I. (eds) (2001) *Well-being in Organizations*, Chichester: Wiley and Sons.

Costa, P.T. and McCrae, R.R. (1992) *NEO-PI-R, Professional Manual*, Odessa, FL: Psychological Assessment Resources.

Cox, T., Griffiths, A. and Houdmont, J. (2003) 'Rail safety in Britain: an occupational health psychology perspective', *Work and Stress*, 17, 103–108.

Daniels, K. and Guppy, A. (1995) 'Stress, social support and psychological well-being in British accountants', *Work and Stress*, 19, 432–447.

Daniels, K. Harris, C. and Briner, R. (2004) 'Linking work conditions to unpleasant affect: cognition, categorization and goals', *Journal of Occupational and Organizational Psychology*, 77, 343–363.

De Jonge, J., Reuvers, M.M.E.N., Houtman, I.L.D., Bongers, P.M. and Kompier, M.A.J. (2000) 'Linear and nonlinear relations between psychosocial job characteristics, subjective outcomes and sickness absence: baseline results from SMASH', *Journal of Occupational Health Psychology*, 5, 256–268.

De Jonge, J. and Schaufeli, W.B. (1998) 'Job characteristics and employee well-being: a test of Warr's Vitamin Model in health-care workers using structural equation modelling', *Journal of Organizational Behaviour*, 19, 387–407.

Deary, I.J., Blenkin, H., Agius, R.M., Endler, N.S., Zealley, H. and Wood, R. (1996) 'Models of job-related stress and personal achievement among consultant doctors', *British Journal of Psychology*, 87, 3–29.

Deming, W.E. (1982) *Quality, Productivity and Competitive Position*, Boston, MA: MIT Press.

Dick, N. and Shepherd, G. (1994) 'Work and mental health: a preliminary test of Warr's model in sheltered workshops for the mentally ill', *Journal of Mental Health*, 3, 387–400.

Ezoe, S. and Morimoto, K. (1994) 'Behavioural lifestyle and mental health status of Japanese factory workers', *Preventative Medicine*, 23, 98–105.

Fineman, S. (2000) *Emotions in Organizations*, 2nd edition, London: Sage.

Firth-Cozens, J. (1992) 'The role of early family experience in the perception of organizational stress – using clinical and organization perspectives', *Journal of Occupational and Organizational Psychology*, 65, 61–75.

French, J.R.P. and Kahn, R.L. (1962) 'A programmable approach to studying the industrial environment and mental health', *Journal of Social Issues*, 18, 2.

Frenkel, S.J., Korczynski, M, Shire, K.A. and Tam, M. (1999). *On the Front Line; Organization of Work in the Information Economy*, London: Cornell University Press.

Funk, S.C. and Houston, B.K. (1987) 'A critical analysis of the Hardiness Scale's validity and utility', *Journal of Personality and Social Psychology*, 53, 572–578.

Ganster, D.C. and Schaubroeck, J. (1991) 'Work stress and employee health', *Journal of Management*, 17, 235–271.

Garden, A.M. (1989) 'Burnout: the effect of psychological type on research findings', *Journal of Occupational Psychology*, 6, 223–234.

Gardner, D.G., van Dyne, L. and Pierce, J.L. (2004) 'The effects of pay level on organization-based self-esteem and performance: a field study', *Journal of Occupational and Organizational Psychology*, 77, 307–322.

Gidron, Y., Davidson, K. and Bata, I. (1999) 'Short-term effects of a hostility-reduction intervention on male coronary heart disease patients', *Health Psychology*, 18, 416–420.

Gilbreath, B. and Benson, P.G. (2004) 'The contribution of supervisor behaviour to employee psychological well-being', *Work and Stress*, 18, 255–267.

Grzywacz, J.G. and Marks, N.F. (2000) 'Reconceptualising the work-family interface: an ecological perspective on the correlates of positive and negative spill-over between work and family', *Journal of Occupational Health Psychology*, 5, 111–126.

Hackman, J.R. and Oldham, G.R. (1976) 'Motivation through the design of work: test of a theory', *Organizational Behaviour and Human Performance*, 16, 250–279.

Herzberg, F. Mausner, B. and Snyderman, B. (1959) *The Motivation to Work*, New York: Wiley.

Houkes, I. Janssen, P.M., de Jonge, J. and Bakker, A.B. (2003) 'Personality, work characteristics, and employee well-being: a longitudinal analysis of additive and moderating effects', *Journal of Occupational Health Psychology*, 8, 20–38.

Jackson, S. and Schuler, R. (1985) 'A meta-analysis and conceptual critique of research on role ambiguity and role conflict in work settings', *Organizational Behaviour and Human Decision Processes*, 36, 16–78.

Jackson, P.R. and Wall, T.D. (1991) 'How does operator control enhance performance of advanced manufacturing technology?', *Ergonomics*, 34, 1301–1311.

Jeurissen, T. and Nyklicek, I. (2001) 'Testing the Vitamin Model of job stress in Dutch health care workers', *Work and Stress*, 15, 254–264.

Jones, F. and Bright, J. (2001) *Stress: Myth, Theory and Research*, Harlow: Pearson Education Limited.

Kahn, R.L, Wolfe, D.M., Quinn, R.P., Snoek, J.D. and Rosenthal, R.A. (1964) *Organizational Stress*, New York: Wiley.

Karasek, R.A. (1979) 'Job demands, job decision latitude, and mental strain: implications for job redesign', *Administrative Science Quarterly*, 24, 285–308.

Karasek, R.A. and Theorell, T. (1990) *Healthy Work*, New York: Basic Books.

Keane, A., Ducette, J. and Adler, D.C. (1985) 'Stress in ICU and non-ICU nurses', *Nursing Research*, 34, 231–236.

Kirjonen, J. and Hanninen, V. (1986) 'Getting a better job: antecedents and effects', *Human Relations*, 39, 503–516.

Kobasa, S.C. (1979) 'Stressful life events, personality and health: an inquiry into hardiness', *Journal of Personality and Social Psychology*, 37, 1–11.

Kompier, M.A.J. (1996) 'Job design and well-being' in M.J. Shabracq, J.A.M. Winnubst and C.L. Cooper (eds) *Handbook of Work and Health Psychology*, pp. 349–369, Chichester: John Wiley and Sons.

Kornhauser, A.W. (1965) *Mental Health of the Industrial Worker: A Detroit Study*. New York: Wiley.

Lawler, E.E. and Finegold, D. (2000) 'Individualizing the organization: past, present and future', *Organizational Dynamics*, 29, 1–15.

Lazarus, R. and Folkman, S. (1982) *Stress, Appraisal and Coping*, New York: Springer Publications.

Leach, D.J., Wall, T.D. and Jackson, P.R. (2003) 'The effect of empowerment on job knowledge: an empirical test involving operators of complex technology', *Journal of Occupational and Organizational Psychology*, 76, 27–52.

Littlewood, S., Case, R., Gater, R. and Lindsey, C. (2003) 'Recruitment, retention, satisfaction and stress in child and adolescent psychiatrists', *Psychiatric Bulletin*, 27, 61–67.

Marmot, A.F., Eley, J., Stafford, M., Stansfeld, S.A., Warwick, E. and Marmot, M.G. (2006) 'Building health: An epidemiological study of "sick building syndrome" in the Whitehall II study', *Occupational and Environment Medicine*, 63, 283–289.

McCrae, R.R. and Costa Jr, P.T. (1990) *Personality in Adulthood*, New York: Guilford.

McCranie, E.W. and Brandsma, J.M. 'Personality antecedents of burnout among middle-aged physicians', *Behavioral Medicine*, 1988, 14, 30–36.

McGregor, D. (1960) *The Human Side of Enterprise*, New York: McGraw-Hill.

Menotti, A. and Seccareccia, F. (1985) 'Physical activity at work and job responsibility as risk factors in coronary heart disease and other causes of death', *Journal of Epidemiology and Community Health*, 39, 325–329.

Michie, S. and Cockcroft A. (1996) 'Overwork can kill?' *British Medical Journal*, 312, 921–922.

Miller, D.M. (1994) 'Gaining control over the work environment', in C.L. Cooper and S. Williams (eds) *Creating Healthy Work Organizations*, Chichester: John Wiley and Sons Ltd.

Miller, S.M., Rodoletz, M., Schroeder, C.M., Mangan, C.E. and Sedlacek, T.V. (1996) 'Applications of the monitoring process model to coping with severe long-term medical threats', *Health Psychology*, 15, 216–225.

Nadaoka, T. Kashiwakura, M., Oija, A., Morioka, Y. and Totsuka, S (1997) 'Stress and psychiatric disorders in local government officials in Japan, in relation to their employment level', *Acta Psychiatrica Scandinavica*, 96, 176–183.

Nemeroff, C.B., Musselman, D.L. and Evans, D.L. (1998) 'Depression and cardiac disease', *Depression and Anxiety*, 8 (Supplement 1), 71–79.

Netterstrom, B. and Juel, K. (1988) 'Impact of work-related and psychosocial factors on the development of ischaemic heart disease among urban bus drivers in Denmark', *Scandinavian Journal of Work and Environmental Health*, 14, 231–238.

Parker, S.K., Wall, T.D. and Cordery, J.L. (2001) 'Future work design research and practice: towards an elaborated model of work design', *Journal of Occupational and Organizational Psychology*, 74, 413–440.

Parker, S.K. and Wall, T.D. (1998) *Job and Work Design: Organizing Work to Promote Well-being and Effectiveness*, San Francisco, CA: Sage.

Payne, R. (1988) 'Individual differences in the study of occupational stress', in C.L. Cooper and R. Payne (eds) *Causes, Coping and Consequences of Stress at Work*, Chichester: John Wiley and Sons.

Pearson, C.A.L. (1992) 'Autonomous work groups: an evaluation at an industrial site', *Human Relations*, 45, 905–936.

Probst, T.M. (2004) 'Safety and insecurity: exploring the moderating effect of organizational safety climate', *Journal of Occupational Health Psychology*, 9, 3–10.

Probst, T.M. and Brubaker, T.L. (2001) 'The effects of job security on employee safety outcomes: cross-sectional and longitudinal explorations', *Journal of Occupational Health Psychology*, 6, 139–159.

Rotter, J.B. (1966) 'Generalized expectancies for internal versus external control of reinforcement', *Psychological Monographs*, 91, 482–497.

Russek, H.I. and Zohman, B. (1958) 'Relative significance of heredity, diet and occupational stress in CHD among young adults', *American Journal of Medical Science*, 235, 266–275.

Schabracq, M.J., Winnubst, J.A. and Cooper, C.L. (2002) *Handbook of Work and Health Psychology*, Chichester: Wiley and Sons.

Schneider, W., and Shiffrin, R.M. (1977) 'Controlled and automatic human information processing. I. Detection, search, and attention', *Psychological Review*, 84, 1–66.

Selye, H. (1956) *The Stress of Life*, New York: McGraw-Hill.

Sloan, G. (1999) 'Good characteristics of a clinical supervisor: a community mental health perspective', *Journal of Advanced Nursing*, 30, 713.

Sparks, K., Faragher, B. and Cooper, C.L. (2001) 'Well-being and occupational health in the 21st century workplace', *Journal of Occupational and Organizational Psychology*, 74, 489–509.

Spector, P.E. Chen, P.Y. and O'Connell B.J. (2000) 'Longitudinal study of relations between job stressors and job strain while controlling for prior negative affectivity and strains', *Journal of Applied Psychology*, 85, 211–218.

Spurgeon, A. and Cooper, C.L. (2000) 'Working time, health and performance', in C.L. Cooper and I.T. Robertson (eds) *Well-Being in Organizations*, Chichester: John Wiley and Sons.

Stansfeld, S., Fuhrer, R. and Shipley, M.J. (1998) 'Types of social support as predictors of psychiatric morbidity in a cohort of British Civil Servants (Whitehall II Study)', *Psychological Medicine*, 28, 881–892.

Stansfeld, S.A., North, F.M. White, I. and Marmot, M.G. (1995) 'Work characteristics and psychiatric disorder in civil servants in London', *Journal of Epidemiology and Community Health*, 49, 48–53.

Stanton, J.M. (2000) 'Reactions to employee performance monitoring: framework, review, and research directions', *Human Performance*, 13, 85–113.

Steptoe, A. (2006) *Depression and Physical Illness*, London: Cambridge University Press.

Terry, D.J. and Jimmieson, N.L. (2001) 'Work control and employee well-being: a decade review', in C.L. Cooper and I. Robertson (eds) *Well-Being in Organizations*, Chichester: John Wiley and Sons.

Vahtera, J., Kivimaki, M. and Pentti, J. (1997) 'Effect of organizational downsizing on health of employees', *Lancet*, 350, 1124–1128.

Warr, (2007) *Work, Happiness and Unhappiness*, Mahwah, NJ: Erlbaum.

Warr, P.B. (1999) 'Well-being and the workplace', in D. Kahneman, E. Diener and N. Schwartz (eds) *Well-being: The Foundations of Hedonic Psychology*. New York: Russell Sage.

Warr, P.B. (1987a) *Work, Unemployment and Mental Health*, Oxford: Clarendon.

Warr, P.B. (1987b) *Psychology at Work*, 3rd edition, London: Penguin.

Watson, D. and Pennebaker, J.W. (1989) 'Health complaints, stress and distress: exploring the central role of negative affectivity', *Psychological Review*, 96, 234–254.

Watson, D., Clark, L.A. and Tellegen, A. (1988) 'Development and validation of brief measures of positive and negative affect: The PANAS Scales', *Journal of Personality and Social Psychology*, 54, 1063–1070.

Watson, D. and Clark, L.A. (1984) 'Negative affectivity: the disposition to experience aversive emotional states', *Psychological Bulletin*, 96, 465–490.

Weinberg, A. and Cooper, C.L. (2003) 'Stress among national politicians elected to Parliament for the first time', *Stress and Health*, 19, 111–117.

Weinberg, A. and Creed, F. (2000) 'Stress and psychiatric disorder in healthcare professionals and hospital staff', *Lancet*, 355, 533–537.

Weiss, H.M. and Cropanzano, R. (1996) 'Affective events theory: a theoretical discussion of the structure, causes and consequences of affective experiences at work', *Research in Organizational Behaviour*, 18, 1–74.

Wyatt, S., Fraser, J.A. and Stock, F.G.L. (1928) *The Comparative Effects of Variety and Uniformity in Work, Industrial Fatigue Research Board Report*, no. 52, London: HMSO.

Wylie, I. (1997) 'The human answering machines', *Guardian*, 26 July.

Zohar, D. (1980) 'Safety climate in industrial organizations: theoretical and applied implications', *Journal of Applied Psychology*, 65, 96–102.

Chapter 4

Adelmann, P.K. (1995) 'Emotional labor as a potential source of job stress', in S.L. Sauter and L.R. Murphy (eds) *Organizational Risk Factors for Stress*, pp. 371–381, Washington, DC: American Psychological Association.

Argyris, C. (1960) *Understanding Organizational Behaviour*, Homewood, IL: Dorsey Press.

Arnold, J., Cooper, C.L. and Robertson, I.T. (1998) *Work Psychology*, 3rd edn, Harlow: Prentice Hall.

Arthur, M.B., and Rousseau, D.M. (1996) 'The boundaryless career as a new employment principle', in M.B. Arthur and D.M. Rousseau (eds) *The Boundaryless Career: A New Employment Principle for a New Organizational Era*, 3–20, Oxford: Oxford University Press.

Ashforth, B.E. and Tomiuk, M.A. (2000) 'Emotional labour and authenticity: views from service agents', in S. Fineman (ed.) *Emotion in Organizations*, 2nd edition, 184–203, London: Sage.

Ashkanasy, N.M., Zerbe, W.J. and Hartel, C.E.J. (2002) *Managing Emotions in the Workplace*, New York: Sharpe.

Brotheridge, C.M. and Lee, R.T. (2003) 'Development and validation of the Emotional Labour Scale', *Journal of Occupational and Organizational Psychology*, 76, 365–379.

Constanti, P. and Gibbs, P. (2004) 'Higher education teachers and emotional labour', *International Journal of Educational Management*, 18, 243–249.

Conway, N., Briner, R.B. and Wylie, R. (1999) 'A daily diary of psychological contracts', Annual Conference of the Division of Occupational Psychology, Leicester: British Psychological Society.

Gakovic, A. and Tetrick, L.E. (2003) 'Psychological contract breach as a source of strain for employees', *Journal of Business and Psychology*, 18, 235.

Giga, S.I. and Cooper, C.L. (2003) 'Psychological contracts within the NHS', *Human Givens Journal*, 10, 38–40.

Glomb, T.M. and Tews, M.J. (2004) 'Emotional labor: a conceptualization and scale development', *Journal of Vocational Behaviour*, 64, 1–23.

Goffman, E. (1959) *The Presentation of Self in Everyday Life*, New York: Anchor Books.

Gorman, H. (2000) 'Winning hearts and minds? Emotional labour and learning for care management work', *Journal of Social Work Practice*, 14, 149–158.

Guest, D., Conway, N., Briner, R. and Dickman, M. (1996) *The State of the Psychological Contract in Employment*, London: Institute of Personnel and Development.

Handy, C. (1989) *The Age of Unreason*, London: Business Books.

Harris, L.C. (2002) 'The emotional labour of barristers: an exploration of emotional labour by status professionals', *Journal of Management Studies*, 39, 4, 553–581.

Hartel, C.E.J., Hsu, A.C.F. and Boyle, M.V. (2002) 'A conceptual examination of the causal sequences of emotional labor, emotional dissonance, and emotional exhaustion: the argument for the role of contextual and provider characteristics', in N.M. Ashkanasy, W.J. Zerbe and C.E.J. Hartel, *Managing Emotions in the Workplace*, pp. 251–275, New York: Sharpe.

Herriot, P. and Pemberton, C. (1995) *New Deals*, Chichester: Wiley.

Hochschild, A.R. (1983) *The Managed Heart: Commercialization of Human Feeling*, Berkeley, CA: University of California Press.

Kinman, G. and Jones, F. (2004) *Working to the Limit*, London: AUT.

Langan-Fox, J. (2001) 'Women's careers and occupational stress', in C.L. Cooper and I. Robertson (eds), *Well-Being in Organizations*, pp. 177–208, Chichester: John Wiley and Sons.

Morris, J.A. and Feldman, D.C. (1996) 'The dimensions, antecedents, and consequences of emotional labor', *Academy of Management Review*, 21, 986–1010.

Peters, T. and Waterman, R.H. (1982) *In Search of Excellence: Lessons from America's Best-Run Companies*, London: Harper and Row.

Rafaeli, A. and Sutton, R.I. (1990) 'Busy stores and demanding customers: how do they affect the display of positive emotion?' *Academy of Management Journal*, 32, 245–273.

Robinson, S.L. and Rousseau, D.M. (1994) 'Violating the psychological contract: not the exception but the norm', *Journal of Organizational Behaviour*, 15, 245–259.

Rousseau, D.M. (2004) 'Psychological contracts in the workplace: understanding the ties that motivate', *Academy of Management Executive*, 18, 120.

Rousseau, D.M. (2003) 'Extending the psychology of the psychological contract; a reply to "putting psychology back into psychological contracts",' *Journal of Management Inquiry*, 12, 229.

Rousseau, D.M. (1995) *Psychological Contracts in Organizations: Understanding Written and Unwritten Agreements*, London: Sage.

Schein, E.H. (1980) *Organizational Psychology*, 3rd edition, Englewood Cliffs, NJ: Prentice-Hall.

Shimmin, S. and Wallis, D. (1994) *Fifty years of Occupational Psychology*, Leicester: British Psychological Society.

Smither, R. (1998) *The Psychology of Work and Human Performance*, New York: Longman.

Strazdins, L. (2002) 'Emotional work and emotional contagion', in N.M. Ashkanasy, W.J. Zerbe and C.E.J. Hartel, *Managing Emotions in the Workplace*, pp. 232–250, New York: Sharpe.

Sunday Times (2006) *The 100 Best Companies to Work For*, London: *Sunday Times*.

Terkel, S. (1972) *Working*, New York: Avon Books.

Turnley, W.H. and Feldman, D.C. (2000) 'Re-examining the effects of psychological contract violations: unmet expectations and job dissatisfaction as mediators', *Journal of Organizational Behaviour*, 21, 1–25.

Van Maanen, J. and Kunda, G. (1989) 'Real feelings: emotional expression and organizational culture', *Research in Organizational Behaviour*, 11, 43–103.

Weinberg, A., Williamson, J. Challis, D. and Hughes, J. (2003) 'What do care managers do? A study of working practices in older peoples' services', *British Journal of Social Work*, 33, 901–919.

Wharton, A.S. (1993) 'The affective consequences of service work: managing emotions on the job', *Work and Occupation*, 20, 205–232.

Chapter 5

Aaras, A., Horgen, G. and Ro, O. (2000) 'Work with the display unit: health consequences', *International Journal of Human-Computer Interaction*, 12, 107–134.

Arnold, J., Sylvester, J., Patterson, F., Robertson, I.,Cooper, C.L. and Burnes, B. (1998) *Work Psychology*, 3rd edition, Harlow: Pearson Education Limited.

Batt, R. (1999) 'Work organization, technology and performance in customer service sales', *Industrial and Labour Relations Review*, 52, 539–564.

Bower, M. (1966) 'Company philosophy: the way we do things around here', in *The Will to Manage: Corporate Success through Programmed Management*, Colombus, OH: McGraw-Hill.

Carayon, P. (1994) 'Effects of electronic performance monitoring on job design and worker stress: results of two studies', *International Journal of Human–Computer Interaction*, 6, 177–190.

Cassidy, S. (2002) 'A social psychological perspective on mobile phone use', *Proceedings of the British Psychological Society*, 11.

Chmiel, N. (1998) *Jobs, Technology and People*, London: Routledge.

Clegg, C., Coleman, P., Hornby, P., McClaren, R., Robson, J., Carey, N. and Symon, G. (1996) 'Tools to incorporate some psychologiclal and organizational issues during the development of computer-based systems', *Ergonomics*, 39, 482–511.

Cooper, C.L. (2000) 'Home is where the tele-rage awaits', *Sunday Times*, 6 February.

Dedobbeleer, N. and Beland, F. (1991) 'A safety climate measure for construction sites', *Journal of Safety Research*, 22, 97–103.

Ekberg, K, Eklund, J., Tuvesson, M., Oertengren, R., Odenrick, P. and Ericson, M. (1995) 'Psychological stress and muscle activity during data entry at visual display units', *Work and Stress*, 9, 475–490.

Finholt, T. and Sproull, L. (1990) 'Electronic groups at work', *Organization Science*, 1, 41–64.

Guardian (2005) 'Bosses say "yes" to home work', 26 May.

Haynes, R.S., Pine, R.C. and Fitch, H.G. (1982) 'Reducing accident rates with organizational behaviour modification', *Academy of Management Journal*, 25, 407–416.

Holman, D., Wall, T.D., Clegg, C., Sparrow, P. and Howard, A. (2002) *The New Workplace*, Chichester: Wiley.

Holman, D., Wall, T.D., Clegg, C., Sparrow, P. and Howard, A. (2004) *The Essentials of the New Workplace*, Chichester: Wiley.

Houtman, I.L.D. (1999) 'The changing workplace', in *Work, Stress and Health 1999: Organization of Work in a Global Economy*, Conference Proceedings (abstracts), March, APA and NIOSH, Washington, DC: American Psychological Association.

HSE (2006) Statistics on fatal and non-fatal accidents by occupational grouping, accessed at http//:www.statistics.gov.uk/STATBASE/ssdataset.asp?vlnk= 3986, 11 August 2006.

Jackson, P.R. and Wall, T.D. (1991) 'How does operator control enhance performance of advanced manufacturing technology?', *Ergonomics*, 34, 1301–1311.

Kelly, J. (1982) *Scientific Management, Job Redesign and Work Performance*, London: Academic Press.

Langan-Fox, J. (2005) 'New technology, the global economy and organizational environments: effects on employee stress, health and well-being', in A-S. Antoniou and C.L. Cooper (eds) *Research Companion to Organizational Health Psychology*, Cheltenham: Edward Elgar.

Liff, S. (1990) 'Clerical workers and information technology: gender relations and occupational change', *New Technology, Work and Employment*, 5, 44–55.

Parker, S.K., Wall, T.D. and Cordery, J.L. (2001) 'Future work design research and practice: towards an elaborated model of work design', *Journal of Occupational and Organizational Psychology*, 74, 413–440.

Parkinson, B. and Lea, M. (2005) 'Video-linking emotions', in A. Kappas (ed.) *Face-to-Face Communication over the Internet: Issues, Research, Challenges*, Cambridge: Cambridge University Press.

Reason, J.T. (1990) *Human Error*, Cambridge: Cambridge University Press.

Reason, J.T. and Mycielska, K. (1982) *Absent-Minded? The Psychology of Mental Lapses and Everyday Errors*, Englewood Cliffs, NJ: Prentice-Hall.

Schein, E. (1992) *Organizational Culture and Leadership*, 2nd edition, San Francisco, CA: Jossey-Bass.

Sparks, K., Faragher, B. and Cooper, C.L. (2001) 'Well-being and occupational health in the 21st century workplace', *Journal of Occupational and Organizational Psychology*, 74, 489–509.

Stanton, J.M. (2000) 'Reactions to employee performance monitoring: framework, review and research directions', *Human Performance*, 13, 85–113.

Symon, G. (2000) 'Information and communication technologies and the network organization: a critical analysis', *Journal of Occupational and Organizational Psychology*, 73, 389–414.

Terry, D.J. and Jimmieson, N.L. (2001) 'Work control and employee well-being: a decade review', in C.L. Cooper and I. Robertson (eds) *Well-Being in Organizations*, Chichester: John Wiley and Sons.

Trice, H.M. and Beyer, J.M. (1984) 'Studying organizational cultures through rites and rituals', *Academy of Management Review*, 9, 653–669.

Trist, E. and Bamforth, K. (1951) 'Some social and psychological consequences of the longwall method of coal-getting', *Human Relations*, 4, 3–38.

Wall, T.D. and Davids, K. (1992) 'Shopfloor work organization and advanced manufacturing technology', in C.L. Cooper and I.T. Robertson (eds) *International Review of Industrial and Organizational Psychology*, vol. 7, 363–398, Chichester: Wiley.

Waterson, P.E., Clegg, C.W., Bolden, R., Pepper, K., Warr, P.B. and Wall, T.D. (1999) 'The use and effectiveness of modern manufacturing practices: a survey of UK industry', *International Journal of Production Research*, 37, 2271–2292.

Wilen, J., Sandstrom, M. and Hansson Mild, K. (2002) 'Subjective symptoms among mobile phone users – a consequence of absorption of radiofrequency fields?', *Bioelectromagnetics Society*, 24th Annual Meeting, Quebec.

Chapter 6

Adler, A. (1933) *What Life Should Mean to You*, London: Unwin Books.

Ambady, N. (1993) 'Half a minute: predicting teacher evaluations from thin slices of non-verbal behaviour and physical attractiveness', *Journal of Personality and Social Psychology*, 64, 431–441.

Bar-On, R. (1997) *The Emotional Intelligence Inventory (EQ-i): Technical Manual*, Toronto: Multi-Health Systems.

Ben Ze'ev, A. (2002) 'Emotional intelligence: the conceptual issue', in N.M. Ashkanasy, W.J. Zerbe and C.E.J. Hartel, *Managing Emotions in the Workplace*, pp. 251–275, New York: Sharpe.

Boyatzis, R.E. (2005) 'Developing leadership through emotional intelligence', in A.-S.G. Antoniou and C.L. Cooper, *Research Companion to Organizational Health Psychology*, pp. 656–660, Cheltenham: Edward Elgar.

Carnegie, D. (1938) *How to Win Friends and Influence People*, Suffolk: The Chaucer Press.

Caruso, D.R. and Wolfe, C.J. (2001) 'Emotional intelligence in the workplace', in J. Ciarrochi, J.P. Forgas and J.D. Mayer (eds) *Emotional Intelligence in Everday Life*, pp. 150–167, Hove: Psychology Press.

Cherniss, C. and Goleman, D. (eds) (2001) *The Emotionally Intelligent Workplace*, Chichester: John Wiley and Sons.

Dawda, D. and Hart, S.D. (2001) 'Assessing emotional intelligence: reliability and validity of the Bar-On Emotional Quotient (EQ-i) in university students', *Personality and Individual Differences*, 28, 797–812.

Dulewicz, V. and Higgs, M. (1999) 'Can emotional intelligence be measured and developed?', *Leadership and Organizational Development Journal*, 20, 242–253.

Dulewicz, V. and Higgs, K. (2001) *EI General and General 360 Degree User Guide*, Windsor: NFER-Nelson.

Einarsen, S. (1996) 'Bullying and harassment at work: epidemiological and psychological aspects', PhD thesis, Department of Psychological Sciences, University of Bergen.

Einarsen, S., Hoel, H., Zapf, D. and Cooper, C.L. (eds) (2003) *Bullying and Emotional Abuse in the Workplace: International perspectives in research and practice*, London: Taylor and Francis.

Elias, M.J., Hunter, L. and Kress, J.S. (2001) 'Emotional intelligence and education', in J. Ciarrochi, J.P. Forgas and J.D. Mayer (eds) *Emotional Intelligence in Everday Life*, pp. 133–149, Hove: Psychology Press.

Fineman, S. (ed) (2000) *Emotion in Organizations*, 2nd edition, London: Sage.

Fletcher, C. (2006) Editorial review. http://www.amazon.com/Hard-Truth-About-Soft-Selling-Profession/dp/093507084, accessed 21 November.

Flury, J. and Ickes, W. (2001) 'Emotional intelligence and empathic accuracy', in J. Ciarrochi, J.P. Forgas and J.D. Mayer (eds) *Emotional Intelligence in Everday Life*, pp. 113–132, Hove: Psychology Press.

Gardner, H.A. (1983) *Frames of Mind*, New York: Basic Books.

Gibbs, N. (1995) 'What's your EQ?' *Time*, 2 October.

Goleman, D. (2000) 'Intelligent leadership', *Executive Excellence*, 3, 17.

Goleman, D. (1998a) *Working with Emotional Intelligence*, London: Bloomsbury.

Goleman, D. (1998b) 'The emotional intelligence of leaders', *Leader to Leader*, 20–26.

Goleman, D. (1995) *Emotional Intelligence*, New York: Bantam Books.

Guardian (1997) 'Met chief: 'Criminals in my force', 7 October.

Hayes, J. (2002) *Interpersonal Skills at Work*, New York: Routledge.

Hoel, H., Cooper, C.L. and Faragher (2001) 'The experience of bullying in the UK, the impact of organizational status', *European Journal of Work and Organizational Psychology*, 10, 443–465.

Hoel, H., Faragher, B. and Cooper, C.L. (2004) 'Bullying is detrimental to health, but all bullying behaviours are not equally damaging', *British Journal of Guidance and Counselling*, 32, 367–387.

Hoel, H., Rayner, C. and Cooper, C.L. (2001) 'Workplace bullying', in C.L. Cooper and I. Robertson (eds) *Well-Being in Organizations*, pp. 55–90, Chichester: John Wiley and Sons Ltd.

Jordan, P.J. Ashkanasy, N.M., Hartel, C.E.J. and Hooper, G.S. (2002) 'Workgroup emotional intelligence: scale development and relationship to team process effectiveness and goal focus', *Human Resource Management Review*, 12, 195–214.

Mayer, J.D. (2001) 'A field guide to emotional intelligence', in J. Ciarrochi, J.P. Forgas and J.D. Mayer (eds) *Emotional Intelligence in Everday Life*, pp. 3–24, Hove: Psychology Press.

Mayer, J.D., Ciarrochi, J. and Forgas, J.P. (2001) 'Emotional intelligence and everyday life: an introduction', in J. Ciarrochi, J.P. Forgas and J.D. Mayer (eds) *Emotional Intelligence in Everday Life*, Hove: Psychology Press.

Mayer, J.D., Caruso, D. and Salovey, P. (1999) 'Emotional intelligence meets traditional standards for an intelligence', *Intelligence*, 27, 267–298.

Miguel-Tobal, J.J. and Gonzalez-Ordi, H. (2005) The role of emotions in cardiovascular disorders, in A-S. Antoniou and C.L. Cooper (eds) *Research Companion to Organizational Health Psychology*, pp. 455–477, Cheltenham: Edward Elgar.

Nemiah, J.C., Freyberger, H. and Sifneos, P.E. (1976) Alexithymia: a view of the psychosomatic process, in O.W. Hill (ed.) *Modern Trends in Psychosomatic Medicine*, vol. 3, pp. 430–439, London: Butterworths.

O'Moore, A.M. and Hillery, B. (1988) 'Bullying in Dublin schools', *Irish Jouranl of Psychology*, 10, 426–441.

Petrides, K.V. and Furnham, A. (2000) 'On the dimensional structure of emotional intelligence', *Personality and Individual Differences*, 29, 313–320.

Quine, L. (1999) 'Workplace bullying in NHS community trust: staff questionnaire survey', *British Medical Journal*, 318, 228–232.

Randall, P. (1997) *Adult Bullying: Perpetrators and Victims*, London: Routledge.

Rayner, C. and Hoel, H. (1997) 'A summary review of literature relating to workplace bullying', *Journal of Community and Applied Psychology*, 7, 181–191.

Salovey, P. and Mayer, J.D. (1990) 'Emotional intelligence', *Imagination, Cognition, and Personality*, 9, 185–211.

Standard (2005) 'Asia slowly shifts to shorter working week', 28 September.

Stansfeld, S., Fuhrer, R and Shipley, M.J. (1998) 'Types of social support as predictors of psychiatric morbidity in a cohort of British Civil Servants (Whitehall II Study)', *Psychological Medicine*, 28, 881–892.

Tanner, J.F. and Dudley, G. (2003) *International Differences – Examining Two Assumptions about Selling*, accessed at http//:business.baylor.edu/web/DEPT/COMM&MKT/SMA2003paper.pdf, 10 August 2006.

Taylor, G.J. (2001) 'Low emotional intelligence and mental illness', in J. Ciarrochi, J.P. Forgas and J.D. Mayer (eds) *Emotional Intelligence in Everday Life*, pp. 67–81, Hove: Psychology Press.

Taylor, G.J. (2000) 'Recent developments in alexithymia theory and research', *Canadian Journal of Psychiatry*, 45, 134–142.

Taylor, G.J. and Bagby, R.M. (2000) 'Overview of the alexithymia construct', in R. Bar-On and J.D.A. Parker (eds) *Handbook of Emotional Intelligence*, pp. 40–67, San Francisco, CA: Jossey Bass.

Taylor, G.J., Parker, J.D.A. and Bagby, R.M. (1999) 'Emotional intelligence and the emotional brain: points of convergence and implications for psycho-analysis', *Journal of the American Academy of Psychoanalysis*, 27, 339–354.

Unison (1997) *Bullying at Work*, Survey report, London: Unison.

Vartia, M. and Hyyti, J. (2002) 'Gender differences in workplace bullying among prison officers', *European Journal of Work and Organizational Psychology*, 11, 113–127.

Vartia, M. (1996) 'The sources of bullying: psychological work environment and organizational climate', *European Journal of Work and Organizational Psychology*, 5, 203–214.

Waldron, V.R. (2000) 'Relational experiences and emotion at work', in S. Fine-man (ed.) *Emotion in Organizations*, 2nd edition, London: Sage.

Weinberg, A. and Creed, F. (2000) 'Stress and psychiatric disorder in healthcare professionals and hospital staff', *Lancet*, 355, 533–537.

Weinberg, A. and Pearson, A. (2005) 'Emotional intelligence among psychology undergraduates – a competitive edge?' *Proceedings of the British Psychological Society*, 14, 2.

Wong, C-S, Foo, M-D, Wang, C-W and Wong, P-M (2006) The feasibility of training and development of emotional intelligence: An exploratory study in Singapore, Hong Kong and Taiwan, *Intelligence*, in press; available online at http://www.sciencedirect.com/science?_ob=ArticleURL&_udi=B6W4m-4KF1HPK_2&_user=494590&_CoverDate=07%2F17%2F2006&_alid=493698576&_rdoc=1&_fmt=full&_orig=search&_cdi=6546&_sort=d&_docanchor=&viewc&_acct=c000024058&_version=1&_urlVersion=0&_userid=494590&md5=666fdo1406027c89c78309101ff3f48c

Zapf, D., Knortz, C. and Kulla, M. (1996) 'On the relationship between mobbing factors and job content, social work environment, and health outcomes', *European Journal of Work and Organizational Psychology*, 5, 215–237.

Zerbe, W.J., Hartel, C.E.J. and Ashkanasy, N.M. (2002) Emotional labor and the design of work, in N.M. Ashkanasy, W.J. Zerbe and C.E.J. Hartel, *Managing Emotions in the Workplace*, pp. 276–284, New York: Sharpe.

Chapter 7

Abdalla, I.A. and Al-Homoud, M.A. (2001) 'Implicit leadership theory in the Arabian Gulf States', *Applied Psychology: An International Review*, 50, 506–531.

Antoniou, A-S,G. (2005) 'Emotional intelligence and transformational leadership', in A-S. Antoniou and C.L. Cooper (eds) *Research Companion to Organizational Health Psychology*, pp. 633–655, Cheltenham: Edward Elgar.

Arnold, J., Sylvester, J., Patterson, F., Robertson, I., Cooper, C.L. and Burnes, B. (2005) *Work Psychology*, 4th edition, Harlow: Pearson Education Limited.

Bain and Co. (1995) 'The Planning Forum, "Management tools and techniques: Survey results summary"', Boston, MA: Bain and Co.

Barling, J., Moutinho, S. and Kelloway, E.H. (2000) *Transformational Leadership and Group Performance: The Mediating Role of Affective Commitment*, Kingston, Ontario: Queen's University.

Bennis, W. (1994) *On Becoming a Leader*, New York: Addison Wesley.

Blake, R.R. and Mouton, J.S. (1964) *The Managerial Grid*, Houston, TX: Gulf Publishing.

Blanchard, K.H. and Johnson, S. (2000) *The One Minute Manager*, New York: HarperCollins.

Bordia, P., Hobman, E., Jones, E., Gallois, C. and Callan, V.J. (2004) 'Uncertainty during organizational change: types, consequences and management strategies', *Journal of Business and Psychology*, 18, 507–532.

Borrill, C.S., Wall, T.D., West, M.A., Hardy, G.E., Shapiro, D.A., Haynes, C.E., Stride, C.B., Woods, D. and Carter, A.J. (1998) *Stress among Staff in NHS Trusts: Final Report*, Institute of Work Psychology, University of Sheffield and Psychological Therapies Research Centre, University of Leeds.

Boyatzis, R. (2005) 'Developing leadership through emotional intelligence', in A-S. Antoniou and C.L. Cooper (eds) *Research Companion to Organizational Health Psychology*, pp. 599–622, Cheltenham: Edward Elgar.

Brodbeck, F.C., Brenk, K., Castel, P., *et al.* (2000) 'Cultural variation of leadership prototypes across 22 European countries', *Journal of Occupational and Organizational Psychology*, 73, 1–29.

Burns, J.M. (1978) *Leadership*, New York: Harper and Row.

Conger, J.A., Kanungo, R.N. and Menon, S.T. (2000) 'Charismatic leadership and follower effects', *Journal of Organizational Behaviour*, 21, 747–767.

Cooper, C.L. and Robertson, I. (eds) (2001) *Well-being in Organizations*, Chichester: Wiley and Sons.

Ekman, P. (2003) *Gripped by Emotion*, New York: Times Books, Henry Holt.

Fiedler, F.E. (1995) 'Cognitive resources and leadership performance', *Applied Psychology: An International Review*, 44, 5–28.

Firth-Cozens, J. (1994) *Stress in Doctors: A Longitudinal Study*, Report for the Department of Health, Leeds: University of Leeds.

Gardner, L. and Stough, C. (2002) 'Examining the relationship between leadership and emotional intelligence in senior level managers', *Leadership and Organization Development Journal*, 23, 68–78.

Goleman, D. (1998) *Working with Emotional Intelligence*, London: Bloomsbury.

Guardian (2005) 'Too many chilled-out entertainers?' 26 May.

Handy, C. (1999) 'The Midas touch: Can it be taught?' *The Times*, 4 October.

Handy, C.B. (1995) *The Empty Raincoat*, London: Random House.

Higgs, M. (2005) 'Leading from the front', *Sunday Times*, 6 February.

Hoel, H. and Cooper, C.L. (2000) *Workplace Bullying in Britain*, Manchester: UMIST.

Hofstede, G. (2001) *Culture's Consequences*, 2nd edition, London: Sage.

Hofstede, G. (1980) *Culture's Consequences: International Differences in Work-Related Values*, London: Sage.

Judge, T.A. and Bono, J.E. (2000) 'Five-factor model of personality and transformational leadership', *Journal of Applied Psychology*, 85, 751–765.

Kapstein, J. (1989) 'Volvo's radical new plant: the death of the assembly line', *Business Week*, 28 August, 92–93.

Karasek, R.A. and Theorell, T. (1990) *Healthy Work*, New York: Basic Books.

Machiavelli, N. (1984) *The Prince*, trans. P. Bondarella, Oxford: Oxford University Press.

Marcus Aurelius (1964) *Meditations*, trans. M. Staniforth, Harmondsworth: Penguin.

Meyer, J. (2002) 'Coaching and counselling in organizational psychology', in M. Schabracq, J.A.M. Winnubst and C.L. Cooper (eds) *The Handbook of Work and Health Psychology*, Chichester: John Wiley and Sons.

Micklethwait, J. and Wooldridge, A. (1996) *The Witch Doctors*, London: Heinemann.

Pearce, J.L. and Henderson, G.R. (2001) 'Understanding acts of betrayal: implications for industrial and organizational psychology', in C.L. Cooper and I. Robertson, *Well-Being in Organizations*, Chichester: John Wiley and Sons.

Peters, T. and Waterman, R.H. (1982) *In Search of Excellence: Lessons from America's Best-Run Companies*, London: Harper and Row.

Pugh, D.S. and Hickson, D.J. (1996) *Writers on Organizations*, 5th edition, London: Penguin.

Sunday Times (2006) 'Modern coaching takes centre stage', 30 April.

Sunday Times (2005) *The 100 Best Companies to Work For*, Supplement.

Weinberg, A. and Creed, F. (2000) 'Stress and psychiatric disorder in healthcare professionals and hospital staff', *Lancet*, 355, 533–537.

Worrall, L. and Cooper, C.L. (2001) 'The long working hours culture', *European Business Forum*, 6, 48–53.

Yukl, G. (1998) *Leadership in Organizations*, 4th edition, Englewood Cliffs, NJ: Prentice-Hall.

Chapter 8

Allen, T. (2001) 'Family-supportive work environments: the role of organizational perceptions', *Journal of Vocational Behaviour*, 58, 414–435.

Bacharach, S.B., Bamberger, P. and Conley, S. (1991) 'Work–home conflict among nurses and engineers: mediating the impact of role stress on burnout and satisfaction at work', *Journal of Organizational Behaviour*, 12, 39–53.

Brough, P. and O'Driscoll, M. (2005) 'Work–family conflict and stress', in A-S. Antoniou and C.L. Cooper (eds) *Research Companion to Organizational Health Psychology*, pp. 346–365, Cheltenham: Edward Elgar.

Brown, G.W. and Harris, T. (1978) *Social Origins of Depression - A Study of Psychiatric Disorder in Women*, London: Routledge.

Bureau of Labor Statistics (1997) 'Workers are on the job more hours over the course of a year', *Issues in Labor Statistics*, Summary, 97, 3, Washington, DC: US Department of Labor.

Carr, D. (2002) 'The psychological consequences of work-family trade-offs for three cohorts of men and women', *Social Psychology Quarterly*, 65, 103–124.

Carlson, D.S. and Kacmar, K.M. (2000) 'Work–family conflict in the organization: do life role values make a difference?' *Journal of Management*, 26, 1031–1054.

Chabot, J. (1992) 'Dual earner families and the care of the elderly in Japan', in S. Lewis, D.N. Izraeli and H. Hootsmans (eds) *Dual Earner Families: International Perspectives*, pp. 172–184, London: Sage.

Cooper, C.L. and Lewis, S. (1998) *Balancing your Career, Family and Life*, London: Kogan Page.

Costa, G., Akerstedt, T., Nachreiner, F., *et al.* (2004) 'Flexible working hours, health and well-being in Europe: Some considerations from a SALTSA Project', *Chronobiology International*, 21.

Eby, L.T., Casper, W., Lockwood, A., Bordeaux and Brinley, A. (2005) 'Work and family research in IO/OB: content analysis and review of the literature', *Journal of Vocational Behaviour*, 66, 124–197.

Frone, M.R. (2003) 'Work–family balance', in J.C. Quick and L.E. Tetrick (eds), *Handbook of Occupational Health Psychology*, pp. 143–162, Washington, DC: American Psychological Association.

Frone, M.R. and Yardley, J.K. (1996) 'Workplace family-supportive programmes: predictors of employed parents' ratings', *Journal of Occupational and Organizational Psychology*, 69, 351–366.

Grandey, A.A., Cordeiro, B.L. and Crouter, A.C. (2005) 'A longitudinal and multi-source test of the work-family conflict and job satisfaction relationship', *Journal of Occupational and Organizational Psychology*, 78, 305–324.

Grandey, A.A. and Cropanzano, R. (1999) 'The conservation of resources model applied to work-family conflict and strain', *Journal of Vocational Behaviour*, 54, 350–370.

Greenhaus, J.H. and Beutell, N.J. (1985) 'Sources of conflict between work and family roles', *Academy of Management Review*, 10, 76–88.

Guardian (2005) 'Suicide blights China's young adults', 26 July.

Guardian (2006) 'Japan to tell its workers: take time off – for the sake of the nation', 17 January.

Haynes, S.G., Eaker, E.D. and Feinleib, M. (1984) 'The effects of unemployment, family and job stress on coronary heart disease patterns in women', in

E.B. Gold (ed.) *The Changing Risk of Disease in Women: An Epidemiological Approach*, pp. 37–48, Lexington, MA: Heath.

Hochschild, A. (1997) *The Time Bind: When Work Becomes Home and Home Becomes Work*, New York: Holt.

ISR (1995) *Employee Satisfaction: Tracking European Trends*, London: ISR.

Kanter, R.M. (1977) *Men and Women of the Corporation*, New York: Basic Books.

Kinnunen, U., Mauno, S., Geurts, S. and Dikkers, J. (2005) 'Work–family culture: theoretical and empirical approaches', in S. Poelmans (ed.) *Work and Family: An International Research Perspective*, pp. 87–120, Mahwah, NJ: Lawrence Erlbaum Associates.

Kushner, K.E. and Harrison, M.J. (2002) 'Employed mothers: stress and balance-focused coping', *Canadian Journal of Nursing Research*, 34, 47–65.

Lancet (1998) 'Prevention and treatment of occupational mental disorders', *Lancet*, editorial, 352, 26 September.

Lewis, S. and Cooper, C.L. (1999) 'The work–family research agenda in changing contexts', *Journal of Occupational Health Psychology*, 4, 382–393.

Luk, D.M. and Shaffer, M. (2005) 'Work and family domain stressors and support: within- and cross-domain influences on work-family conflict', *Journal of Occupational and Organizational Psychology*, 78, 489–509.

MacEwen, K.E. and Barling, J. (1994) 'Daily consequences of work interference with family and family interference with work', *Work and Stress*, 8, 244–254.

Major, V.S., Klein, K.J. and Ehrhart, M.G. (2002) 'Work time, work interference with family, and psychological distress', *Journal of Applied Psychology*, 87, 427–436.

Matsui, T., Ohsawa, T. and Onglatco, M.L. (1995) 'Work–family conflict and stress-buffering effects of husband support and coping behaviour among Japanese married working women', *Journal of Vocational Behaviour*, 47, pp. 178–192.

Mauno, S., Kinnunen, U. and Pyykko, M. (2005) 'Does work–family conflict mediate the relationship between work–family culture and self-reported distress? Evidence from five Finnish organizations', *Journal of Occupational and Organizational Psychology*, 78, 509–531.

Noor, N.M. (2002) 'The moderating effect of spouse support on the relationship between work variables and women's work–family conflict', *Psychologia: An International Journal of Psychology in the Orient*, 45, 12–23.

O'Driscoll, M.P., Poelmans, S., Spector, P.E., Kalliath, T., Allen, T.D., Cooper, C.L. and Sanchez, J.I. (2003) 'Family-responsive interventions, perceived organizational and supervisor support, work–family conflict, and psychological strain', *International Journal of Stress Management*, 10, 326–344.

Phelan, J. Schwartz, J.E., Bromet, E.J., Dew, M.A., Parkinson, D.K., Schulberg, H.C., Dunn, L.O., Blane, H. and Curtis, E.C. (1991) 'Work stress, family stress and depression in professional and managerial employees', *Psychological Medicine*, 21, 381–392.

Rout, U., Cooper, C.L. and Kerslake, H. (1997) 'Working and non-working mothers: a comparative study', *Women in Management Review*, 12, 264–275.

Sennett, R. (1998) 'Why good workers make bad people', *New Statesman*, 9 October, 15–27.

Shellenbarger, S. (1992) 'Lessons from the workplace: how corporate policies and attitudes lag behind workers' changing needs', *Human Resource Management*, 31, 157–169.

Snow, D.L., Swan, S.C., Raghavan, C., Connell, C.M. and Klein, I. (2003) 'The relationship of work stressors, coping and social support to psychological symptoms among female secretarial employees', *Work and Stress*, 17, 241–263.

Standard (2005) 'Asia slowly shifts to shorter working week', 28 September.

Tausig, M. and Fenwick, R. (2001) 'Unbinding time: alternate work schedules and work–life balance', *Journal of Family and Economic Issues*, 22, 101–119.

Thomas, L.T. and Thomas, J.T. (1990) 'The ABCs of child care: building blocks of competitive advantage', *Sloan Management Review*, 31, 31–41.

Thompson, C., Beauvais, L. and Lyness, K. (1999) 'When work–family benefits are not enough: the influence of work–family culture on benefit utilization, organizational attachment and work–family conflict', *Journal of Vocational Behaviour*, 54, 392–415.

Weinberg, A. and Cooper, C.L. (2003) 'Stress among national politicians elected to Parliament for the first time', *Stress and Health*, 19, 111–117.

Weinberg, A. and Creed, F. (2000) 'Stress and psychiatric disorder in healthcare professionals and hospital staff', *Lancet*, 355, 533–537.

Worrall, L. and Cooper, C.L. (2001) 'The long working hours culture', *European Business Forum*, 6, 48–53.

Chapter 9

Appleby, L., Amos, T., Doyle, U., Tomenson, B. and Woodman, M. (1996) 'General practitioners and young suicides: a preventative role for primary care', *British Journal of Psychiatry*, 168, 330–333.

Aron, A., Aron, E.N. and Coups, E.J. (2005) *Statistics for the Behavioural and Social Sciences*, 3rd edition, Upper Saddle River, NJ: Prentice Hall.

Bar-On, R. (2002) *Bar-On Emotional Quotient Inventory: Technical Manual*, New York: Multi-Health Systems.

Beck, A.T., Ward, C.H., Mendelson, M., Mock, J. and Erbaugh, J. (1961) An inventory for measuring depression. *Archives of General Psychiatry*, 4, 561–571.

Birdi, K.S., Warr, P.B. and Oswald, A. (1995) 'Age differences in three components of employee well-being', *Applied Psychology: An International Review*, 44, 345–373.

Borrill, C.S., Wall, T.D., West, M.A., Hardy, G.E., Shapiro, D.A., Haynes, C.E., Stride, C.B., Woods, D. and Carter, A.J. (1998) *Stress among Staff in NHS*

Trusts: Final Report, Institute of Work Psychology, University of Sheffield and Psychological Therapies Research Centre, University of Leeds, Sheffield: University of Sheffield.

Bowling, A. and Ebrahim, S. (2005) *Handbook of Health Research Methods: Investigation, Measurement and Analysis*, Maidenhead: McGraw Hill.

Brief, A.P., Burke, M.J., George, J.M., Robinson, B.S. and Webster, J. (1988) 'Should negative affectivity remain an unmeasured variable in the study of job stress?' *Journal of Applied Psychology*, 73, 193–198.

British Medical Association (1993) *The Morbidity and Mortality of the Medical Profession*. London: BMA.

Brodman, K., Erdmann, A.J.J., Lorge, I. and Wolff, H.G. (1949) 'The Cornell Medical Index: an adjunct to medical interview', *Journal of the American Medical Association*, 140, 530–534.

Ciarrochi, J. Chan, A., Caputi, P. and Roberts, R. (2001) 'Measuring emotional intelligence', in J. Ciarrochi, J.P. Forgas and J.D. Mayer (eds) *Emotional Intelligence in Everday Life*, pp. 25–45, Hove: Psychology Press.

Clarkson, P. and Lynch, S. (1998) 'Screening for depression in primary care: a review of current instruments and their use in detection', *Primary Care Psychiatry*, 4, 4, 179–188.

Cohen, P.Y. and Spector, P.E. (1991) 'Negative affectivity as the underlying cause of correlations between stressors and strains', *Journal of Applied Psychology*, 76, 398–407.

Cooper, C.L. and Marshall, J. (1978) *Understanding Executive Stress*, London: Macmillan.

Cooper, C.L., Sloan, S.J. and Williams, S. (1988) *Occupational Stress Indicator*. Windsor: NFER-Nelson.

Daniels, K., Brough P., Guppy, A., Peters-Bean, K.M. and Weatherstone, L. (1997) 'A note on modification to Warr's measures of affective well-being at work', *Journal of Occupational and Organizational Psychology*, 70, 129–138.

Dulewicz, V. and Higgs, K. (2005) *Emotional Intelligence Questionnaire*, London: ASE.

Davey Smith, G., Macleod, J., Hart, C., Heslop, P. and Metcalfe, C. (2001) 'Psycho-social stress, lifestyle and socio-economic inequalities in morbidity and mortality', *Research Findings from the Health Variations Programme*, September, Lancaster: ESRC.

Faragher, B., Cooper, C.L. and Cartwright, S. (2004) 'A shortened stress evaluation tool (ASSET)', *Stress and Health*, 20, 189–201.

Fletcher, B.C. (1988) 'The epidemiology of occupational stress', in C.L. Cooper and R. Payne, *Causes, Coping and Consequences of Stress*, pp. 3–50. Chichester: Wiley.

Furnham, A. and Henderson, M. (1983) 'Response bias in self-report measures of general health', *Personality and Individual Differences*, 4, 519–525.

Garden, A. (1989) 'Burnout: the effect of physiological type on research findings', *Journal of Occupational Psychology*, 62, 223–234.

George, J.M. and Jones, G.R. (1996) 'The experience of work and turnover intentions: interactive effects of value attainment, job satisfaction and positive mood', *Journal of Applied Psychology*, 81, 318–325.

Goldberg, D. and Williams, P. (1988) *A User's Guide to the General Health Questionnaire*, Windsor: NFER-Nelson.

Goleman, D., Boyatzis, R. and the Hay Group (2006) *Emotional Competence Inventory*, London: Hay Group.

Howton, K., Fagg, J., Simkin, S., Harriss, L. and Malmberg, A. (1998) 'Methods used for suicide by farmers in England and Wales: the contribution of availability and its relevance to prevention', *British Journal of Psychiatry*, 173, 320–324.

Jamison, K.R. (1999) *Night Falls Fast: Understanding Suicide*, New York: Vintage Books.

Jones, F. and Bright, J. (2001) *Stress: Myth, Theory and Research*, Harlow: Pearson Education Limited.

Kasl, S. and Amick, B. (1995) 'Work stress', in S. Kasl (ed.) *Research Methods in Stress and Health Psychology*, pp. 239–266, Chichester: Wiley.

Lazarus, R.S., DeLongis, A, Folkman, S. and Gruen, R. (1985) 'Stress and adaptational outcomes: the problem of confounded measures', *American Psychologist*, 40, 770–779.

Lewis, G., Pelosi, A.J., Araya, R. and Dunn, G. (1992) 'Measuring psychiatric disorder in the community: a standardized assessment for use by lay interviewers', *Psychological Medicine*, 22, 465–486.

Lindeman, S., Laura, E., Hakko, H. and Lonnqvist, J. (1996) 'A systematic review on gender-specific suicide mortality in medical doctors', *British Journal of Psychiatry*, 168, 274–279.

Magnus, K., Diener, E., Fujita, F. and Pavot, W. (1993) 'Extraversion and neuroticism as predictors of objective life events; a longitudinal analysis', *Journal of Personality and Social Psychology*, 65, 1046–1053.

Maslach, C. and Jackson, S. (1986) *The Maslach Burnout Inventory*, Palo Alto, CA: Consulting Psychologists Press.

Mayer, J.D., Salovey, P. and Caruso, D.R. (2002) *Mayer–Salovey–Caruso Emotional Intelligence Test*, New York: Multi-Health Systems.

Mitra, A., Jenkins, G.D. and Gupta, N. (1992) 'A meta-analytic review of the relationship between absence and turnover', *Journal of Applied Psychology*, 77, 879–889.

Mullarkey, S., Wall, T.D., Warr, P.B., Clegg, C.W. and Stride, C.B. (eds) (1999) *Measures of Job Satisfaction, Mental Health and Job-Related Well-Being*, University of Sheffield: Institute of Work Psychology, Sheffield: Institute of Work Psychology, University of Sheffield.

Petrides, K.V. and Furnham, A. (2001) 'Trait emotional intelligence: psychometric investigation with reference to established trait taxonomies', *European Journal of Personality*, 15, 425–448.

Robson, C. (2004) *Real-World Research*, Oxford: Blackwell.

Siegrist, J., Peter, R., Georg, W., Cremer, P. and Siedel, D. (1991) 'Psychosocial and biobehavioural characteristics of hypertensive men with elevated atherogenic lipids', *Atherosclerosis*, 86, 211–218.

Siegrist, J., Matschinger, H., Cremer, P. and Siedel, D. (1988) 'Atherogenic risk in men suffering from occupational stress', *Atherosclerosis*, 69, 211–218.

Spector, P.E. and O'Connell, B.J. (1994) 'The contribution of personality traits, negative affectivity, locus of control and Type A to the subsequent reports of job stressors and strains', *Journal of Occupational and Organizational Psychology*, 67, 1–11.

Spector, P.E., Dwyer, D.J. and Jex, S.M. (1988) 'Relation of job stressors to affective, health and performance outcomes: a comparison of multiple data sources', *Journal of Applied Psychology*, 76, 46–53.

Stansfeld, S.A. and Marmot, M.G. (1992) 'Social class and minor psychiatric disorder in British civil servants: a validated screening survey using the General Health Questionnaire', *Psychological Medicine*, 22, 739–749.

Stansfeld, S.A., North, F., White, I, and Marmot, M.G. (1995) 'Work characteristics and psychiatric disorder in civil servants in London', *Journal of Epidemiological Community Health*, 49, 48–53.

Tomas, V. (ed.) (1957) *Charles S. Peirce: Essays in the Philosophy of Science*, New York: Liberal Arts Press.

Wall, T.D., Bolden, R.I., Borrill, C.S., Golya, D.A., Hardy, G.E., Haynes, G., Rick, J.W., Shapiro, D.A. and West, M.A. (1997) 'Minor psychiatric disorder in NHS Trust staff: occupational and gender differences', *British Journal of Psychiatry*, 171, 519–523.

Warr, P.B. (1990) 'The measurement of well-being and other aspects of mental health', *Journal of Occupational Psychology*, 63, 193–210.

Warr, P.B. (1999) 'Well-being in the workplace', in D. Kahneman, E. Diener and N. Schwartz (eds) *Well-being: The Foundations of Hedonic Psychology*, 392–412, New York: Russell Sage.

Weinberg, A. and Cooper, C.L. (2003) 'Stress among national politicians elected to Parliament for the first time', *Stress and Health*, 19, 111–117.

Weinberg, A., Cooper, C.L. and Weinberg, A. (1999) 'Workload, stress and family life in British Members of Parliament and the psychological impact of reforms their working hours', *Stress Medicine*, 15, 79–87.

Weinberg, A. and Pearson, A. (2005) 'Emotional intelligence among psychology undergraduates – a competitive edge?' *Proceedings of the British Psychological Society*, 14, 2.

Zigmond, A.S. and Snaith, R.P. (1983) 'The hospital anxiety and depression scale', *Acta Psychiatrica Scandinavia*, 67, 361–370.

Chapter 10

Alberti, R.D. and Emmons, M.L. (1970) *Your Perfect Right: A Guide to Assertive Behaviour*, New York: Impact.

Bernin, P., Theorell, T., Cooper, C.L., Sparks, K., Spector, P.E., Radhadkrishnan, P. and Russinova, V. (2003) 'Coping strategies among Swedish female and male managers in an international context', *International Journal of Stress Management*, 10, 376–391.

Brown, S.P., Westbrook, R.A. and Challagalla, G. (2005) 'Good cope, bad cope: adaptive and maladaptive coping strategies following a negative critical negative work event', *Journal of Applied Psychology*, 90, 792–798.

Brown, J.A.C. (1964) *Freud and the Post-Freudians*, Harmondsworth: Penguin.

Cacioppo, J.T. and Gardner, W.L. (1999) 'Emotion', *Annual Review of Psychology*, 50, 191–214.

Carver, C.S., Scheier, M.F. and Weintraub, J.K. (1989) 'Assessing coping strategies: a theoretically based approach', *Journal of Personality and Social Psychology*, 56, 267–283.

Clow, A. (2001) 'The physiology of stress', in F. Jones and J. Bright (2001) *Stress: Myth, Theory and Research*, pp. 47–62, Harlow: Pearson Education Limited.

Cohen, S. and Wills, T.A. (1985) 'Stress, social support and the buffering hypothesis', *Psychological Bulletin*, 98, 310–357.

Cooper, C.L., Cooper, R.D. and Eaker, L.H. (1988) *Living with Stress*, London: Penguin.

Cooper, C.L. and Williams, S. (1996) *Occupational Stress Indicator Version 2.0*, Windsor: NFER-Nelson.

Costa, J.P.T., Somerfield, M.R. and McRae, R.R. (1996) 'Personality and coping: a reconceptualization', in M. Zeidner and N.S. Endler (eds) *Handbook of Coping*, New York: John Wiley and Sons.

Dewe, P.J. and Guest, D.E. (1990). Methods of coping with stress at work: a conceptual analysis and empirical study of measurement issues. *Journal of Organizational Behaviour*, 11, 135–150.

Galinsky, T.L., Swanson, N.G., Sauter, S.L., Hurrell, J.J. and Schleifer, L.M. (2000) 'A field study of supplementary rest breaks for data-entry operators', *Ergonomics*, 43, 622–638.

Hayashi, M. and Hori, T. (1998) 'The effects of a 20-minute nap before post-lunch dip', *Psychiatry and Clinical Neurosciences*, 52, 203–4.

Jamner, L.D. and Leigh, H. (1999) 'Repressive defensive coping, endogenous opioids and health: how a life so perfect can make you sick', *Psychiatry Research*, 85, 17–31.

Jones, F. and Bright, J. (2001) *Stress: Myth, Theory and Research*, Harlow: Pearson.

Kanarek, R. (1997) 'Psychological effects of snacks and altered meal frequency', *British Journal of Nutrition*, Supplement 1, 105–120.

Kreitzman, L. (1999) *The 24 Hour Society*, London: Profile Books.

Langrish, S. (1981) 'Assertiveness training', in C.L. Cooper (ed.) *Improving Interpersonal Relations*, Epping: Gowen Press.

Lazarus, R. (1993) 'Coping theory and research: past, present and future', *Psychosomatic Medicine*, 55, 234–247.

Lazarus, R. and Folkman, S. (1984) *Stress, Appraisal and Coping*, New York: Springer Publications.

Leff, J. and Vaughan, C. (1981) 'The role of maintenance therapy and relatives' expressed emotion in relapse of schizophrenia: a two-year follow up', *British Journal of Psychiatry*, 139, 102–104.

Linley, A., Joseph, S., Harrington, S. and Wood, A.M. (2006) 'Positive psychology: past, present and (possible) future', *The Journal of Positive Psychology*, 1, 3–16.

Looker, O. and Gregson, T. (1994) 'The biological basis of stress management', *British Journal of Guidance and Counselling*, 22, 13–26.

Norgate, S. (2006) *Beyond 9 to 5*, London: Orion.

Snow, D.L., Swan, S.C., Raghavan, C., Connell, C.M. and Klein, I. (2003) 'The relationship of work stressors, coping and social support to psychological symptoms among female secretarial employees', *Work and Stress*, 17, 241–263.

Sonnentag, S. and Bayer, U-V. (2005) 'Switching off mentally; predictors and consequences of psychological detachment from work during off-job time', *Journal of Occupational Health Psychology*, 10, 393–414.

Strazdins, L. (2002) 'Emotional work and emotional contagion', in N.M. Ashkanasy, W.J. Zerbe and C.E.J. Hartel, *Managing Emotions in the Workplace*, pp. 232–250, New York: Sharpe.

The England Cricket Team (2005) *Ashes Victory*, London: Orion.

Theorell, T., Alfredsson, L. Westerholm, P. and Falck, B. (2000) 'Coping with unfair treatment at work – what is the relationship between coping and hypertension in middle-aged men and women?' *Psychotherapy and Psychosomatics*, 69, 86–94.

Thomas, K.W. (1992) Conflict and negotiation processes in organizations, in M.D. Dunnette and L.M. Hough (eds) *Handbook of Industrial and Organizational Psychology*, 2nd edition, Palo Alto, CA: Consulting Psychologists Press.

Weiss, H.M. and Cropanzano, R. (1996) 'Affective events theory: a theoretical discussion of the structure, causes and consequences of affective experiences at work', *Research in Organizational Behaviour*, 18, 1–74.

Chapter 11

Adkins, J.A., Quick, J. C., and Moe, K. O. (2000) 'Building world-class performance in changing times', in L. R. Murphy and C. L. Cooper (eds),

Healthy and Productive Work: An International Perspective, pp. 107–131, London: Taylor and Francis.

Alexander Consulting Group (1989) *Employee Assistance Program Financial Offset Study*, Westport, CT: Alexander and Alexander.

Arnetz, B.B. (1996) 'Techno-stress: a prospective psychophysiological study of the impact of a controlled stress-reduction program in advanced telecommunication systems design work', *Journal of Occupational Environmental Medicine*, 38, 53–65.

Arthur, A.R. (2002) 'Mental health problems and British workers: a survey of mental health problems in employees who receive counselling from Employee Assistance Programmes', *Stress and Health*, 18, 69–74.

Arthur, A.R. (2000) 'Employee assistance programmes: the emperor's new clothes of stress management', *British Journal of Guidance and Counselling*, 28, 549–559.

Arthur, A.R. (1999) 'Employee assistance programmes present challenges and opportunities for clinical psychologists', Paper presented at Division of Clinical Psychology, British Psychological Society Annual Conference, Belfast.

Aust, B. and Ducki, A. (2004) 'Comprehensive health promotion interventions at the workplace: experiences with health circles in Germany', *Journal of Occupational Health Psychology*, 9, 258–270.

Benson, H. (1976) *The Relaxation Response*, New York: Morrow.

Benson, H. (1993) 'The relaxation response', in D. Goldman and J. Gurin (eds) *Mind/Body Medicine*, New York: Consumer Reports Books.

Berridge, J. and Cooper, C.L. (1993) 'Stress and coping in U.S. organizations: the role of the Employee Assistance Programme', *Work and Stress*, 7, 89–102.

Berridge, J., Cooper, C.L. and Highly-Marchington, C. (1997) *Employee Assistance Programmes and Workplace Counselling*, Chichester: Wiley.

Blaze-Temple, D. and Howat, P. (1997) 'Cost benefit of an Australian EAP', *Employee Assistance Quarterly*, 12, 1–24.

Bond, F.W. and Bunce, D. (2000) 'Mediators of change in emotion-focused and problem-focused worksite stress management interventions', *Journal of Occupational Health Psychology*, 5, 156–163.

Borrill, C.S., Wall, T.D., West, M.A., Hardy, G.E., Shapiro, D.A., Haynes, C.E., Stride, C.B., Woods, D. and Carter, A.J. (1998) *Stress among Staff in NHS Trusts: Final Report*, Institute of Work Psychology, University of Sheffield and Psychological Therapies Research Centre, University of Leeds.

Bunce, D. and West, M.A. (1996) 'Stress management and innovation interventions at work', *Human Relations*, 49, 209–224.

Carroll, M. (1996) *Workplace Counselling*, London: Sage.

Cooper, C.L. and Cartwright, S. (1994) 'Healthy mind; healthy organization – a proactive approach to occupational stress', *Human Relations*, 47, 455–471.

Cooper, C.L. and Sadri, G. (1991) 'The impact of stress counselling at work', in P.L. Perrewe (ed.) Handbook of job stress (special issue), *Journal of Social Behaviour and Personality*, 6, 411–423.

Cuthell, T. (2004) 'De-stressing the workforce', *Occupational Health*, 56, 14–17.

Daily Telegraph (2002) 'Judges tighten rules on stress payouts', 6 February, 1–2.

Daley, A.J. and Parfitt, G. (1996) 'Good health – is it worth it? Mood states, physical well-being, job satisfaction and absenteeism in members and non-members of a British corporate health and fitness club', *Journal of Occupational and Organizational Psychology*, 69, 121–134.

Dishman, R.D. (1988) *Exercise Adherence: Its Impact on Public Health*, Champaign, IL: Human Kinetics Books.

Egan, G. (1986) *The Skilled Helper*, 3rd edition, Monterey, CA: Brooks/Cole.

Elkin, A. and Rosch, P. (1990) 'Promoting mental health in the workplace: the prevention side of stress management', *Occupational Medicine: State of the Art Review*, 5, 739–754.

Ellis, A. (1977) 'The basic clinical theory of rational-emotive therapy', in A. Ellis and R. Grieger (eds) *Handbook of Rational-Emotive Therapy*, New York: Springer-Verlag.

Elo, A.L., Leppanen, A. and Sillanpaa, P. (1998) 'Applicability of survey feedback for an occupational health method in stress management', *Occupational Medicine*, 48, 181–188.

Erfurt, J.C., Foote, A. and Heirich, M.A. (1992) 'The cost-effectivness of worksite wellness programs for hypertension control, weight loss, smoking cessation and exercise', *Personnel Psychology*, 45, 5–27.

Fingret, A. (1994) 'Introducing a mental heath policy in the workplace', in C.L. Cooper and S. Williams (eds) *Creating Healthy Work Organizations*, pp. 97–114, Chichester: Wiley.

Freedy, J.R. and Hobfoll, S.E. (1994) 'Stress inoculation for reduction of burnout: a conservation of resources approach', *Anxiety, Stress and Coping*, 6, 311–325.

Giga, S.I., Cooper, C.L. and Faragher, B. (2003a) 'The development of a framework for a comprehensive approach to stress management interventions at work', *International Journal of Stress Management*, 10, 280–296.

Giga, S., Faragher, B. and Cooper, C. (2003b). 'Part 1: Identification of good practice in stress prevention/management', in J. Jordan, E. Gurr, G. Tinline, S. Giga, B. Faragher, and C. Cooper (eds), *Beacons of Excellence in Stress Prevention*, Health and Safety Executive Contract Research Report No. 133, pp. 1–45, Sudbury: HSE Books.

Health Education Authority (1997) *Organizational Stress: Planning and Implementing a Programme to Address Organizational Stress in the NHS*. London: HEA.

Highley, J.C. and Cooper, C.L. (1993) 'Evaluating employee assistance/counselling programmes', *Employee Counselling Today*, 5, 13–18.

Jackson, P.R. and Wall, T.D. (1991) 'How does operator control enhance performance of advanced manufacturing technology?', *Ergonomics*, 34, 1301–1311.

Jacobsen, E. (1938) *Progressive Relaxation*, Chicago, IL: University of Chicago Press.

Kerr, J.H. and Vos, M.C.H. (1993) 'Employee fitness programmes, absenteeism and general well-being', *Work and Stress*, 7, 179–190.

Kompier, M.A.J., Cooper, C.L. and Geurts, S.A.E. (2000) 'A multiple case study approach to work stress prevention in Europe', *European Journal of Work and Organizational Psychology*, 9, 371–400.

Lancet (1998) 'Prevention and treatment of occupational mental disorders: Editorial', *Lancet*, 352, 999.

Lee, C. and Gray, J.A. (1994) 'The role of employee assistance programmes', in C.L. Cooper and S. Williams, *Creating Healthy Work Organizations*, pp. 214–241, Chichester: John Wiley and Sons.

MacDonald, S., Lothian, S. and Wells, S. (1997) 'Evaluation of an employee assistance program at a transportation company', *Evaluation and Program Planning*, 20, 495–505.

Masi, D.A. (1997) 'Evaluating employee assistance programs', *Research on Social Work Practice*, 7, 378–390.

Masi, D.A. and Jacobson, J.M. (2003) 'Outcome measurements of an integrated employee assistance and work-life program', *Research on Social Work Practice*, 13, 451–467.

McClellan (1989) 'Cost–benefit analysis of the Ohio EAP', *Employee Assistance Quarterly*, 5, 67–85.

Meichenbaum, D. (1977) *Cognitive-Behaviour Modification*, New York: Plenum Press.

Michie, S. and Sandhu, S. (1994) 'Stress management for clinical medical students', *Medical Education*, 28, 528–533.

Miller, D.M. (1994) Gaining control over the work environment, in C.L. Cooper and S. Williams (eds) *Creating Healthy Work Organizations*, pp. 197–213, Chichester: Wiley.

Murphy, L.R. (1996) 'Stress management techniques: secondary prevention of stress', in M.J. Schabracq, J.A.M. Winnubst and C.L. Cooper, *Handbook of Work and Health Psychology*, pp. 427–441, Chichester: John Wiley and Sons.

Nytro, K., Saksvik, P. O., Mikkelsin, A., Bohle, P. and Quinlan, M. (2000) 'An appraisal of key factors in the implementation of occupational stress interventions', *Work and Stress*, 14, 213–225.

O'Driscoll, M.P. and Cooper, C.L. (1995) 'Sources and management of excessive job stress and burnout', in P.B. Warr (ed.) *Psychology at Work*, pp. 188–223, London: Penguin.

Parkes, K.R. and Sparkes, T.J. (1998) 'Organizational interventions to reduce work stress: are they effective?' *Health and Safety Contract Research Report No. 193*, Sudbury: HSE Books.

Perrewe, P.L. and D.C. Ganster, D.C. (1989) 'The impact of job demands and behavioural control on experienced job stress', *Journal of Organizational Behaviour*, 10, 213–229.

Quick, J. (1979) 'Dyadic goal setting and role stress in field study', *Academy of Management Journal*, 22, 241–252.

Randall, R., Griffiths, A. and Cox, T. (2005) 'Evaluating organizational stress-management interventions using adapted study designs', *European Journal of Work and Organizational Psychology*, 14, 23–41.

Reddy, M. (1993) '"EAPS and counselling services is organisations: an ICAS Report and Policy Guide", in M. Reddy, EAPS and their future in the UK: History repeating itself?', *Personnel Review*, 23, 7, 60–78.

Sallis, J.F., Trevorrow, T.R., Johnson, C.C., Hovell, M.F. and Kaplan, R.M. (1987) 'Worksite stress management: a comparison of programmes', *Psychology and Health*, 1, 237–255.

Schabracq, M.J., Winnubst, J.A.M. and Cooper, C.L. (2002) *The Handbook of Work and Health Psychology*, Chichester: John Wiley and Sons.

Schreurs, P.J.G., Winnubst, J.A.M. and Cooper, C.L. (1996) 'Workplace health programmes', in M.J. Schabracq, J.A.M. Winnubst and C.L. Cooper, *Handbook of Work and Health Psychology*, pp. 463–481, Chichester: John Wiley and Sons.

Schweiger, D. M. and DeNisi, A. S. (1991) 'Communication with employees following a merger: a longitudinal field experiment', *Academy of Management Journal*, 34, 110–135.

Sijbrandji, B., Olff, M., Reitsma, J.B., Carlier, I.V.E. and Gersons, B.P.R. (2006) 'Emotional or educational debriefing after psychological trauma: randomised controlled trial', *British Journal of Psychiatry*, 189, 150–155.

Sutherland, V.J. (2005) 'An organizational approach to stress management', in A-S. Antoniou and C.L. Cooper (eds) *Research Companion to Organizational Health Psychology*, pp. 198–208, Cheltenham: Edward Elgar.

Sutherland, V. J. and Cooper, C. L. (1990) *Understanding Stress*, London: Chapman and Hall.

Tmag (2006) 'Quality showcase', *Toyota magazine*, March issue 119, 1.

Trice, H.M. and Schonbrunn, M. (1981) 'A history of job-based alcoholism programs 1900-1955', *Journal of Drug Issues*, 11, 171–198.

Van Den Burgh, N. (2001) *Emerging Trends for EAPs is the 21st Century*, New York: Haworth Press.

Van der Klink, J.J.L., Blonk, R.W.B., Schene, A.H. and van Dijk, F.J.H. (2001) 'The benefits of interventions for work-related stress', *American Journal of Public Health*, 92, 270–276.

Voit, S. (2001) 'Work-site health and fitness programs: impact on the employee and employer', *Work*, 16, 273–286.

Weinberg, A. and Cooper, C.L. (2003) 'Stress among national politicians elected to Parliament for the first time', *Stress and Health*, 19, 111–117.

Weinberg, A. and Creed, F. (2000) 'Stress and psychiatric disorder in healthcare professionals and hospital staff', *Lancet*, 355, 533–537.

Williams, S. (1994) 'Ways of creating health work organizations', in C.L. Cooper and S. Williams, *Creating Healthy Work Organizations*, Chichester: Wiley pp. 7–23.

Chapter 12

Ashkanasy, N.M., Hartel, C.E.J. and Zerbe, W.J. (2002) 'What are the management tools that come out of this?' in N.M. Ashkanasy, W.J. Zerbe and C.E.J. Hartel, *Managing Emotions in the Workplace*, pp. 285–296, New York: Sharpe.

Ashkanasy, N.M., Zerbe, W.J. and Hartel, C.E.J. (2002) *Managing Emotions in a Changing Workplace*, in N.M. Ashkanasy, W.J. Zerbe and C.E.J. Hartel, *Managing Emotions in the Workplace*, pp. 3–24, New York: Sharpe.

Basch, J. and Fisher, C.D. (2000) 'Affective events emotions matrix: a classification of work events and associated emotions', in N.M. Ashkanasy, C.E.J. Hartel and W.J. Zerbe (eds) *Emotions in the Workplace: Research, Theory and Practice*, pp. 36–48, Westport, CT: Quorum Books.

Cherniss, C. and Goleman, D. (2001) *The Emotionally Intelligent Workplace*, Oxford: John Wiley and Sons.

Di Renzo, G-D. (1998) 'Premature births among full-time working women', Paper at Tommy's Campaign conference, 7 September.

Draganski, B., Gaser, C., Busch, V., Schuierer, G., Bogdahn, U. and May, A. (2004) 'Neuroplasticity: changes in grey matter induced by training', *Nature*, 427, 311–312.

Gardner, H. (1983) *Frames of Mind: The theory of multiple intelligences*, New York: Basic Books.

Gardner, H. (1993) *Multiple Intelligences: The theory in practice*, New York: Basic Books.

Goleman, D. (1995) *Emotional Intelligence*, New York: Bantam Books.

Guardian (2006) 'Immobile office workers given DVT warning', 9 May.

Holman, D., Wall, T.D., Clegg, C.W., Sparrow, P. and Howard, A. (2004) *The Essentials of the New Workplace*, Chichester: John Wiley & Sons.

Kaati, G., Bygren, L.O. and Edvinsson, S. (2002) 'Cardiovascular and diabetes mortality determined by nutrition during parents and grandparents' slow growth period', *European Journal of Human Genetics*, 10, 682–688.

Monk, C.S., Nelson, E.E., Woldehawariat, G. *et al.* (2004) 'Experience-dependent plasticity for attention to threat: behavioral neurophysiological evidence in humans', *Biological Psychiatry*, 56, 607–610.

Pembrey, M., Bygren, L.O., Kaati, G.P., *et al.* (2005) 'Sex-specific, sperm-moderated transgenerational responses in humans', *European Journal of Human Genetics*, 14, 159–166.

Terkel, S. (1970) *Working*, New York: Avon Books.

Index